TEA

TEA
Wine's Sober Sibling

MARIËLLA ERKENS

© 2022

Uitgeverij Terra is part of Uitgeverij TerraLannoo bv
P.O. Box 23202
1100 DS Amsterdam
The Netherlands
info@terralannoo.nl
terra-publishing.com

 @terrapublishing
 @terrapublishing

© 2022 Mariëlla Erkens
theesommelier.me

Author: Mariëlla Erkens
Recipes: Mariëlla Erkens a.o.
Designs cover and interior: Natasha Tastachova
Photography: Harold Pereira
Portrait on back cover: D&R Fotografie
Styling: Nicole de Werk
Food styling: Mariëlla Erkens
Editor: Alex Ahearn

First print, 2022

ISBN 978 90 8989 932 3
NUR 440

All rights reserved. No part of this publication may be reproduced and/or made public by means of printing, photocopying, microfilm or by any other means, without the prior written permission of the publisher. This edition has been compiled with the utmost care. Neither the maker nor the publisher, however, is liable for any damage as a result of any inaccuracies and/or omissions in this publication.

This book uses paper that is certain to have not caused forest destruction. Terra believes it is important to use natural resources in an environmentally friendly and responsible manner.

CONTENTS

8	PREFACE	
10	INTRODUCTION	
12	CHAPTER 1	Wine and tea
26	CHAPTER 2	The basics
46	CHAPTER 3	Taste and flavor
60	CHAPTER 4	Tea and food pairing
69	CHAPTER 5	Recipes with three tea suggestions
130	CHAPTER 6	Cooking with tea: theory and recipes
135	CHAPTER 7	Recipes with tea as an ingredient
184	CHAPTER 8	Chocolate and tea
200	CHAPTER 9	Cheese and tea
210	CHAPTER 10	Tea mixology
219	CHAPTER 11	Tea in cafes and restaurants
227	CHAPTER 12	Tea production
239	CHAPTER 13	Tea and health
	APPENDIX	
246	Technical information about water	
248	Flavor wheel	
251	Example forms for tasting notes	
256	Tasting notes and food pairing	
276	Tea characteristics	
284	Index recipes	
286	Index	
288	Addresses of teashops and tea institutes	
294	Bibliography	
296	Acknowledgments	

PREFACE

"Why would you want to serve tea with food?
It is a question I am often asked, and it is usually followed by, "after all, there is nothing better than wine to pair with food. That is what we have done for centuries." Well, sure. That is the general consensus in the Western part of the world. However, in Eastern countries people have been drinking tea with their meals for thousands of years for the very same reason, so why not accept both possibilities?
That is what I did a decade ago and I am very happy I did, as it enriched my life as a whole and my meals in particular. It also broadened my professional scope. In 2010, while working as a chef, I visited a wholesale store to buy produce, and was invited to join a workshop on single origin tea and food pairing. Before then, I had no idea about the endless possibilities of tea, and like most people I knew, I drank tea out of habit. That afternoon completely changed my thoughts about tea. I was awestruck by how tea could taste and how wonderfully it could enhance food. I started reading as much as I could about tea and signed up for a three-year tea sommelier course at the International Tea and Coffee Academy in the Netherlands. Gradually, I started to do more tea training and consultation work. After four years, my professional cooking career took more and more of a backseat. Nowadays, I only cook for pleasure.
I am also a teacher, with a speciality in tea and food pairing, at various institutions, so I decided to bundle all of the knowledge that I have gained over the years into a handbook. Although, I realize that my knowledge does not even remotely start to cover all that there is to know about tea.

All of this information can be rather overwhelming for someone new to tea, so I have included a variety of experiments, tips and examples in this book to help you along the way. This will give you the tools for putting your newly found knowledge into practice. There is a section with over 60 recipes, each with matching tea advice in three categories: budget tea, specialty tea and high-end tea. Most of the recipes have options for a vegetarian or vegan alternative. In the appendix you will also find lists of examples of tea and food combinations without recipes. In addition, there are pairings with cheese and chocolate, recipes for tea cocktails and descriptions of the most common teas and their tasting notes.

This book is for people with various levels of knowledge. It is for anyone, from beginners to advanced tea lovers, tea connoisseurs, chefs, amateur chefs, sommeliers, food lovers, and anyone looking for the best options for non-alcoholic alternatives to wine. It is also a highly practical handbook for people in the catering and hospitality sector, and it can be used in hospitality training courses.

All knowledge starts with a theory, but practice makes perfect. Understanding tea is so much more than theory, and you will really learn to appreciate it by tasting it, as often as possible, prepared in different ways. After all, the proof is in the pudding.

INTRODUCTION

Let us be honest, to most people, steeping tea generally means absentmindedly dunking tea bags in piping hot, tap water, which has been boiled several times already and as such acquiring a flat, unpleasant flavor. Once the tea is ready for drinking, the very few flavors that do manage to break through the suffocating actions of calcium, magnesium and other dissolved solids, will get drowned in milk and sugar, and will never even get near our taste buds.
No wonder tea steeped like that tastes rather boring and always the same, and it is no surprise that most people drink it distractedly, gulping it down without paying any attention to what they are drinking. They think this is what tea is supposed to taste like, and one cannot blame them.
The fact is that most people simply do not know how a good cup of tea ought to be steeped.
For this reason, the unique flavors of each tea will never get a chance to surface.
For those who do take the time, love and effort to discover tea's many possibilities, there is a world of delight to discover. Once you have the knowledge and you master skills, steeping your cup of tea will never be the same again, I can promise you that.

People often think that tea is a hassle, but it is just a matter of acquiring the proper knowledge, just like all those other things we are not familiar with yet.
For example, not so long ago, the average Westerner's knowledge about wine, tea and coffee was:
- Wine is red, or white, sometimes pink and it sparkles when there is a party.
- Tea should be taken with milk and sugar.
- Coffee is usually a powder which you dissolve in hot water and mix with milk and sugar.

Since then, our collective knowledge about wine and coffee has increased enormously, and many supermarkets now stock very high-quality coffee and wine. In general, people know the names of the most common wines and drink them regularly, just like they routinely order espresso, macchiato, cappuccino or caffè latte. Now it is tea's turn. Apart from the well-known teas, like English Breakfast, Earl Grey or green tea, there are thousands of different kinds of loose-leaf tea, in all sorts of qualities. Do not let this put you off, as there is no need to know them all. Buy yourself only

a few different types of tea, maybe five or six, in small quantities, about 50 g (or 2 oz) each, or buy a sample set. See which ones you like best and start from there.
You could even start with just one tea if that would be easier for you. All it takes is time and practice, and all that matters is your own opinion. There is no right or wrong. If you like a certain tea, then that is perfect, no matter the quality or flavor. If you do not like a certain tea, no matter how fancy or special, just do not drink it. Expensive tea (or wines, for that matter) do not automatically agree with everybody's taste buds. It is all a matter of personal taste, which needs to be discovered.

Considering the growing number of people who want to drink less alcohol or no alcohol at all, it is becoming increasingly necessary for restaurants to offer alcohol-free beverages to accompany and complement food. Soft drinks and water do not add anything to the food experience, in fact; they do the very opposite. Many chefs and sommeliers are now going out of their way to develop non-alcoholic cocktails, herbal mixes, hip lemonades and flavored waters. It is all quite creative, sure, but those drinks do not have the same effect on food as wine, beer and tea have.

In short
Wine, beer or tea are the only good solutions for a complete flavor experience.
A combination of all three is also an option, of course. For those who do not drink alcoholic drinks, tea is the best alternative.

I have been working with tea and its distinctive flavors on a daily basis since 2010, tasting teas both with and without food and writing lots and lots of recipes. The grand total of these efforts is incorporated in this book. However, my suggestions are just that: suggestions, based on my taste. Consider this a handbook that will help you develop your own taste in tea and food pairing. Once you have tackled the basics, take it from there and start to develop your own style. Experiment, do the unexpected. The worst thing that can happen is a disappointing result. By using this book, you will learn how to bring the best out of tea, with or without food. Read on!

CHAPTER 1

Wine and tea

Tea has more in common with wine than you may think. In fact, tea and wine could almost be sister and brother, considering the many similarities they share, the effect they may have on food, the way of growing the product, the importance of terroir, the decisive hand of the tea master, the hand-picking, the similar aromas and so on. The only two things they do not have in common are alcohol and acidity.
If getting slightly intoxicated is your goal, then go ahead and choose wine. If you prefer to stay clear-headed, tea is definitely a better option. The choice is yours. If you cannot choose between them, then drink them both.

THE TERROIR OF TEA
Terroir (terre, French for earth) is of great importance for the flavor development of both tea and wine.
Terroir means the composition of the soil in terms of minerals, acidity, rock, sand, clay, etc. Is the soil rich or poor in nutrients? Terroir also refers to questions such as: Where does the bush grow in terms of geography? At what altitude? How much sun does it get per day? How much rain does the area get? What is the average temperature? Is it foggy at night or not? Is the air humid or dry?
All these factors together determine the terroir and have a definite impact on the final product. An example is Cabernet Sauvignon red wine from France, Chile, and South Africa. They are all made with the same grape but have different terroirs.
When you taste these wines, it will soon become clear that each one has a different taste and slightly different characteristics. Although you will also note that they have the same grape variety in common.
Do the same test with tea, for example, with the oolong tea generally called Tieguanyin (also known as; Ti Kuan Yin, and Tieguanyin, Tiekuanyin). This is a good choice, as it is made from the Tieguanyin cultivar of Camellia sinensis and is produced in China, Taiwan and Thailand, always with the same cultivar, but with different terroirs. Cultivar is short for the phrase cultivated variety.

> **Test:**
> Please do prepare each of the teas in exactly the same way to taste the variations between the terroirs. The difference in temperature, amount of tea or steeping time could cause the teas to not taste the same. You will notice that, just like the Cabernet Sauvignon in the previous example, the three teas all have the specific taste characteristics of Tieguanyin while maintaining their own unique character because of the terroir.

THE NAMES OF TEA AND WINE
Many teas are named after their cultivar (e.g., Tieguanyin, Jin Xuan #12 and Bai Hao Yin Zhen) or the tea-producing region they are from (e.g., Ali Shan, Darjeeling and Assam), or after the way they were produced (e.g., Matcha, powdered tea, and Hōjicha, roasted tea). In China, some names are poetic and do not necessarily correspond to a particular region or cultivar, while others do, such as Long Jing. Its name means "Dragon Well," and a tea can only be called Long Jing when made with the specific cultivar, grown in a restricted area and precisely processed, resulting in a specific flat sword-like shape of the leaf. However, names may also have other sources. Taiwanese Baozhong translates to "wrapped variety" or "the wrapped kind," because in the past, Baozhong was wrapped and packaged in paper. In short, tea names can be quite confusing.

That said, the same applies to wine, as some wines are named after a particular grape variety used to make them (e.g., Chardonnay, Sauvignon Blanc, Cabernet Franc), and others are named after their origin. Beaujolais wine is usually made with Gamay grapes and is named after the region, instead of the grape variety used. Chablis is another example of this, as the wine is Chablis and is always made with 100% Chardonnay grapes. Many wines are often blends, with strict rules concerning the percentage of each grape variety. A lot of teas are also blends; for example, many Japanese teas are very often blended to sheer perfection. Other well known blends are English Breakfast, Irish Breakfast, Prince of Wales and Earl Grey. My advice: do not focus too much on the origin for now and just follow your taste buds.

WHERE TO START

For a novice, it might be overwhelming to find the right combination, as there are thousands of wines and teas to choose from. To get you started, I have created a table comparing some of the most well-known teas and wines based on their main aromas, texture and intensity. Please bear in mind that two identical types of teas or wines from different origins could have another flavor profile, due to variables in climate, soil, another time in the year for harvesting, or the farmer's own method of processing the grapes or leaves. This overview is meant as a starting point so as not to get lost in the forest of possibilities. Once you know your way around, and feel confident and adventurous, follow your own path into the exciting world of tea and food. Whatever you do, remember to take notes. They are the pebbles that will show you the way.

TEA AND WINE

SIMILARITIES BETWEEN TEA AND WINE	🫖	🍷
Stimulates appetite	●	●
Cleanses the mouth after each bite	●	●
Blends well with food, producing harmony	●	●
When combined it may lead to a new flavor	●	●
Enhances the flavor of the food	●	●
Stimulates digestion	●	●
Drink and food bring out the best in each other	●	●
Drink and food remain like they are; respecting each other	●	●
Assertive drink becomes more balanced when paired with food	●	●
Flavor of final product depends on the condition of the plant	●	●
Flavor of final product depends on the soil characteristics	●	●
Flavor of final product depends on location and altitude	●	●
Flavor of final product depends on rainfall and sunlight	●	●
Flavor of final product depends on the skills of the maker	●	●
Some age really well as flavor and texture improve with age	●	●
DIFFERENCES IN QUALITIES BETWEEN TEA AND WINE		
May cause drunkenness		●
May cause drowsiness		●
Provokes a clear state of mind, wakefulness, sharper focus	●	
May be too dominant regarding acidity		●
May be too dominant regarding astringency	●	
May have a diuretic effect (due to caffeine)	●	

WHAT TEA CAN DO TO YOUR TASTE BUDS

Tea, like wine, may have a flavor-enhancing or altering effect on food. Wine, however, can be quite dominant and sometimes even clash with the food or lessen its flavor. Tea is much more forgiving in that respect. The worst that can happen with a bad choice of tea and food pairing would be a powerful drying effect in the mouth or a dampening one on the overall flavor, but it does not get much worse than that. Usually tea intensifies the flavors of the food. This is partly due to the temperature of the tea, but is mainly caused by the many flavor and aroma components in tea reacting with those in the food.

Drinking tea with food can enhance, accentuate, or balance some of the flavors of the food. I have tested this by drinking both warm water and warm tea at the same temperature with the same food. The effect of the warm water was way less intense than that of the warm tea. With the water, the flavor of the food was actually washed away very quickly, whereas: with the tea, the flavor was both enhanced and prolonged.

TEA PRODUCTION

There are many similarities between wine and tea production. Wine is made from the grapes of the *Vitis vinifera* vine, whereas tea is made from the leaves of the *Camellia sinensis* plant. There are over 10.000 grape varieties that make up the world of wine, although there are 300 or so that are really interesting to make wine with. A similar fact applies to tea.

The tea plant has two main varieties: *Camellia sinensis sinensis* and *Camellia sinensis assamica*. From those two varieties, tea farmers and researches develop *cultivars* or **culti**vated **vari**eties to have desirable qualities (e.g., frost and drought resistance, etc.). The production process dictates the final color of a tea; for example, black, green or white. More about tea production and the various types of tea follows in the next chapter.

In theory, you could make red, white and rosé wine from any vine with red grapes. In reality, certain grape varieties are better suited for white or red than the other species. This also applies to the various tea varieties.

A tea farmer could produce all six types of tea with any cultivar, the six types being green, yellow, white, oolong, black and post-fermented tea (you can read more about the differences between these types in Chapters 2 and 12). There are tea gardens, where in the past only black tea was made, now they produce green, white and oolong teas as well with occasionally spectacular results.

A few years ago, I visited the Glenburn Tea Estate, a beautiful tea garden in Darjeeling. They had just won the first prize at a world championship with their Silver Needle white tea. This type of tea is made from only the buds of the tea plant and originates in China and is still produced there, according to centuries-old tradition. On the Glenburn Tea Estate, they produce a similar tea with an entirely different variety and terroir. Their Silver Needle tasted sweet, fruity, floral, round, soft, complex and very well balanced. It must have been quite a triumph for them to rob China of that title, which is comparable to a wine maker from Chile instead of France winning a gold medal for a Sauvignon Blanc.

WHICH TEA TO HAVE WITH YOUR FOOD

Of course, it is not imperative to always search for the perfect match. You may simply not have the time or the energy to do this. It is not always necessary, either. Often enough, one simply drinks the wine one happens to have or orders the house wine at a restaurant.

In Japan, Hōjicha, an everyday roasted green tea, mostly made of the twigs of the tea plant, is usually served with food. Sometimes, Sencha, green tea, is served, regardless of which dish is ordered. In Taiwan, roasted oolong is

the standard tea to serve with food. In many Chinese restaurants, you will be served a Jasmine tea alongside your dish. Even though those teas are usually served with food, they may not always be the best pairings. Compare it with drinking any choice of table wine with your dishes. The chance is small that you will experience a perfect match, sometimes they even clash, but we simply do not always have the time or knowledge to search for a perfect wine or tea to pair with our food and that is ok. When we do have time and knowledge though, the right combination could lead to a very special experience, an uplifting of the senses, true and pure joy. A taste bud party, whether it is done with wine or tea.

SOME OF THE SIBLINGS UP AND CLOSE
Examples of matching teas and wines

WHITE TEA	
Tea varieties	Grape varieties
CHINA	
Bai Hao Yin Zhen, *Fujian, China*; smooth, rich, creamy, sweet, vegetal, floral, sweets, fruity, grains; grass, hay, pink rose, vanilla, apricot, toasted brioche with apricot jam, S	**Torrontés Riojano**, *Calchaqui Valleys, N-Argentina*; smooth, neutral to dry, sweet, fruity, floral; apricot, peach, melon, honey, lily, white flowers, rose, S
Bai Mudan, *Fujian, China*; smooth, mellow, rich, later bright, sweet, floral, fruity, sweets, nutty, grains, honeysuckle, lily, peach, apricot, melon, honey, hay, toasted bread, M	**Roussanne**, *Central Coast, California, U.S.A.*; smooth, rich, silky, sweet, sour, fruit, floral; lanolin, apricot, pear, lemon, white flowers, almond, orange blossom, S
Yue Guang Bai, *Yunnan, China*; smooth, rich and bright, sweet, earthy, fruity, spices, floral, sweets, henna, caramel, wood, sweet tobacco, apricot, honeysuckle, honey, vanilla, L	**Viognier**, *Yarra Valley, Australia*; dry, rich and bright, sweet and sour, fruity, mineral, spices, floral, peach, apricot, green plum, red apple, rock, nutmeg, geranium, jasmine, honey, M-L
INDIA	
Spicy White, *first flush, Kurseong valley, Darjeeling, India*; dry, bright, crisp, sweet, bitter, floral, fruity, vegetal, herbaceous; white flowers, muscatel grape, capsicum, hay, M	**Silvaner d'Alsace**, *trocken, Rheinhesssen, Germany*; dry, bright, fruity, vegetal, floral, citrus, grape, grass, white flowers, M
KENIA	
White Whisper, *Silver Needle, Nyeri region, Kenya*; smooth, bold, rich, later bright, sweet, vegetal, floral, fruity, nutty, grains; grass, honey suckle, peach, almond, toasted brioche, M	**Viognier**, *N-Rhône, France*; smooth, bold, bright, sweet, sour, fruity, floral, nutty, spices, nectarine, a hint of citrus, pineapple, mango, honeysuckle, rose, almond, anise, honey, M-L

GREEN TEA	
CHINA	
Anji Bai Cha, *Zhejiang Province, China*; smooth, rich, sweet, slightly sour, umami, dairy, floral, nutty, sweets, vegetal, fruity; butter, honey suckle, magnolia, macadamia nut, honey, snow peas, melon, citrus, strawberry jam, S-M	**Sémillon**, *Bordeaux, France*; smooth, dry, sour, bright, floral, fruity, nutty, grains, sweets; orange blossom, white flowers, honeysuckle, citrus, green apple, white peach, melon, lemon zest, a hint of nut, butter on toast, honey, beeswax, S
Long Jing, *Zhejiang Province, China*; smooth, rich, later a bit bright, round, creamy, sweet, umami, vegetal, fruity, grains, nutty, maritime; peas, corn, chestnut, raw courgette, toast, cookies, macadamia, oyster, M	**Melon de Bourgogne**, *Muscadet, Bourgogne, France*; dry, bright, fruity, floral, maritime, grains, nutty; pear, citrus, green apple, white flowers, shellfish, bread, almond, M

GREEN TEA	
Tea varieties	Grape varieties
CHINA	
Bi Luo Chun, *Dong Shan, Jiangsu Province, China*; smooth, rich, later dry and bright, sweet, slightly bitter, umami, vegetal, fruity, grains, nutty, spices, mineral; courgette, edamame, candied lemon, plum, toast, cookies, hazelnut, aniseed, flint, M	**Müller-Thurgau,** *Willamette Valley, W-Oregon, USA*; dry, bright, slightly sweet, light; fruity, floral, mineral, peach, citrus, rose, elderflower, flint, M
Tai Ping Hou Kui, *Tai Ping County, Anhui Province, China*; smooth, rich, later dry and bright, sweet, slightly bitter, umami, vegetal, fruity, nutty, herbaceous; peas, green beans, asparagus, green bell pepper, pear, guava, almond, a hint of eucalyptus, honey, M	**Sauvignon Blanc,** *Marlborough, New Zealand*; dry, bright, fruity, vegetal, herbaceous, floral; citrus, papaya, melon, green bell pepper, peas, asparagus, grass, elderflower, geranium, M
Gunpowder, *Zhejiang Province, China*; neutral-bright, dry, sweet, bitter, sour, fruity, floral, earthy, vegetal, herbaceous, grains, nutty, fruity, mineral, metal; citrus, lily, pot soil, wood, broccoli, sage, cookies, almonds, flint, smoke, steel, M-L	**Aligoté,** *Burgundy, France*; bright, dry, fruity, floral, herbaceous, mineral, metal; apple, citrus, unripe peach, white flower, sage, rosemary, smoke, steel, M-L
JAPAN	
Sencha, *Kochi, Shikoku, Japan*; smooth to dry, rich and bright, sweet, bitter, umami, vegetal, herbaceous, maritime, fruity; grass, spinach, cucumber, parsley, basil, seaweed, citrus, peach, melon, M	**Melon de Bourgogne,** *Muscadet, Bourgogne, France*; dry, bright, fruity, floral, maritime, grains, nutty; pear, citrus, green apple, white flowers, shellfish, bread, almond, M
Hōjicha, *Tsukigase, Nara prefecture, Japan*; roasted tea, smooth and dry, rich, sweet, umami, nutty, grains, fruity, vegetal, herbaceous, maritime, earthy; caramel, honey, toasted almond, filter coffee, toast, pear, roasted corn, fennel, seaweed, cedar wood, M	**Grillo,** *Sicily, Italy*; full, fruity, floral, nutty, mineral, maritime, herbaceous, citrus, peach, pear, melon, orange blossom, almond, thyme, honey, M
Kamairicha, *Ureshino, Saga Prefecture, Japan*; slightly dry, ends smooth and bright, sweet, slightly bitter, umami, floral, sweets, grains, vegetal, herbaceous, fruity, dairy; freesia, oatmeal cookies, asparagus, cucumber, parsley, melon, buttered toast, M-L	**Grauburgunder,** *Baden-Württemberg, Germany*; dry, full, vegetal, floral, fruity, nutty, dairy, honeysuckle, citrus, pear, pineapple, melon, almond, butter, M
Gyokuro, *Fujieda, Shizuoka, Japan*; smooth, rich, ends bright and dry, umami, sweet, vegetal, herbaceous, mineral, animal, fruity, dairy, maritime; grass, spinach, courgette, cucumber, parsley, sage, beef stock, honeydew melon, butter, shell food, seaweed, L-XL	**Cortese,** *Piedmont, N-Italy*; smooth and dry, bright, fruity, maritime, herbal, nutty, red apple, lemon, honeydew melon, shell food, grassy, almond, L

GREEN TEA	
Tea varieties	Grape varieties
JAPAN	
Kabusecha, *Wazuka, Kyôto prefecture, Japan*; smooth, round, rich, mellow, umami, sweet, vegetal, herbaceous, fruity, dairy, maritime; fennel, spinach, braised courgette, dill, honeydew melon, peach, butter, seaweed, oyster, L-XL	**Chardonnay,** *Meursault, France*; oaked, smooth and dry, creamy, dairy, fruity, nutty, floral, spices, sweets, vegetal; butter, cream, pear, apple, nectarine, melon, citrus, pineapple, mango, peach, lime, hazelnut, wild flowers, orange-blossom, vanilla, clove, cinnamon, L
KOREA	
Woojeoncha, *Jeju, Korea*; smooth, ends a bit dry, rich, creamy, sweet, umami, vegetal, fruity, nutty, dairy, mineral, maritime; spinach, cabbage, cucumber, wood, citrus, honeydew melon, hazelnut, butter, rock, seaweed, M	**Chenin Blanc,** *Stellenbosch, Helderberg, South Africa*; smooth, dry, round, fruity, vegetal, sweets, mineral, yellow apple, passion fruit, persimmon, citrus, hay, white cabbage, honey, ginger, honeydew melon, rock, M
VIETNAM	
Snow Shan Green, *Ban Lien, Lao Cai, N-Vietnam*; neutral to dry, bright, sweet, umami, bitter, fruity, floral, vegetal, herbaceous, mineral; grapes, gooseberry, lychee, wild flowers, kale, green bell pepper, sage, cedar wood, flint, M-L	**Sauvignon Blanc,** *Loire, France*; dry, bright, fruity, vegetal, herbaceous, floral, mineral; citrus, gooseberry, honeydew melon, green bell pepper, asparagus, grass, nettle, elderflower, flint, M

YELLOW TEA	
CHINA	
Mo Gan Huang Ya, *Mo Gan Shan, Zhejiang Province, China*; neutral, neutral, sweet, bitter, floral, mineral, earthy, sweets, vegetal, nutty; honeysuckle, beeswax, hay, sandalwood, honey, sweet corn, hazelnut, M	**Marsanne,** *N-Rhône, France*; smooth, bright, fruity, floral, sweets, mineral, nutty; tropical fruit, honeysuckle, tropical wood, honey, beeswax, hazelnut, M-L
Huo Shan Huang Ya, *Huo Shan County, Anhui Province, China*; smooth, bright, sweet, sour, umami, vegetal, fruity, earthy, grains, nutty, mineral; sweet corn, chestnut, steamed carrot, red apple, pear, chocolate, honey, hay, toasted oats, hazelnut, beeswax, M	**Chardonnay,** *Alto Adige, Italy*; oaked, dry, full, dairy, fruity, nutty, mineral, sweets, creamy, butter, aged, honey, peach, hazelnut, vanilla, citrus, beeswax, L
Huang Da Cha, *Jinzhai County, Anhui Province, China*; smooth, ends dry, rich, sweet, umami, vegetal, earthy, fruity, grains, nutty, sweets; spinach, hay, buttered toast with strawberry jam, charcoal, hazelnut, caramel, chocolate, M	**Blanc de Blancs,** *Chardonnay, Napa Valley, California, USA*; oaked and aged, full, smooth, rich, dairy, fruity, nutty, grains; butter, baked apple, roasted hazelnuts, buttered toast, M-L
Jun Shan Yin Zhen, *Jun Shan, Hunan, China*; smooth, rich, ends bright, sweet, vegetal, floral, herbaceous, fruity, sweets; hay, chestnut, chamomile, honeysuckle, tarragon, eucalyptus, honeydew melon, muscatel grape, honey, M	**Chardonnay,** *Willamette Valley, Oregon, USA*; oaked, dry and smooth, rich, fruity, buttery, floral, nutty, vegetal, herbaceous; honeydew melon, apricot, peach, pear, yellow apple, buttered toast, chamomile, lily, honeysuckle, rose, hay, fresh tarragon, olive oil, L

LIGHT OOLONG	
Tea varieties	Grape varieties
TAIWAN	
Wen Shan Baozhong, *Taipei County, Taiwan*; smooth and dry, rich and bright, sweet, slightly bitter, dairy, floral, fruity, vegetal, herbaceous, grains, nutty, spices; butter, rose, honeysuckle, citrus, peach, lychee, grass, coriander, mint, cookies, almond, ginger, M	**Gewurztraminer,** *Alsace, France*; off-dry, smooth and dry, rich and bright, floral, fruity, spices; rose, honeysuckle, lychee, peach, pepper, ginger, cardamom, M
Si Ji Chun, *Nantou, Taiwan*; smooth, rich and bright, sweet, bitter, a bit sour, floral, herbaceous, vegetal, sweets, fruity, nuts, dairy; honeysuckle, jasmine, coriander, snow pea, vanilla, caramel, citrus, nectarine, melon, coconut, almond, cream, butter, M	**Riesling,** *Washington State, USA*; off-dry, floral, fruity, mineral; jasmine, citrus, apple, peach, melon, beeswax, flint, M
Qing Xin, *Li Shan, Taiwan*; smooth and dry, rich and bright, sweet, bitter, floral, vegetal, dairy, herbaceous, fruity, sweets; hyacinth, rose, orchid, hay, cucumber, butter, coriander, peach, red apple, pear, honey, M	**Chenin Blanc,** *Stellenbosch, Helderberg, South Africa*; smooth, dry, round, fruity, vegetal, sweets, mineral; yellow apple, passion fruit, persimmon, citrus, hay, white cabbage, honey, ginger, honeydew melon, rock, M
Jin Xuan #12, *Alishan, Taiwan*; smooth, silky, rich, sweet, slightly bitter, dairy, floral, fruity, vegetal, herbaceous; butter, cream, custard, vanilla, lily, orchid, honeysuckle, gardenia, peach, pear, apple, apricot, grass, broccoli, oregano, M-L	**Chardonnay,** *Mendocino, California, U.S.A*; oaked, aged, dry and smooth, rich, fruity, dairy, grains, floral, nutty, vegetal, herbaceous; apricot, peach, pear, yellow apple, buttered brioche toast, honeysuckle, lily, sage, L
Dong Ding, *Mei Shan, Nantou, Taiwan*; smooth and dry, rich and bright, sweet, slightly bitter, nutty, mineral, floral, sweets, vegetal, herbaceous, fruity, dairy; hazelnuts, toast, smoke, orchid, gardenia, vanilla, honey, yam, mint, peach, melon, cream, butter, M-L	**Pinot Gris,** *Alsace, France, oaked*; off dry; smooth and dry, rich and bright, fruity, floral, mineral, sweets, nutty, spices, dairy; pear, apricot, peach, melon, honeysuckle, gravel, smoke, honey, vanilla, almond, clove, cinnamon, ginger, butter, M-L
CHINA	
Tie Guan Yin, *light roast, Anxi, China*; smooth and dry, bright, sweet, sour, bitter, floral, vegetal, herbaceous, fruity, mineral, metallic; orchid, gardenia, rose, grass, green bean, broccoli, mint, green apple, red fruit, citrus, apricot, wood, camphor, silver, M	**Sauvignon Blanc,** *Pouilly Fumé, Loire Valley, France*; dry, crisp, bright, fruity, floral, herbaceous, vegetal, mineral; gooseberry, citrus, green apple, melon, elderflower, iris, fresh herbs, asparagus, grass, green bean, flint, M
DARK OOLONG	
TAIWAN	
Dong Fang Mei Ren, *Hsinchu County, Taiwan*; sweet, smooth, ends a bit dry, rich, sweets, floral, fruity, earthy, mineral, spices; honey, elderflower, rose, geranium, grapes, red currant, citrus, apricot, lychee, wood, rock, cinnamon, M	**Cserszegi Fűszeres,** *Hungary*; dry to off-dry, smooth, rich, fruity, floral, mineral, spices, grape, peach, lychee, elderflower, rose, rock, white pepper, M

DARK OOLONG	
Tea varieties	Grape varieties
TAIWAN	
Tie Guan Yin, *heavy roast, Longten, Taiwan;* smooth, rich, a bit bright, sweet, bitter, fruity, sweets, earthy, grains, floral, nutty, spices; cherry, plum, stone fruit, red apple, dried fruit, pear, honey, caramel, dark wood, smoke, toast, cinnamon, L	**Aglianico,** *Campania, Italy;* aged; full, smooth, rich, fruity, mineral, animal, earthy, spices; red cherry, plum, dried fig, smoke, game, leather, cacao, cedar wood, mushroom, pepper, cinnamon, L
CHINA	
Mi Lan Xiang Feng Huang Dan Cong, *Chaozhou, Guangdong province, China;* smooth, ends a bit dry, rich, sweet, umami, fruity, vegetal, floral, earthy, grains, sweets; pear, dried apricot, raisins, plum, yam, orchid, honeysuckle, cocoa, licorice, wood, toast, honey, M-L	**Bobal,** *Valencia, Spain;* soft, smooth, rich, fruity, sweets, earthy, blackberry, cherry, pomegranate, licorice, cocoa, wood, M
Da Hong Pao, *Wuyi Shan, Fujian, China;* smooth, ends a bit dry, rich, sweet, sour, umami, fruity, floral, sweets, earthy, herbaceous, grains, nutty, spices, mineral; peach, prune, orchid, caramel, cacao, tobacco, sandalwood, pine, bread, hazelnut, cinnamon, clove, rock, L-XL	**Touriga Nacional,** *Douro Valley, Portugal;* oak aged; full, bold, lush, dry, rich, fruity, floral, sweets, herbaceous, earthy, spices, mineral, plum, prune, blueberry, violet, vanilla, licorice, toasted marshmallow, mint, cocoa, nutmeg, cinnamon, wet slate, gravel, L-XL

BLACK TEA	
INDIA AND NEPAL	
Darjeeling, *first flush, Darjeeling, India;* dry, bright, crisp, sweet, bitter, fruity, sweets, grains, vegetal, herbaceous, floral; muscatel grape, pear, vanilla, brioche, asparagus, freshly cut grass, mint, coriander, wild flowers, pink rose, S-M	**Torrontés Riojano,** *Calchaqui Valleys, N-Argentina;* smooth, neutral to dry, sweet, fruity, floral; apricot, peach, melon, honey, lily, white flowers, rose, S
Nepalese black, *first flush, Hile, Dhankuta, Nepal;* smooth and dry, bright, crisp, sweet, slightly sour, fruity, sweets, earthy, nutty, floral; muscatel grape, pear, citrus, honey, woody, hay, hazelnut, field flowers, orange blossom, M	**Muscat d'Alsace,** *France;* dry, bright, fruity, floral; citrus, grape, pear, orange blossom, M
Darjeeling, *second flush, Darjeeling, India;* neutral-dry, bright, crisp, floral, fruity, herbaceous, spices, orange blossom, muscatel grapes, yellow plum, citrus, wood, cinnamon, clove, M-L	**Gewürztraminer,** *Pfalz, Germany;* dry, bright, fruity, floral, spices; lychee, citrus, mango, melon, rose, ginger, cinnamon, clove, M-L
Nilgiri, *Blue Mountains, India;* smooth, bright, sweet, fruity, floral, earthy, mineral, spices; raisins, red fruit, blackberry, fig, plum, orchid, wood, soil, rock, cinnamon, M	**Gamay,** *Fleurie, France;* light, off-dry, bright, floral, fruity, earthy, spices, violet, iris, peony, rose, strawberry, raspberry, cherry, plum, black currant, soil, granite, cardamom, cinnamon, vanilla, M

BLACK TEA	
Tea varieties	Grape varieties
INDIA AND NEPAL	
Nepalese Imperial Black, *second flush, Hile, Dhankuta, Nepal;* smooth, rich and bright, umami, sweet, fruity, grains, sweets, spices, earthy, vegetal; citrus, strawberry, grapes, toast, honey, milk chocolate, cinnamon, clove, wood, pumpkin, yam, bell pepper, M-L	**Merlot,** *Mendoza, Argentina;* dry, rich, fruity, earthy, spices, vegetal, blackberry, raspberry, strawberry, plum, cherry, chocolate, cedar wood, clove, green bell pepper, M
Assam, *second flush, Assam, India;* dry, rich, robust, bold, sweet, bitter, umami, fruity, grains, sweets, earthy, animal, spices, herbaceous; raisins, citrus, toast, honey, cedar wood, malt, soil, leather, clove, oregano, XL	**Tempranillo,** *Rioja Reserva, Spain;* oak, dry, rich, fruity, sweets, earthy, animal, herbaceous; cherry, fig, red fruit, vanilla, cedar wood, tobacco, leather, dill, XL
CHINA	
Lapsang Souchong, *unsmoked, Wuyishan, Fujian, China;* smooth, rich, sweet, umami, vegetal, mineral, earthy, sweets, fruity, floral; yam, pebbles, pine wood, mushroom, honey, molasses, chocolate, plum, lychee, orchid, rose, M-L	**Merlot,** *Margaret River, Australia;* dry, rich, fruity, earthy, spices, sweets, cherry, red currant, blackberry, plum, cedar wood, bay leaf, vanilla, chocolate, dried herbs, M
Dian Hong, *Yunnan, China;* smooth, rich, sweet, umami, earthy, sweets, fruity, nutty, spices; wood, malt, honey, molasses, raisins, black currant, black plum, dried apricot, a hint of citrus, walnut, clove, L	**Pinotage,** *Stellenbosch, South Africa;* aged, dry, bold, full, rich, earthy; fruity, spices; wood, sweet pipe tobacco, dry earth, oak, cedar, licorice, smoke, black plum, blackberry, raspberry, rooibos, coffee, clove, XL
Keemun, *Qimen County, China;* smooth, ends a bit dry, rich, sweet, umami, fruity, floral, grains, animal, sweets, earthy; stone fruit, dried fruit, cherry, orchid, rose, chocolate, toast, leather, malt, smoke, L	**Zinfandel,** *Paso Robles, California;* smooth, rich, round, juicy, fruity, spices, sweets, vegetal, earthy; black cherry, plum, raspberry, strawberry jam, yellow raisin, violets, pepper, vanilla, chocolate, fennel, cigar, oak, smoke, XL
Lapsang Souchong, *smoked, Wuyishan, Fujian, China;* smooth, rich, umami, sweet, bold, robust, mineral, earthy, sweets, fruity; smoked pine, charcoal, resin, rock, incense, tar, dark chocolate, dried fruit, brandy, XL	**Shiraz,** *Valle del Elqui, Chile;* dry, rich, fruity, spices, earthy, animal, sweets, mineral; red fruit, black cherry, pepper, vanilla, coffee, licorice, smoke, meaty, chocolate, flint, XL
SRI LANKA	
Ceylon Nuwara Eliya, *Sri Lanka;* dry to astringent, brisk, bright, sour, fruity, earthy, herbaceous, spices; citrus, plum, peach, raisins, cedar wood, soil, mint, eucalyptus, clove, M	**Cinsault,** *Provence, France;* dry, bright, slightly saline, clean, floral, fruity, spices, smoke, violets, red fruit, citrus, peach, pepper, cinnamon, clove, cardamom, M
Ceylon Pusselawa, *Sri Lanka;* a bit smooth, dry, bright, sour, bitter, floral, fruity, earthy; rose, citrus, plum, malt, wood, M-L	**Malbec,** *Cahors, France;* dry, bright, floral, fruity, spices, earthy, rose, plum, red cherry, raspberry, blueberry, anise, M

BLACK TEA	
Tea varieties	Grape varieties
SRI LANKA	
Ceylon Uva, *Sri Lanka*; smooth and dry, mellow, bright, sweet, sour, herbaceous, fruity, earthy; plum, honey, eucalyptus, mint, citrus, pine wood, tobacco, camphor, malt, L-XL	**Cabernet Sauvignon,** *Coonawarra, S- Australia*; dry, bright and rich, fruity, herbaceous, earthy; black fruit, dried fruit, eucalyptus, mint, cedar wood, licorice, mushroom, tobacco, XL
KENIA	
Kericho, *Western Highlands, Kenia*; dry, slightly astringent, bright, sour, sweet, bitter, earthy, vegetal, sweets, fruity; exotic wood, fennel, chocolate, citrus, red fruit, malt, L	**Zinfandel,** *Paso Robles, California*; smooth, rich, round, juicy, fruity, spices, sweets, vegetal, earthy; black cherry, plum, raspberry, strawberry jam, yellow raisin, violets, pepper, vanilla, chocolate, fennel, cigar, oak, smoke, XL
MALAWI	
Satemwa Black, *Shire Highlands Malawi*; rich, smooth and dry, robust, sour, bitter, umami, earthy, fruity, spices; malt, wet leaves, cacao, citrus, orange, dried fruit, pepper, XL	**Blaufränkisch,** *Austria*; dry, rich, fruity, sweets, earthy, spices; black cherry, blackberry, dark chocolate, wet soil, pepper, cardamom, XL
TAIWAN	
Ruby #18, *Sun Moon Lake, Nantou County, Taiwan*; smooth, rich, sweet, earthy, herbaceous, fruity, sweets, spices; exotic wood, mint, plum, peach, honey, cinnamon, M	**Pinot Gris,** *Germany*; neutral to dry, neutral to bright, full, fruity, floral, sweets, spices; lychee, peach, red apple, pear, lily of the valley, white flowers, honeysuckle, honey, cinnamon, M-L
Honey Black #13, *Nantou County, Taiwan*; smooth, rich, sweet, fruity, sweets; lychee, plum, honey, chocolate, M	**Tinta Negra Mole,** *Madeira, Portugal*; smooth, rich, sweet, fruity; honey, jam, wood, caramel, black fruit, M
JAPAN	
Benifûki Wakoucha, *Takachiho, Japan*; rich, smooth, later dry, sweet, umami, floral, fruity, grains, earthy, mineral; orchid, orange blossom, peach, grapes, red fruit, cherry, barley, baked oats, cedar wood, oak, resin, L-XL	**Cabernet Sauvignon,** *Napa Valley, California*; dry, rich, fruity, herbaceous, earthy, mineral, floral, spices; blackberry, strawberry, cherry, black currant, plum, dried fruit, graphite, cedar wood, oak, tobacco, licorice, sage, violet, cinnamon, clove, XL

POST-FERMENTED TEA	
CHINA	
Sheng (raw) Pu Erh, *Lincang, Yunnan Province, China*; aged: neutral to smooth, rich and bright, sweet, sour, bitter, umami, earthy, vegetal, animal, herbaceous, spices, floral, fruity; hay, wood, forest leaves, pipe tobacco, mushrooms, stable, sage, mint, eucalyptus, pepper, citrus, stewed apple, M-L	**Pinot Noir,** *Mendocino County, California, U.S.A*; dry, austere, rich, fruity, floral, herbaceous, earthy, cherry, violet, oak, mushroom, licorice, wet leaves, tobacco, clove, vanilla, caramel, L-XL

POST-FERMENTED TEA	
Tea varieties	Grape varieties
CHINA	
Shu (cooked) Pu Erh, *Yunnan Province, China;* smooth, round, rich, sweet, umami, earthy, animal, sweets, vegetal; henna, moss, clay, wet leaves, stable, tobacco, caramel, molasses, wood, L-XL	**Mourvèdre,** *Bandol, France;* full, dry, rich, strong, fruity, earthy, spices, animal; blackberry, red berries, red plum, olives, farmyard, tobacco, pepper, wild game, XL
JAPAN	
Goishicha, *Otoyo town, Kochi Prefecture, Japan;* dry to neutral, rich and bright, sour, umami, sweet, dairy, animal, earthy, fruity, vegetal, herbaceous; buttermilk, yoghurt, goat stable, straw, soil, balsamic vinegar, sour cherry, citrus, dried fruit, sour plum, purslane, lemongrass, verbena, M-L	**Sangiovese,** *Tuscany, Italy;* dry, medium to full, acidic, fruity, vegetal, herbaceous, earthy; sour cherry, plum, red fruit, roasted tomato, oregano, coffee, sweet balsamic, leather, L-XL

PRESSED WHITE TEA, AGED IN A DRIED MANDARIN

CHAPTER 2

The basics

Not everything we call "tea" is actually "tea". Tea is made of the leaves or stems of the tea plant: the *Camellia sinensis*. If it is not made from the *Camellia sinensis* plant, then it is not a tea but an herbal infusion. The French have a separate name for this: tisane, making the distinction between tea and herbal infusion. In English, we call it herbal tea, but strictly speaking, this is not the correct term because there is no *Camellia sinensis* in it.

For example, rooibos does not come from *Camellia sinensis* and therefore is not tea, but an herbal infusion.

The same applies to rose hip, fennel, mint, nettle and verbena, among others. Furtermore, tea always contains caffeine (theine), while an infusion does not. Three exceptions to this rule are yerba maté, guayusa and Guaraná, as these three herbal infusions do contain caffeine and quite a lot of it at that.

THE DIFFERENT FAMILY MEMBERS OF THE CAMELLIA SINENSIS

The tea plant has two main varieties:
- *Camellia sinensis sinensis*
- *Camellia sinensis assamica*

The genealogy of plants can be determined on a molecular and even genetic level. Scientists have discovered several other varieties belonging to the Camellia Theaceae family, amongst them:
- *Camellia cambodia* (no western name as yet, contains caffeine)
- *Camellia taliensis* ("Purple Buds"; low in caffeine)
- *Camellia ptilophylla* (no caffeine)
- *Camellia crassicolumna* (Hongyacha in Chinese; Yabao in the West; no caffeine)

The last three examples on the list contain practically no caffeine, a fact which puzzles scientists, as caffeine is the natural pesticide of *Camellia Theaceae* plants and is important for its survival.

Since these three types are not as yet being commercially exploited and are still being intensively studied, this book focuses on the two types of tea that have been used for hundreds, if not thousands, of years.

CAMELLIA SINENSIS SINENSIS

In the wild, the *Camellia sinensis sinensis* plant can grow up to four meters high, but on plantations it is kept small, about 1 meter high. This, of course, makes plucking the leaves much easier than from a ladder high up in a tree. Additionally, a plant needs a lot of energy for its trunk and branches to grow. If a tea plant's height is kept low, more of its energy will be used for the leaves, which means more leaves and a higher yield.

Westerners call this family by its Latin name, *sinensis* (which means "Chinese"), while the Chinese call it *Cháhuá*, which means "tea flower." This is confusing, because tea is always made from the leaves and stems of the plant, never from the flowers, but maybe the name tea flower is meant in a poetical sense.

The sinensis variety has small, soft leaves and a fine, complex aroma and it thrives most comfortably in a temperate climate, preferably high up in the mountains, between 600 and 2,500 meters altitude.

CAMELLIA SINENSIS ASSAMICA

The *assamica* variety can grow up to 20 meters in the wild and thrives best in tropical climate. Its towering height makes plucking leaves even more difficult, so the *sinensis assamica* is usually kept short as well, up to one meter.

The Chinese call this variety *Da Ye*, which means "big leaf". And the name says it all, as the *sinensis assamica* has much larger, coarser,

YABAO TEA

thicker and tougher leaves than *sinensis sinensis*. It is more robust, and in general more resistent to plagues and insects than *sinensis sinensis*.

The varieties *Camellia sinensis sinensis* and *Camellia sinensis assamica* are often crossbred, in order to produce hybrid plants with specific desirable characteristics, like higher yield, a stronger immune system, easier pluck, and a specific flavor profile.

CONDITIONS FOR A HEALTHY TEA PLANT
In general, the *Camellia sinensis* plant thrives under the following conditions:
- Rainfall: 125 - 250 cm (49.2 - 98.4 inches) per year
- Level of humidity in the air: 75 - 85%
- Temperature: averagely 18 - 25°C (64 - 77°F) during the growing season. Some cultivars and varieties are frost and drought resistant
- Soil: rich, airy, preferably loam
- pH value of the soil: quite acidic: 5 - 6.5
- Altitude: preferably a minimum of 600 m (~ 2,000 ft), though exceptions do exist

TEA GARDENS AROUND THE WORLD
There are thriving tea gardens to be found in not so obvious countries with very different conditions than those in the classic tea countries; England, Scotland, the Netherlands, France, Switzerland, Italy, Portugal, Georgia, USA and New Zealand, to name a few. Especially the one in the Netherlands seems odd, as the Netherlands lie below sea level. Where does the preferred minimum of 600 m (~ 2,000 ft) altitude fit in there? Yet the tea produced by Dutch tea garden *Het Zuyderblad*, is of an exceptionally good quality. The same goes for various tea gardens situated near a coastline all over the world; for example, Oritaen tea garden, located on the southern coast of Kyushu island, Japan. The garden lies 100 meters above sea level and produces excellent teas. This indicates that lots of rain and good soil are of greater importance to the *Camellia* plant than altitude.
From the two *Camellia* varieties and their many, many cross breeds, six main types of tea may be produced:

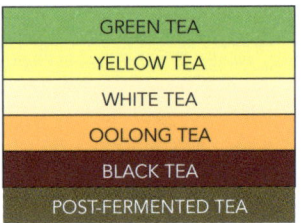

These names refer to the processing of the tea leaf. Tea leaves are always green on the tree or bush. You will find an extensive explanation of the production of these six tea types in chapter 12. All six have their own specific characteristics, flavors and steeping methods. Read more about all this on pages 276 - 281.

Pu-Erh is the best known of the post-fermented teas, so I will use that name throughout the book. Pu-Erh is always post-fermented, but not all post-fermented tea comes from Pu-Erh, which is the town and surrounding areas where this type of tea originates from in Yunnan, China. Compare this to the name champagne: not all sparkling wine is champagne, but champagne is always sparkling and always comes from the Champagne area in France.

BASIC KNOWLEDGE OF TEA
After water, tea is the most popular drink in the world, and people have been drinking (and eating) tea for thousands of years. It is rather strange that in the West, where tea is known since the 17th century, we still do not know how to steep it properly. It is simply taken for granted, and no one seems to care what it tastes like. Have tea with breakfast or in the afternoon, add lots of milk and sugar, dip a biscuit in it and gulp it down or drink it when ill. That is what tea is for most people — a missed opportunity of gigantic proportion. Tea actually has lots more to offer with its myriad of different flavors, as you can also cook with it, combine it with savory or sweet food, drink it hot or cold and mix it with other ingredients in cocktails, ice tea and other cold drinks.

Tea has the ability to amaze and overwhelm, bring pleasure, calmness and focus; most importantly, tea has many different flavors and aromas, and by flavors I do not mean melon, strawberry or forest fruit; I mean the innate flavors of tea itself. To allow all these wonderful flavors to release themselves, it is absolutely essential to know how to steep tea properly. Without basic steeping knowledge, a major amount of the complexity of tea is lost.
So, that is where we shall start, with the basics.

HOW TO STEEP TEA PROPERLY?
- Use the right water
- Get the temperature right
- Use the appropriate amount of dry tea
- Steep for a sufficient time

This may sound more complicated than it actually is. If you think about it, you also serve wine from a correctly opened bottle, at the right temperature, in a proper glass, and poured at the right level. It is just a matter of knowing the basics and acting on that knowledge. Okay, you will need to practice, but if you do so regularly, you will soon be steeping a perfect cup of tea without having to think twice. Just like riding a bike.

THE RIGHT WATER
Tea is 99.9 percent water. It is therefore essential that the water is fresh and of good quality, meaning soft and with a neutral pH level. Cold tap water might be safe to drink, but it is usually hard. How hard, that depends on the soil composition which varies by area. Sandy soil, for example, has softer groundwater than lime-rich soil. The harder the water, the more dramatic its effect on the taste of hot tea (or coffee). Another devastating effect on its flavor is caused by the level of alkalinity. Soft, neutral tasting water brings out the beautiful flavors in tea. Later on in this book the chemical side of water is explained more extensively. For now, I will only focus on what will happen with tea if you prepare it with the wrong kind of water.

THE HARDNESS OF WATER
When water is heated to 65°C (149°F) or higher, which is usually the case when making tea, limestone is created: magnesium and calcium will clump together and thus form the infamous limescale in taps, irons, kettles and coffee machines. The calcium and magnesium ions like to cling to anything that is in their path: the walls of the boiler, for example, but also the essential oils in the tea leaf. This inhibits the fine aromas of tea to release themselves, as they are stuck to those ions.
The effect on tea is this:
- an unpleasant smell
- while tea is cooling off, a murky film develops at the surface
- hard water that has not been boiled causes scum on tea
- brown stains stick to the insides of cups, glasses, and teapot
- the tea gets dark and cloudy very quickly
- hard water brings a flat, bitter, and sometimes even soapy flavor

> So, if you get served a cup of tea that looks cloudy and dark, tastes flat and leaves a thick brown ring in the cup, then rest assured that it is not the tea that is bad, but the water.
>
> Filtered water does not need to be brought to the boil first. It will remain bright and clear, because there is too little calcium in it to cause foam and turbidity.

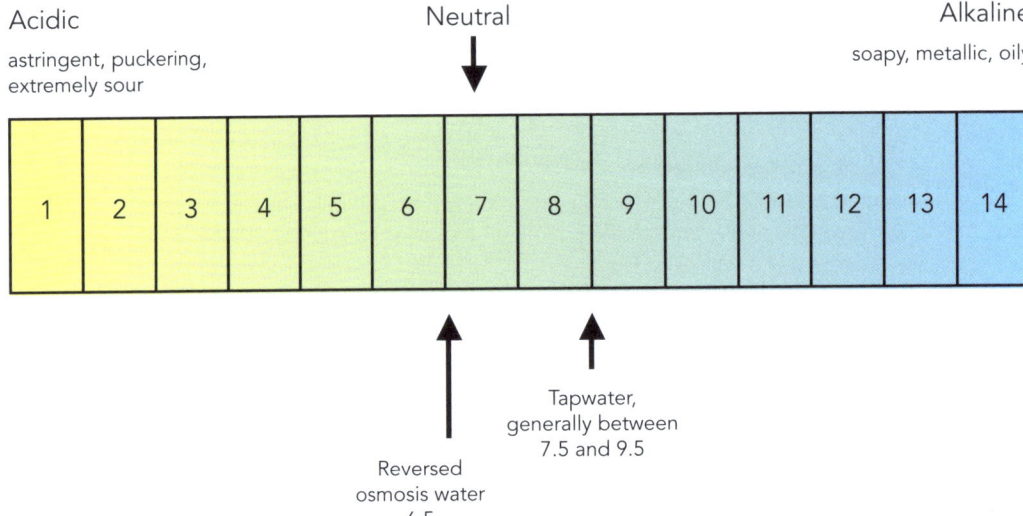

PH VALUE

Another vital factor for the taste of tea is the pH value; this is the level of acidity in the water, or the concentration of acid or hydrogen ions (H^+) versus the level of alkalinity. HCO_3 is the bicarbonate ion and is the main alkaline factor in water. This ion is able to neutralize free acid ions and as such makes the water less acidic, more alkaline.

For a good tasting tea you want the pH value to be as neutral as possible, because alkalinity can cause a bitter, soapy, salty, and sometimes metallic, unclean and greasy taste. The higher the number of the pH value, 7 and up, the more alkaline the water (Less H+), the lower that number, 6 or less, the more acidic the water (More H+). pH value is measured on a scale of 0 - 14, with 7 representing neutral. If the number is higher than 7, the water will taste alkaline and if it is lower than 7, the water will taste acidic.

Heating makes water more alkaline, because the acidic component in the water, CO_2, evaporates. This has an impact on the taste of the tea. Cold water with a pH value of 6.5 becomes 7 when boiled: the ideal level for tea, because it is neutral. Unfortunately, most tap water has a pH value of 8 or higher.

TAP WATER AND TEA

Every country has its own way of grading its tap water. In Germany and the Netherlands, the values are given in Degrees German (°D). In the UK in Degrees English (°E) and in France in Degrees French (°f). In the US they measure in PPM and GPG. As all these systems have different values, it is impossible to advise you on the hardness of the water in your area. Check with your local water supplier and do not forget to ask about the pH value of your tap water!

FILTERED WATER

So now you know that tap water is almost never soft, but most bottled water is not either, although there are some exceptions to the rule. The best and cheapest solution to obtain filtered water for your tea is by means of a good quality water filter. There are several options. It is important to choose the right one because there is a lot of difference in the end result. How soft does the water become, and what about the alkalinity after filtering? On the next page you will find a number of possibilities.

SOFTENING WATER

If you descale your water with an ion exchanger, it is important to know which one is suitable for tea and which one is not.

THE SALT SOFTENER

This type of ion exchanger is often used in areas with very hard water and is connected to the pipe through which the water enters the house. This type of softener works with salt: sodium. It exchanges sodium ions with calcium and magnesium ions. As a result, you do not get limescale in the water when heated above 65°C (149°F). Perfect for keeping your household machines and tiles free of limescale, but this water is not suitable for tea at all. Although it looks clear enough because there is no calcium in the water to cause cloudiness, the added salts (sodium, or Na) have turned the filtered water more alkaline. Heating increases this alkalinity even more, with the result that the tea still tastes flat and soapy, sometimes even metallic or musty.

THE HYDROGEN SOFTENER

This type of softener is placed close to the tap where the filtered water should come from because this is only used for softening water that is meant for coffee, tea and possibly for cooking vegetables. A good example is a 4-step filter which has the following features:
- an ion exchanger that exchanges calcium and magnesium ions against hydrogen (H+)
- a carbon filter
- coarse particle filtration
- and a very fine-grained end filter

Bonus: this system also has an adjustable bypass for the perfect adjustment for the desired hardness.

The advantage of this method is that not only the amount of calcium and magnesium is reduced, but that the hydrogen also causes the alkalinity to be reduced. H+ (hydrogen) is self-acidic.

Not all calcium and magnesium ions disappear with this filtering method, which is less of a problem than using water with a high level of alkalinity. A little bit of calcium and magnesium sometimes improves certain teas, especially some light oolongs.

FILTER JUG

If you do not want to go that far, you can get by with a water filter jug. It is very important to pick one with the appropriate kind of filter, as not all filters produce water that is suitable for tea. The best filters contain both an H+ ion exchanger and a carbon filter, ensuring the removal of chlorine and other flavor and odor-disrupting substances.

THE REVERSE OSMOSIS FILTER SYSTEM

This method provides the cleanest and softest water, this is how it works:
- Water is pressed under high pressure by a particularly fine-mesh membrane.
- Solids, hydrogen carbonate (HCO_3), organic substances, viruses and bacteria dissolved in the water do not get through the membrane.
- CO_2 however is a gas and does pass the membrane, making the water less alkaline by adding its H+.
- These residues are separated from the clean water after filtering.
- The dirty water is discharged into the drain.
- The clean water is diverted to the tap.

There are large reverse osmosis systems for sale that are suitable for the catering industry. For domestic use, there are smaller systems that fit in your kitchen cabinet or on your kitchen counter. They are for sale at specialty stores.

SOFT WATER   TAP WATER   COFFEE MACHINE WATER

BOTTLED WATER

If you prefer using mineral water, always take a close look at the label before you buy.
Read the levels of calcium (Ca), magnesium (Mg) and hydrogen carbonate (HCO_3) carefully. The higher these levels, the worse for your tea. Look for levels of:

- Ca (calcium): 5 mg per liter or lower (0.00017 oz per 34 fl.oz)
- Mg (magnesium) 2 mg per liter or lower (0.00007 oz per 34 fl.oz)
- HCO_3 (hydrogen carbonate): 20 mg per liter or less (0.0007 oz per 34 fl.oz)

If the level of dry residue is mentioned on the label, then make sure it reads 50 mg per liter or below. (0.0017 oz per 34 fl.oz) In the appendix on page 246 you can read a more detailed explanation of what dry residue is and what it does. But even without knowing the meaning, you should remember this: the higher the dry residue level on the label, the worse the tea will taste.

Making tea with bottled water is expensive, polluting and requires a lot of lugging around. My advice: buy a good water filter.

BALANCE IS THE KEYWORD

The right balance between water hardness and the tea depends on each individual's taste. It may be that you prefer tea made with relatively or even very hard water. You may of course continue to prepare your tea that way, because one cannot argue about taste. But it cannot do any harm either to experiment with other hardnesses to expand your taste library. For example by doing the tests with water and tea that are in this book on page 43. If that is not your cup of tea, too nerdy maybe, but you do not exactly like tea made with hard water either, then just stick to filtered water with a neutral pH level and your tea will be fine.

WATER TEMPERATURE

So, as you have learned above, using the right water is the most important thing for the taste of a cup of tea, with the ideal being soft, water with a pH value of 6 - 6.5.

But there is more to a good tasting cup of tea than just the water. The temperature of the water in combination with the steeping time is also essential. The right water temperature for tea depends on the type of tea you are using. Black tea handles high temperatures very well, but green tea becomes bitter when steeped with water that is too hot. If you steep green tea for only a few seconds, then boiling or very hot water is possible. In that case you will need to use a higher dosage of tea leaves and much less water, or else the tea will taste too thin.

This is the Eastern way of tea steeping. More about this on page 39.

HOW TO GET THE RIGHT TEMPERATURE FOR YOUR TEA

You will find kettles on the market with different temperature settings. My advice to you is: look for the best quality appliance. The lower-cost variants often deviate in the temperature they reach as soon as you put less than a liter in the boiling pot, and can vary with around ten degrees difference or even more. Good kettles will heat the water to the exact degree. These do not come cheap, but are worth every penny. Some slightly lower-cost kettles have temperature intervals of 5°C (4°F), and that works fine too.

If you do not want to invest in a kettle with different temperature options, you could also try the following suggestions:

BOILING AND SUBSEQUENTLY COOLING WATER FOR TEA

- Bring a liter (34 fl.oz) of soft and fresh* water to the boil.
- Use two teapots.
- As soon as large bubbles start to form on the water surface, turn off the kettle.
- Pour the water into one of the teapots, and allow it to cool.
- As soon as the water has reached 85°C (184°F), usually after about 3 minutes, pour the water. into the other teapot, this way the temperature drops down to 80°C (176°F).

*With fresh I mean water that has not already been boiled. Many people turn on their kettle again and again, without throwing away the old water first. When water is boiled several times, it loses oxygen and therefore its vitality. On top of that, it becomes more and more alkaline, resulting in a flat and often unpleasant taste. Therefore, only ever boil the amount of water you need.

Of course, when you use half the amount of water, the timing stated above is shorter:
- Bring 500 ml (17 fl.oz) of soft and fresh water to the boil
- Use two teapots
- As soon as large bubbles start to form on the water surface, turn off the kettle
- Pour the water into one of the teapots and allow to cool
- The temperature will drop quickly to 88°C (190°F)
- After one minute of waiting, it will lower to 83°C (181°F)
- After 2 ½ minutes, it has dropped to 80°C (176°F)

1 liter (34 fl.oz)	100°C (212°F)	after 10 sec	95°C (203°F)
		after 60 sec	90°C (194°F)
		after 180 sec	85°C (185°F)

500 ml (17 fl.oz) (in a teapot of 1 liter (34 fl.oz)	100°C (212°F)	after 10 sec	90°C (194°F)
		after 70 sec	85°C (185°F)
		after 150 sec	80°C (176°F)

If the timing is too much of a hassle for you, just add cold water:
to 1 liter of boiling hot water: 200 ml (to (34 fl.oz: 6.76 fl. oz)
or for 500 ml of boiling hot water: 100 ml (17 fl.oz: 3.4 fl. oz)

Did you know that…
- …In the old days, people used to boil tea water for a long time in order to precipitate the limescale? The water did become softer and clearer, because the limescale subsided to the bottom, but because the oxygen evaporated, the water became more alkaline at the same time, resulting in a flat, soapy and greasy taste. Not to be continued, if you ask me.

- …Most mineral waters are much too hard for tasty tea? They contain a lot of minerals, which add flavor but usually also contribute to the hardness of water. Only mineral water with a dry residue level of <50 mg per liter (0.0017 oz per 34 fl.oz) is suitable for tea. This level can be found on the label.

Tip
If the resulting tea turns out too bitter, then simply adjust the temperature to make it cooler. If it tastes too flat, then use a higher temperature. Once you have found the perfect temperature to suite your palate, write it down on a piece of tape and stick it on the tea tin. That way, you will not forget it!

INTERESTING TEMPERATURE SHORT CUTS WITH GOOD RESULTS

AMBIENT BREW
Tea steeped with water at ambient temperature is another interesting way to serve tea with food. I learned this type of brewing from Timothy d'Offay's excellent book about tea, *Easy Leaf Tea*. He advises to use 12 grams (0.42 oz) of leaf tea with 750 ml (25 fl. oz) of water at room temperature for about 40 minutes or so. The only drawback for this system is, that you or your guest cannot really adjust its flavor to taste, except for adding water if they consider the tea too strong. In my opinion, some teas need an even higher amount of tea leaf when combined with food. Apart from that, tastes differ: what is too strong for one might well be too weak for another. Although Timothy's recipe definitely is very practical and efficient, I personally prefer my cold brew tea extract method, both in and out of home (see below and page 36 - 37). This method is more versatile; you can mix the extract with hot, cold, iced or sparkling water, adding extract or water to your liking.

COLD BREW
Tea can also be steeped with cold water in the fridge, but when you use this method, bear in mind that steeping time takes at least 4 hours, and ideally 8 or more. The advantage of cold brew is that the flavors have plenty of time to develop fully, without turning the tea astringent, which is often the case when tea is steeped hot, even more so when then cooling off. Bitter flavors need a very high temperature, in order to release themselves. That is the reason why green tea often tastes bitter when steeped with boiling water: the bitters are easily released and take control.
Because of the slower process, cold steeped tea has much more time to develop its innate flavors, texture and aromas. The components of a tea will release themselves at varying times, without turning the tea bitter or astringent. The taste can become very complex, although this also depends on the quality of the tea. If there is not much flavor in the tea to begin with, then you could wait forever, but it will never become complex. What is not in it to start with, cannot come out. Cold brew does not work well for tightly pressed teas, like Pu-Erh cakes. These are best steeped in hot or boiling water.

RECIPE FOR COLD BREW
The idea is, to make a very strong cold brew by pouring relatively little water over relatively a lot of tea in a jar, e.g., 500 ml (17 fl. oz) of water over 20 g (0.78 oz) of tea leaves. Close the jar firmly, label it and place in the fridge. After 8 hours, strain the liquid into another jar, or bottle.

To make tea, either hot or cold, you simply pour a bit of the tea extract into a glass or cup and add either hot or cold water to taste. This tea extract saves you a lot of last minute stress and the taste is very good. The strained extract may be kept in the fridge up to three days. However, freshly steeped tea is usually preferable, especially when done so with care and knowledge, with the best result coming from the Eastern style of steeping. However, when serving tea with food, the cold brew version is best, as it is stress-free and easier to serve, while still tasting very good. Bonus: the tea almost never becomes bitter, not even after cooling off. You could serve both the extract and the hot water separately in elegant carafes and pour the mixture for the guests, explaining to them that they can adjust the amount of tea and water to their own taste. Another way of serving is not straining the leaves at all, but showing their beauty inside the carafes. Do bear in mind that you will need a proper strainer inside the bottle, as things might turn out quite messy if leaves slip out while pouring the extract.

COLD BREW HOT TEA

Preparation cold brew
STEP 1

A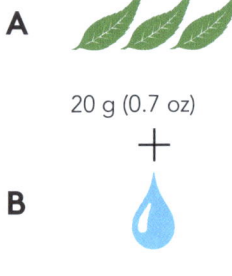

20 g (0.7 oz)

+

B

500 ml (17 fl. oz)

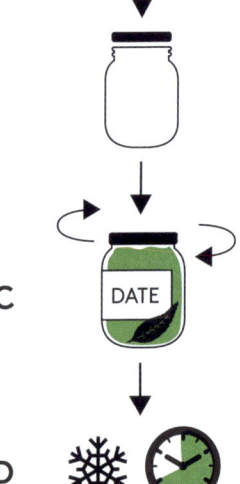

C

D

Min 6 h

STEP 2

A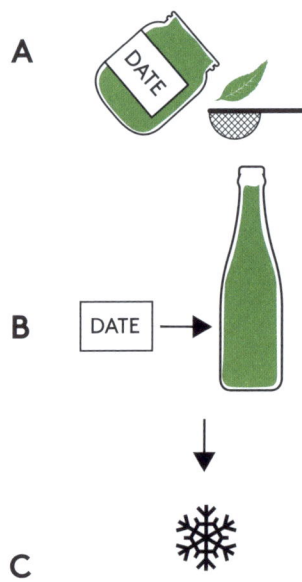

B

C

Keeps at least
10 days unopened.
After opening 3 days.

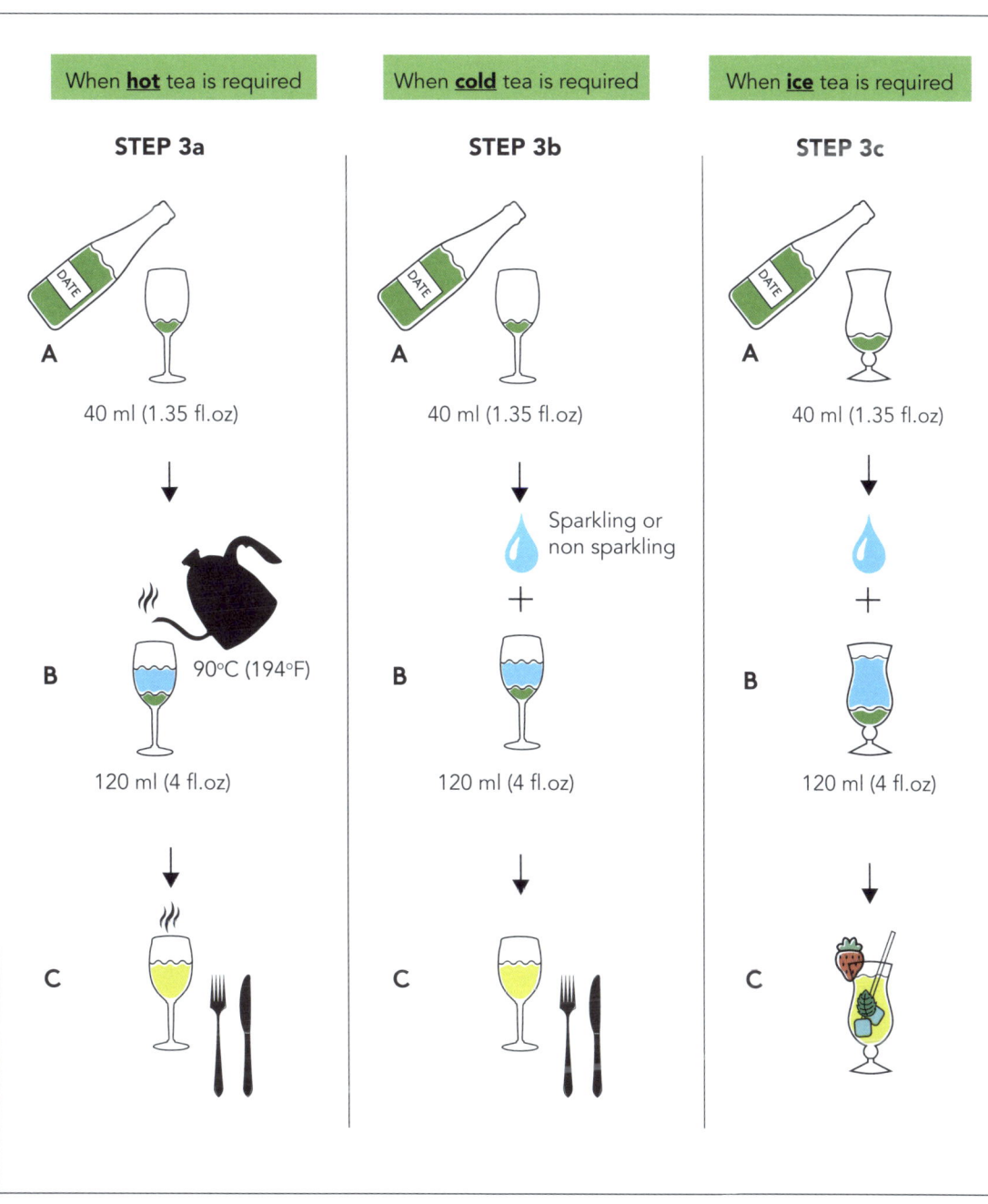

AMOUNT OF TEA AND STEEPING TIMES

How much tea to use and how long to steep your tea depends on the method of steeping. This could be the Eastern way, as is done in China, Japan, Taiwan, Korea or Thailand, or the Western way, as in Europe, India, the Americas, Africa, New Zealand and Australia.

STEEPING TEA WESTERN STYLE

The standard method uses about 10 g per liter (0.35 oz per 34 fl.oz), but tastes do differ widely. Start off with 10 g (0.35 oz) and adjust the weight to your taste if you find the tea too weak or too strong. If you work with tea bags, 10 g (0.35 oz) usually equals 5 bags. The higher the temperature, the easier it is for the bitter molecules to dissolve in the water. Movement and steeping time also lend a hand in this. If you move the tea bag through the water up and down or side to side, your tea will become bitter as the motion pushes bitter molecules out of the tea bag into the water. The combination of extended steeping time with very hot water has the same effect. If you leave the bag in the water for more than 4 minutes and squeeze the bag firmly above the cup, all the bitters are then in your cup. Do you love that? Then by all means, keep doing it. But if you prefer that your tea does to not taste bitter, try not to move the bag, use filtered water with a neutral pH value at a lower temperature and let the tea steep for no longer than 3 minutes. If you steep your tea like that, then you will soon discover that sugar and or milk is no longer necessary.

TABLE WESTERN METHOD

Tea type	Amount of water	Weight	Temperature	Time	Amount of steeps
Japanese green tea	1 L (34 fl.oz)	10 g (0.3 oz)	50 - 70°C (122 -158°F)	2 min	2
Chinese green and yellow tea	1 L (34 fl.oz)	10 g (0.3 oz)	75 - 83°C (167-181°F)	2½ min	2 - 3
White tea	1 L (34 fl.oz)	10 g (0.3 oz)	85 - 95°C (185 - 203°F)	3½ min	2 - 3
Oolong	1 L (34 fl.oz)	10 g (0.3 oz)	85 - 95°C (185 -203°F)	2½ min	2 - 3
Black tea	1 L (34 fl.oz)	10 g (0.3 oz)	85 - 95°C (185 - 203°F)	2½ min	1
Pu-Erh tea	1 L (34 fl.oz)	10 g (0.3 oz)	100°C (212°F)	2 min	3*

* Rinse twice with boiling water

> If you use tea bags, allow them to sit quietly, Do not move them around. Motion promotes bitter molecules from the tea leaf to release themselves into the water. The same applies to boiling water.

STEEPING TEA EASTERN STYLE

In countries in East Asia, a relatively high amount of tea and little water is used, with a shorter steeping time. Also, no more tea is made than will be served in one round. The tea can be steeped several times, even up to 10 times this way and tastes subtly different with each round. The Chinese name for this way of preparing and serving tea is Gong fu cha, which translates to "making tea with skill". And that is exactly what it is. The teapots and cups are small; they contain no more than three sips. Eastern style style tea drinking is not about quenching thirst, but about enjoying the taste and the many aromas of the tea. There are many different shapes and types of teapots, and each type of tea requires a different shape or material. Because the sizes of the vessels differ and each tea and region has its own recipe, giving an overview is impossible. I will only use a few examples. It is important that you should always use fresh and soft, filtered water, no matter the style of steeping you are doing.

TABLE EASTERN METHOD

Tea type	Amount of water	Weight	Temperature*	Time*	Amount of steeps
Japanese green tea	150 ml (5 fl. oz)	5 - 10 g (0.17 - 0.35 oz)	50 - 70°C (122 -158°F)	2 min - 30 sec	2 - 3
Chinese green and yellow tea	100 ml (3.4 fl.oz)	3 - 7 g (0.10-0.24 oz)	75 - 83°C (167 - 181°F)	1 min - 30 sec	3 - 4
White tea	100 ml (3.4 fl.oz)	3 - 7 g (0.10-0.24 oz)	85 - 95°C (185 - 203°F)	½ min 40 sec	4 - 8
Oolong	100 ml (3.4 fl.oz)	3 - 7 g (0.10-0.24 oz)	85 - 95°C (185 - 203°F)	1 min 40 sec	4 -10
Black tea	100 ml (3.4 fl.oz)	3 - 7 g (0.10-0.24 oz)	85 - 95°C (185 - 203°F)	½ min - 30 sec	2 - 3
Pu-Erh tea	100 ml (3.4 fl.oz)	5 g (0.17 oz)	100°C (212°F)	15 sec - 45 sec	** > 10

* The higher the temperature, the shorter the steeping time
** Rinse twice with boiling water

PU-ERH TEA

It is best to steep Pu-Erh in the Eastern style, because Pu-Erh comes into its own when you steep it multiple times. Pu-Erh should always be rinsed first. Pour boiling water over the tea and let it steep for about 10 seconds. Next, strain the tea and discard the water.

The first serving after rinsing usually has less taste than the following steeps. More flavor is released with each steep. This also applies to tea rolled into tight balls, such as Tieguanyin, Jasmine pearls or Gunpowder. The leaf must first unfold in order to be able to release its aromas and flavors.

STEEPING TEA WESTERN STYLE VERSUS EASTERN STYLE

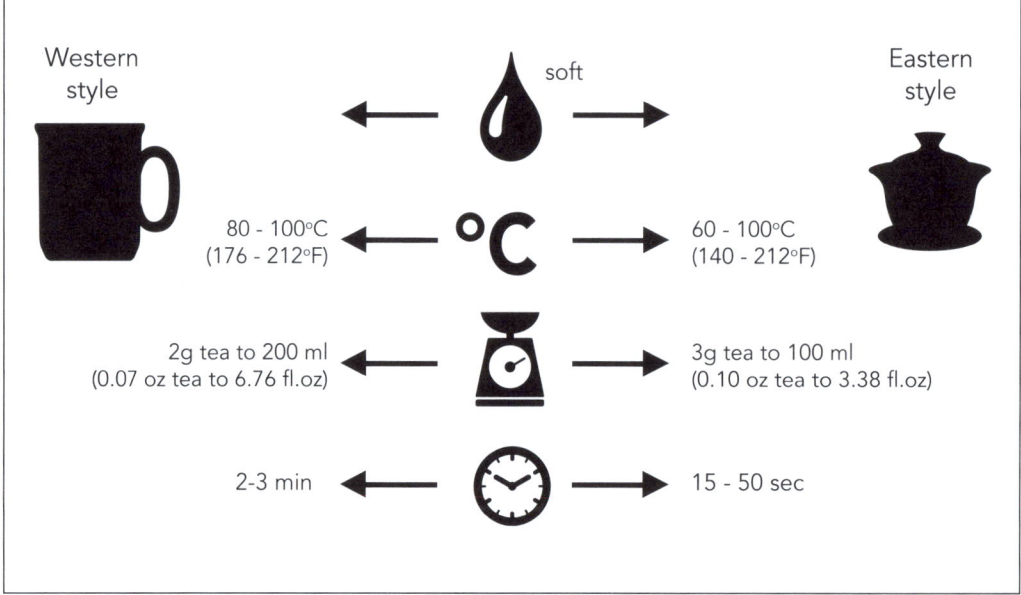

Tip
Have no time for preparing your cup of tea this mindfully with scale and right temperature? Here are two other options:
A. Make a cold brew strong tea extract the night before you want to drink it. (See pag 35 for recipe). Then, when you would like to drink a cup of tea, pour some of the extract into a cup and add boiling water to taste.
B. Always use fresh and soft, filtered water with a neutral pH value with a temperature of 90°C (194°F)
Use a shorter steeping time for green tea than for black. Use a teaspoon for measuring.

41

THE QUALITY OF THE TEA

The quality of the tea makes a big difference in taste, especially with the complexity and depth of flavor. The bigger the leaves or parts of leaves, the more flavors may be preserved, and the smaller the tea leaf particles, the more flavors will have been lost in the production process. Does this mean that tea bags are bad by definition? Absolutely not. They might be, but it is not a given. However, if the tea bags are very cheap, then you can be sure that the tea inside has little flavor, but the same can be said for very cheap loose leaf tea. In other words, it is not the tea bags that define the quality of the tea, but the content.

TEA BAGS

Tea bags were invented for convenience. Usually, the tea inside them is like sand, or dust: the smallest particles after cutting the tea leaves. For more details about the different sizes of tea leaf and the inherent definitions of quality, see pages 233 - 234.

The smaller the particles, the faster the colors and flavors release themselves into the water. Also, the less space is needed for the packaging and sending. However, nowadays you may also find tea bags with bigger pieces of tea leaf inside. As those particles are bigger, they need more space and therefore are usually packed in bigger bags, often in a pyramid shape. When a tea leaf comes into contact with water, it may expand up to three or four times its original volume, so bigger space is needed for the proper release of flavors and aromas. The more space the tea has to extend itself, the more flavor it can release. This leads to the obvious conclusion that when tea is loose in the teapot, the leaves have the most space, and will be able to fully release all their aromas and flavors, provided that the water is soft and fresh, with a neutral pH.

Consequently, the bigger tea leaf, even when packed in bigger bags, still does not have enough space for full flavor release, as it is confined to the limited space within the pyramid bag. If tea is being made with dust, tea bags are the most practical, as tea dust will give off its flavors very fast and even might turn bitter when loose in the pot. Tea made of dust is best prepared with tea bags. Tea made of bigger leaves is best steeped loose in the pot.

BEWARE:

Bottled water is usually hard; it is not called mineral water for nothing. However, there are some bottled waters that do contain water soft and neutral enough for tea. Always look at the labels for the following information: dry residue 50 mg per liter or less (0.0017 oz per 34 fl.oz or less).

WHAT IS THE BEST WAY TO STORE YOUR TEA?

In order to keep your tea's aromas at their best, always make sure you keep it far away from anything with a strong odor, such as spices, herbs, coffees, soap etc. Tea readily absorbs odors and I imagine you really do not want your tea to taste like soap or coffee. So, always remove it from the packaging as soon as you arrive home with it, unless it is sealed and or vacuum packed in odorless packaging, like coated bags. If you can smell the tea through the packaging, then it is essential that you transfer the tea as soon as possible to a canister with a solid lid, preferably a double lidded canister or tin. If you leave tea inside paper bags, closed off with a pin, you will be ruining the tea, as it will lose most of its own aromas and adopt those of its surroundings, which is a complete waste of the tea. The same goes for tea bags in cardboard boxes. If they are vacuum packed and sealed: no worries. If not: transfer them asap to their own tin.

WHAT KIND OF CANISTER?

Stainless steel or tin are always the best options, preferably with double lids. Glass is transparent, which affects the aromas in a very bad way, unless you store the airtight jars in a dark place, like a drawer or a cupboard, of course. However, when left out in the light, the aromas will diminish quickly. Never use plastic containers, as the tea will start to taste like plastic over time.

Test 1
Why fresh and filtered water is quintessential. Do this following test, and you will taste why:

- Use two identical tea bags, of the same flavor. Which flavor you choose is up to you.
- Use two identical glasses.
- Hang one tea bag in each glass.
- Bring 200 ml (7.76 fl.oz) of filtered water with a neutral pH value to the boil in one pan and the same amount of your regular tap water in another. The pans need to be clean and odorless.
- Pour the boiling water from the pans simultaneously over the tea bags in the two glasses, so one type of water in one, and the other type of water in the other.
- Steep for between 2½ and 3 minutes, without moving the bags around at all. Let them sit still in the glasses.
- After the required time, remove both tea bags simultaneously and put them aside.
- Stir both teas a bit and now look at them. What is the difference?
- Smell both teas: what is the difference?
- After a few minutes, when cooled off enough to be drinkable without burning your lips, taste both of them. Start with the tap water tea. Slurp it and suck in some oxygen, as you would do when tasting wine. Do the very same with the other tea. What is the difference?
- Taste both of them again when they have cooled off quite a bit. Look, smell and taste each one: what are the differences?

Test 2
Why movement of tea bags is bad for the taste.

Try the same test again, but this time, use the very same water for both teas. Again: same tea, same glasses, both boiling water (the very same water), each steeping for 2½ to 3 minutes. The difference this time is motion: in one glass, move the tea bag up and down and back to forth, as most people do with tea bags. Do not touch the tea bag in the other glass at all. Let it steep without any motion whatsoever. Repeat as above: look, smell, taste. Then wait for the tea to cool down. Then wait again until it is much cooler. Note the differences.

Please note: this is not about liking or disliking what you observe, as what we like or do not like, is subjective. It is about clinically noting the differences, without judgment.

HOW TO STEEP TEA BEST?

- With the right water: fresh, soft, neutral pH

Calcium < 5
Magnesium < 2
HCO3- < 17

- and the right amount of dry tea

- at the right temperature

- with sufficient steeping time

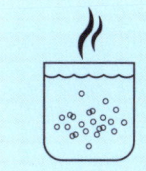
Tip
No need to bring soft water to a boil.

- preheat the pot with boiling water

- discard the water

- add the correct amount of tea leaf

- pour soft water of the right temperature into the pot

- set a timer for the desired steeping time

- pour the tea through a strainer into another pot

CHAPTER 3

Taste and flavor

Most people find it difficult to explain what they taste. How can you describe a taste in an objective and understandable way? How do you dissect a taste in a universal way? Peter Klosse, a Dutch gastronomy professor and the founder of Taste - The Academy for Scientific Taste Evaluation, has led scientific analysis and research into flavors for over 30 years. Klosse's main focus is with developing a system towards a universal flavor model in order to come to a better understanding and a scientific approach of how taste works as a whole, the full experience, so to speak. I have used his book *The Essence of Gastronomy: Understanding the Flavor of Foods and Beverages*, which he wrote together with master chef Angelique Schmeink, as the basis for my tasting notes regarding tea and food.

TOOLS

I have adapted and simplified his theory for analyzing tea and its effect on food, as it is not my goal to copy his book here; that would make this book on tea too extensive to grasp. For an in depth dive into his theory, I refer you to his book, as it is a must for anyone who wants to know more about the theoretical and scientific side of food and drinks. The very same goes for Harold McGee's fascinating book by the way: *Nose Dive: A Field Guide to the World's Smells*. Highly recommended.

I have translated my conclusions from Peter's book into a graph consisting of two flavor wheels. The wheels contain five analyzing tools: *textures, flavor types, tastes, main aromas and intensity*. Each of these tools are divided into cool, crisp, dry, astringent, bright, (the blue circle) and warm, smooth, rich, (the red circle) and indicators of the flavor intensity: XS to XL, which are not assigned to a color, as they do not have such properties.

This chapter also includes several charts to help you analyse tea and food. Of course, this does not mean that you have to use these tools every time prior to putting the kettle on. Relax! The idea is that they are just tools meant to help you develop a language to identify what you are tasting. At a certain point, you will no longer need a system to define what you actually taste. Your brain will automatically identify and specify what you taste as soon as you take a sip or bite. Over time, with experience, a true library of flavors and combinations will be stored in your brain, and you will be able to combine tea and food together without thinking. Your brain will get to know which tea or wine to choose with a certain food. However, if you have just begun to discover tea, these tools may come in very handy, as they will guide you through your analysis.

TAKE YOUR PICK

If you want to find out which drink goes best with your food, there are several options:

A. The adventurous option: you simply serve what is available. The chance that it will become a successful match is very small, but who knows, you might just hit the jackpot with your choice.

B. The careful option: you only serve what you are sure will work. You may have seen reviews about certain combinations, or maybe you have already tried and approved that specific combination. So, with this option, you stick to that combination and turn a blind eye to any other ideas, with the fear of being wrong. This works well for conservative and cautious minds.

C. The I-am-interested-but-a-bit-lazy option: you look in books or online to see which wine, tea or beer best suits your dish. The chance of success is quite high, but how certain can you be that the author of that book or article tasted the very same dish/wine/beer/tea that you have in mind? If a recipe is cooked by a hundred different people, you have a hundred different dishes in terms of taste and presentation. Although this method will point you in the right direction, you may still end up with a mismatch.

D. The I-want-to-really-dive-into-this-like-an-expert option (i.e., the nerdy option): you analyse your food and the drinks you have in mind by simply trying them out first. You write down what you taste in terms of effects on a tasting note form. This enables you to use your notes to adjust the recipes in order to make your combination a success, even if it is not quite what you expected. For example, you use less of the ingredients that become too dominant when combined with tea. You adapt the recipe by changing the temperature of the tea, or by adjusting the amount of tea leaves, or by shortening/lengthening the steeping time. If the combination is simply too far off, you just try again, with another tea. This sounds like a lot of work, but it can actually be great fun and very zen. The chance of finding a great match becomes very real when using this method. The more you practice, the quicker you will master it. As soon as you do, you will notice that you do not need to take notes anymore because your brain already knows what to do. You have mastered it, just like how a chef automatically knows what works together and what does not and how long a certain food needs preparing, frying, cooking, and so on.

If you chose option A: close this book and just jump in!

If you chose option B: choose any recipe you like from this book and cook it exactly the way it is described and serve the recommended tea with it. If you are disappointed with the result, remember that nothing ever tastes the same and that all suggestions are just suggestions. There is no guarantee that the pairings will suit your palate. Just shrug it off and and think about what you could change to make the combination suit your taste better. If all else fails, give the book away.

If you chose option C: focus on chapters 1, 2, 5 and 7 and pages 36 - 37, 256 - 272.

If you chose option D: please read on, trigger your curiosity, and try out and discover as much as possible!

TASTES AND SENSES

We use and need our five senses in order to fully taste what we eat or drink. As the saying goes, we also eat with our eyes, so in order to get a complete experience of what we eat and drink, we use not only our sense of taste. We also use the other four senses. Food should look attractive and preferably mouthwateringly good. It should also sound and feel appealing. Crisps, for example, must be crispy and crunchy. Soggy crisps are awful, and even if they taste exactly the same, we will discard them when they are soft. The smell and taste of what we eat are equally important and directly linked to our memory.

THE KEY FACTORS TO DEFINE FLAVOR ARE:
A. *Senses*
B. *Tastes*
C. *Texture (mouthfeel)*
D. *Flavor type*
E. *Intensity*

A. The five senses are:
- Sight
- Hearing
- Taste
- Smell
- Touch

B. The five basic tastes are:

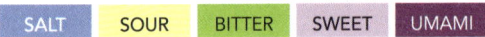

SALT   SOUR   BITTER   SWEET   UMAMI

Umami is a Japanese term for the fifth taste, coined by Japanese scientist Ikeda in 1907. He discovered this taste in typical Japanese products like miso and soy sauce. It is not easy to translate this into another language as it covers several meanings, like savory, intense and strongly flavored. Western examples of umami are mushrooms, anchovies, olives, dried tomatoes, stock, Parmesan cheese, Worcestershire sauce and Marmite/Vegemite. Several other tastes, like fat, metallic, and soap, to name a few, are still waiting to be officially recognized as separate tastes by the International Organization for Standardization. It took them over 45 years to accept umami as an official taste, so my guess is that it will take some time before the list of tastes expands. Which is a shame, really, as it limits our ways of expressing what it is we actually taste.
I mention metal and soap in my flavor wheels, but placed them under main aromas, since they are not official tastes as yet.

TASTES IN TEA
Which taste is dominant? Tea contains several tastes. The most common tastes in tea are sweet, bitter and umami. You will encounter acidity less often, usually with teas that have citrus or berry notes, or in post-fermented teas. You will not find saltiness in tea. If any does exist, then it is very faint, like a hint of salt, just like with wine. Tea may taste slightly savory, but that is not salty, it is umami.

HOW TASTING WORKS
When we eat or drink something, our taste buds, which are located everywhere in the mouth, register these tastes and send the neurologic information to the brain. This goes very fast, in less than a nanosecond. The brain translates the data then into something we understand: this tastes sweet, or salty, or bitter. The five tastes are objective, and everyone tastes them as they are. We say that tastes differ, but that does not apply in this case. Everyone registers sugar as sweet, not as salt, sour, bitter or umami.
However, the intensity of how we experience tastes does differ. Some people experience a bite out of a lemon as extremely refreshing, while others cringe at the thought alone. Whether we like what we taste or not is subjective. You may love or hate the taste of broccoli, yet it is the very same broccoli.

MEMORY
Memory is a very important factor in our perception of taste, especially for our decision whether we like something or not. For example, if you have a pleasant childhood memory of broccoli, you will still like having that as a grown up, as it subconsciously transports you back to those happy days. If you have a bad memory, for example, if you got very sick one day after having eaten broccoli, you will probably not want to eat it anymore.
In other words, our memories are crucial for our appreciation for, or rejection of, food.

> So, our perception of taste as a whole is really the sum of sensory perceptions and memories and is therefore always unique.

AROMAS

In addition to the five tastes, we also register aromas, which are subdivided in this book into main aromas and sub-aromas. An average human being is capable of registering around 5,000 different aromas.

When we smell odors, we call it orthonasal perception of aromas, which occurs as we inhale them through our nose, from where they move up into the olfactory system in our brain, right above the nose, for processing.

When we eat something, our chewing causes the cells of that food to tear, and the cellular juices are then released. Those juices are carriers of the innate aromas and flavors, and we can actually taste the aromas after chewing. After passing through the mouth, they move up to the olfactory system through the open connection between the mouth cavity and the nose, located in the back of the throat, called the retronasal channel. This way of perceiving aromas is called retronasal perception. If you have a cold, this passage will mostly be clogged, which will inhibit you from tasting very much. The aromas simply cannot move through the channel properly, and as a result, cannot fully reach the brain for processing.

AROMAS IN TEA

Over 30,000 compounds can be found in tea, of which scientists have now analyzed and named nearly 4,000. Many of these substances react with each other, and this may lead to certain aromas developing. Just like in wine, many aromas can be detected in tea, such as wood, peach, apple, chocolate, tobacco, leather, to name just a few. These aromas are not added to wine or tea, it is simply that the aroma reminds you.

As mentioned earlier in this chapter, I have designed a flavor wheel based on Peter Klosse's theory for flavor analysis. The idea is that the wheel will be a tool to help you determine what flavors and aromas you may perceive in tea. More on this on the next pages and 248 - 249. Similar tools are used in the wine, coffee and cocoa industries.

To keep things simple, I have used main groups of aromas in most of the charts and graphs. On the following pages you can read more about specific aromas and sub-aromas. For example, floral is a general description and part of a main group. Rose would be a sub-aroma. Fruity is a main group, and apple would be in the sub-aroma group, and green apple even more so.

C. Texture:

The next important factor that contributes to what we taste is texture. Food and drinks can be dry, crisp, astringent, neutral or smooth. Astringency means contraction and it is a texture that is often caused by acidic or bitter flavors. That is why we automatically associate astringency with acidity and bitterness. Imagine an unripe apple, which is sour and astringent. The taste is sour; the texture is astringent. On the other side of the texture spectrum you will find smooth; a bit of honey immediately coats your mouth with a sticky layer of sweetness and therefore feels soft, smooth, sometimes even velvety, or just sticky. Sometimes the aftertaste of honey is a bit sharp, a bit dry at the back of the throat. Other examples of a smooth sensation in the mouth are butter, oil, cream, starch, gelling agents such as gelatine and agar-agar. Starch in itself is dry. However, as soon as you mix it with liquid, such as saliva, water, milk or wine, it becomes silky and smooth (e.g., béchamel sauce). The flour is dry when added to the butter, but once hot milk is mixed in, it becomes soft and creamy. Another example of smooth is a ripe and juicy peach. It makes your mouth water, eliminating any dryness. Umami is often full and creamy, although it may also be slightly astringent and creamy at the same time, like with Parmesan cheese. It may be neutral to slightly astringent, too, as in olives, Marmite and anchovies.

Do the Texture test
Imagine eating a spoonful of cream. How does it feel in your mouth? Now imagine something acidic, for example, a lemon or a green apple. How does that feel?
The cream has a full, round, silky, sticky and sweet texture; whereas the lemon or apple has a contracting, crunchy or dry texture with an acidic sensation. The mouthfeel or texture that you get from something acidic and often from bitter flavors is called astringency. The taste is acidic, or bitter and the texture is astringent.

If you drink black tea that has been steeping for a long time and made with a high quantity of tea leaves, the dominant taste will be bitter, and the texture will be astringent.

The chemical compounds in the tea link with the proteins that are present in the oral mucosa, and by doing so, they absorb the fluid (saliva) present in the mouth. Consequence: a drying sensation. Astringency may also cause a refreshing sensation. The sensation often becomes unpleasant with bitter flavors.

A similar process may take place with wine. In young red wine, this astringency is caused by certain polyphenols, called tannins. In tea the culprits are also polyphenols, but of a different kind, as tannins do not occur in tea. You can read more about this in chapter 13.

Pepper, ginger, wasabi (the green paste often served with sushi) and mustard are not flavors but sensations; they irritate the mucous membrane in your mouth, which leads to a very specific, tingling sensation: burning, hot, sharp. Your nose and tongue may respond strongly to it. Just eat a bit of wasabi or mustard, and you will know exactly what I mean.

SUMMARY OF THE TEXTURE
The tactile aspect of tasting is called texture, or mouthfeel. This could be astringent, dry or smooth, both dry and smooth or neither dry nor smooth: neutral.
With tea, the first sensation is often smooth, soft, and this gradually changes to neutral and then onto dry, with a fresh and dry aftertaste. However, the other way around is also possible.

DRY
- Crisp
- Chewy
- Sharp
- Astringent
- Tingling cold

SMOOTH
- Juicy
- Supple
- Round
- Creamy
- Tingling warm

D. The flavor types are:
- Bright
- Neutral
- Both
- Rich

In addition to texture, there is flavor type. Everything we eat and drink can be divided into bright, rich, both or neutral. By rich, I mean the counterpart of bright, refreshing. Rich stands for intense, full, deep, warm, heavy, round, complex, and is akin to a smooth texture. Bright stands for light, refreshing, crisp, dry, cool, and is akin to a dry or astringent texture.

BRIGHT

Citrus fruit, strawberry, pineapple, raw onion, buttermilk, yoghurt, sparkling water, parsley, coriander, dill, chives, raw snow peas, raw carrot, green apple, red pepper, pepper, cucumber, tomato, raw leek, pickled herring, spring onions, pickles, fresh goat cheese.
Examples of bright tea: green tea, some light oolongs, Darjeeling first flush.

RICH

Ripe banana, mango, peach, apricot, blackberries, blueberries, fig, date, whole milk, cream, thyme, rosemary, oregano, caramelized onion, apple, eggplant, stewed zucchini, stewed leek, smoked fish, fatty cheese, mature cheese, sheep's cheese, honey.
Examples of rich tea: some white, green and black tea, yellow tea, dark oolong, Pu-Erh.

  BRIGHT   RICH   NEUTRAL

Basil, sage, bay leaf, sour cream, unripe banana.

Examples of bright and rich or neutral tea: yellow tea, some green tea, some white tea, some lightly oolongs, Ceylon black tea.

THE FLAVOR TYPE SUMMARIZED
- Bright
- Rich
- Bright and rich
- Not bright, not rich: neutral

TASTES SUMMARIZED

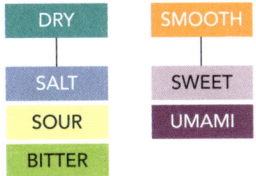

SOME EXAMPLES:

COOL

Refreshing, bright, dry, crisp or astringent tastes, flavors and aromas:
sour: citrus, vinegar, lemon, orange, kiwi, pineapple, red current, raspberry, strawberry, red cherry, green apple, yoghurt, buttermilk
salt: seawater, salt
bitter: tobacco, chicory, grapefruit, raw white almond, endive, aspirin, caffeine
floral: bergamot, perfume
fruity: citrus, berries, passionfruit, green apple

WARM

Rich, round, silky, smooth, warming and sweet tastes, flavors and aromas:
sweet: sugar, honey, molasses, brown sugar, palm sugar, syrup, caramel hard, caramel soft, cream, ripe stone fruits such as peach, apricot, mango, papaya, pear, plums, black cherries
umami: seaweed, sea, broth, meat, grilled chicken, dried tomato, old cheese, dried mushrooms, miso, olive, anchovies
earthy: clay, mud, hay, wet leaves, moss, forest, henna, soil, mushrooms, young wood, old wood, tropical wood, spruce wood, cypress, potatoes, sweet potato, pumpkin, beet, parsnip, celery root, turnip, Jerusalem artichoke
animal: stable, petting zoo, leather, wet dog, musk, birdcage, fish
synthetic, fire, mineral: petroleum, petrol, plastic, tar, burnt wood, ash, smoke, rock, pebble, flint, wet rocks, concrete
floral: rose, tulip, orchid, lily of the valley, lilac, hyacinth, narcissus, mimosa, chrysanthemum, iris, lilies, soap, honeysuckle, linden flower
vegetal: grass, spinach, cabbage, peas, corn, green beans, broad beans, endive, sorrel garden herbs such as parsley, chives, coriander, basil, rosemary
dairy: butter, milk, cream, cheese, full yoghurt
fruit: mango, peach, apricot, grapes, pear, red apple, dried fruit
nuts and seeds: chestnut, hazelnut, walnut, beech nut, apple seeds
grains: cookies, cake, toasted bread, bread dough, whole grain bread
spices: cinnamon, cloves, anise, ginger, pepper, fennel, cumin

E. Intensity:
With this, I mean the amount or level of flavor present in a specific food or tea. Peter Klosse calls it the volume of a dish. For example, boiled white rice has a much lower level of intensity than fried rice. The boiled rice whispers, whereas the fried rice makes itself heard. The same goes for dairy:
- Watered down milk   >   **XS** very low intensity
- low-fat milk   >   **S** low intensity
- semi-skimmed milk   >   **M** average intensity
- whole milk   >   **L** high intensity
- whipped cream   >   **XL** very high intensity

This applies within the dairy group. If you compare whipped cream with fried onions, you have a completely different story.

If something tastes rather bland, it has a low intensity, which could be increased by adding herbs, spices, salt, umami, or by changing the cooking technique. Poached chicken tastes way less intense than grilled chicken. Grilling, baking or roasting causes a Maillard reaction to occur in food. The food turns brown, as certain sugars and amino acids in the ingredient interact due to the use of high temperatures, at least 140°C (285°F). This process intensifies the flavor, like with barbecued meat. The umami components become dominant. You can read more about cooking techniques and their effects on intensity in chapter 4, on page 62 - 63.

I use the terms XS, S, M, L or XL to indicate the level of flavor intensity, but you can also use +++ or - - -, points (1-5) circles or stars, smileys or whatever feels easy to use.

There are three more descriptions that can be used in analyzing tea, terms also used in describing the effect of wine: complexity, the finish and the length.

COMPLEXITY

The more aromas and tastes present, and the longer the length, the more complex a tea is. If a tea tastes primarily sweet with only honey notes, it is a lot less complex than a tea that has sweet notes of honey and also some bitter or umami notes of grapefruit, cocoa, cinnamon, cloves, roasted nuts and soft fruit. However, it is not very important whether or not you can name those sub-aromas. Having this knowledge may help you analyse the complexity of the tea, but it is not absolutely necessary. Do not worry about mastering this quickly. It is more important to determine the main aroma group, the texture, the taste(s) and the flavor type. Sometimes the first thing you will recognize is a sub-aroma. This recognition may also help you to understand what you are tasting. For example, if the first thing you taste is spinach, then you could look it up in either the flavor wheels or in the list of main aromas on page 55. You will see that spinach is part of the neutral and vegetal section, and is most likely a component of green tea. Also on pages 276 - 281, there is a list with teas and their flavor profiles. Under green tea, you will find some teas that have spinach as a sub-aroma.

FINISH

This describes how the experience ends. A sip or bite may result in a pleasant, cleansing finish, or a sticky one, or spicy and so on. It is the sensation that lingers after the flavor has disappeared.

LENGTH

This describes the length of time that flavors linger in your mouth once you have swallowed, in other words: the aftertaste. The longer this takes, the higher the quality of the tea, as it shows its depth and strength, its complexity. This only goes for a pleasant sensation, of course. A tea with a highly unpleasant aftertaste that stays with you for a long time, is not considered to be of high quality.

HOW TO DETERMINE A TEA'S FLAVOR PROFILE

This is what I do: I look at the five factors that determine the profile:
- Texture
- Flavor type
- Taste
- Main notes
- Intensity

With these tools I decide in which flavor wheel the flavors and tastes fit or, when in both, which one is dominant.
I use colored circles that refer to the colors of the flavor wheels (see page 57).
I then add up the blue, grey and red circles that I came up with and divide them by the amount of factors used. That way I know which wheel is more dominant: warm, cold or neutral. I do not count intensity. It is important for the overall experience of tasting, but is an independent factor and has nothing to do with the blue, red or grey.

I use 5 circles per factor: 1 circle represents only a bit of that specific factor, 5 circles represent a lot of a certain characteristic. For example:

Darjeeling first flush:

TEXTURE
| SMOOTH | O O |
| DRY | O O O |

FLAVOR TYPE
| RICH | O |
| BRIGHT | O O O O |

TASTES
| SWEET | O O O |
| BITTER | O O |

MAIN NOTES
Floral, fruity, grainy, vegetal, herbaceous
O O O O O

INTENSITY   M

The total of factors used: 4
Total in red wheel: O 8
Total in blue wheel: O 12
8 O: 4 factors = 2 O
12 O: 4 factors = 3 O
Total score: O O O O O

Conclusion: Darjeeling first flush is a rather dry, bright, slightly sweet type of tea.

The flavor profile of Darjeeling first flush is:
dry, slightly smooth, bright, sweet, slightly bitter, floral, fruity, grainy, vegetal, herbaceous, M

In short
Taste is what the brain registers through the taste buds in the mouth:
sweet, salt, bitter, sour or umami.
Aroma is what the brain registers through the nose. It is what we smell.
Texture is what happens in our mouth; does the mouth salivate or become dry? Is there a puckering sensation or rather a silky, smooth one? This adds to the overall evaluation of what we taste.

Flavor is a combination of texture, taste(s) and aroma(s), passed onto the brain via nose and mouth.

Analyzing flavor with flavor wheels

This tool is especially useful if you are not yet able to describe what it is exactly you are tasting, smelling and feeling. There are example forms in the back of this book, on page 251 - 253. You can use the forms as a guideline when you want to write down what you taste, step by step. They will help you categorize your sensations. There are example forms for tea and food pairing, which can also be used when pairing cheese or chocolate with tea. The idea is that you taste attentively and write down your thoughts on the form. If you cannot think of any words yet, take a look at the flavor wheel to help you find the words to describe what it is that you taste, smell and feel.

Example

How to fill out the form for tea and food pairing, chocolate in this case.

Suppose you eat a piece of dark chocolate that is initially very dry but becomes a bit smoother the longer it stays in your mouth. Under the heading *Texture* you should tick off four circles "dry" and one "smooth".

If the dominant taste is sour, with a bit of umami, then tick off 4 circles "sour" and 1 "umami" under the heading *Tastes*.

If it tastes quite to very rich, but ends a bit bright, then you should tick off four circles "rich" and one circle "bright" under the heading *Flavor Type*.

If the acidity makes you think of lemons, then write down under the heading *Main Aromas*: "fruit", and add: "Sub aroma: lemon".

Next, determine the level of intensity, the volume. Does the chocolate taste very strong or intense? Then tick off four or maybe five circles under the heading *Intensity*.

Then add up all points, and divide them by the number of tools that you have used.

In this case:

1. texture: 4 circles dry (blue) - 1 smooth (red) = 4 blue, 1 red
2. flavor type: 1 circle bright (blue) - 4 circles rich (red) = 1 blue, 4 red
3. tastes: sour (blue) 4 circles - umami (red) 1 circle = 4 blue, 1 red
4. intensity: 4 or 5 circles, color irrelevant, as this is only about intensity: L-XL

So you end up with a total of 9 blue - *6 red*: blue is quite dominant.

The flavor profile in this case is: dry, rich, sour, fruity, citrus, L-XL

DRY RICH SOUR

Analyzing which aromas you taste

With this table you can analyse the aromas. It is a tool for when you are not sure how to describe what you are tasting, just like with the flavor wheels on the next page, but this time in a chart. For example: you taste something that you cannot quite put your finger on. You are familiar with it but cannot remember exactly what it is. Let us say you are eating the very chocolate bar from the previous example. You detect something fruity and bright, acidic. Search in the chart under the heading Main notes to see if you can find a description that fits what you taste. You see fruit in the list. Bingo! Fruit is what you were looking for. What to do with bright? Look to the right of fruit under the heading Bright to work out which fruit you are tasting. Citrus is refreshing, bright, and now you realize. Yes, that is what I taste; lemon!

Chart with overview of aroma categories and sub aromas

MAIN NOTES	SUB NOTES RICH	SUB NOTES BRIGHT	SUB NOTES NEUTRAL	SUB NOTES RICH AND BRIGHT
Floral	Rose, orchid, lily of the valley, lilac, hyacinth, mimosa, iris, lily, gardenia, orange blossom, jasmin, honeysuckle, linden flower	Freesia	Tulip, daffodil	Chrysanthemum, nasturtium
Earthy	Soil, clay, mud, wet leaves, moss, forest, old wood, tropical wood, cedar wood, mushroom, henna, potato, yam, pumpkin, beetroot, parsnip, turnip, celery root, artichoke, truffle, Jerusalem artichoke	Eucalyptus tree, spruce	Blond wood, hay	Silage, cypress, wet hay
Animal	Leather, wet dog, musk, bird cage, zoo	Goat stable		Farm, pigsty
Nutty	Hazelnut, chestnut, appleseed, macadamia nut, pecan, pine nut, sunflower seed, beechnut			Walnut
Synthetic, fire	Petrol, oil, tar, plastic, flint, camphor, sulphur, tarmac, charcoal, smoke, ashes, campfire, gas, cigar, tobacco			
Mineral		Flint	Rock, slate, pebbles, chalk, flint	
Metal	Pewter, lead	Steel, iron, silver	Copper	Gold
Sweets	Honey, caramel, licorice, cough drops, maple syrup, molasses, toffee, chocolate, cake, vanilla	Fruit candy	Malt	Cacao, unsweetened
Vegetal	Cabbage, peas, corn, fava bean	Grass, green pepper, cucumber, sorrel, spring onion, fennel, radish, tomato	Spinach, string beans, endive, purslane, courgette, aubergine, straw	Bell pepper, leek, garlic, snow peas
Herbaceous	Rosemary, thyme, sage, oregano	Parsley, chives, dill, coriander, mint, tarragon	Bay leaf	Basil
Grains	Toast, oats, dough, brioche, sourdough, wholemeal bread, rye			
Fruit	Mango, peach, apricot, pear, dried fruit, plum, persimmon	Citrus, red fruit, passion fruit, green apple	Unripe banana	Grapes, pineapple, red apple, melon
Dairy	Butter, cream, whole milk, cheese	Buttermilk, yoghurt, soft goat cheese, kefir	Semi-skimmed milk, curd cheese, white cheese	Sour cream, Greek yoghurt, crème fraîche
Spices	Cinnamon, clove, ginger, pepper, cumin, nutmeg, mace	Anise seed, fennel seed	Galangal, caraway seeds	Cardamom, coriander seeds
Maritime				Seaweed, fish, shellfish, beach

Analyzing flavor with flavor wheels

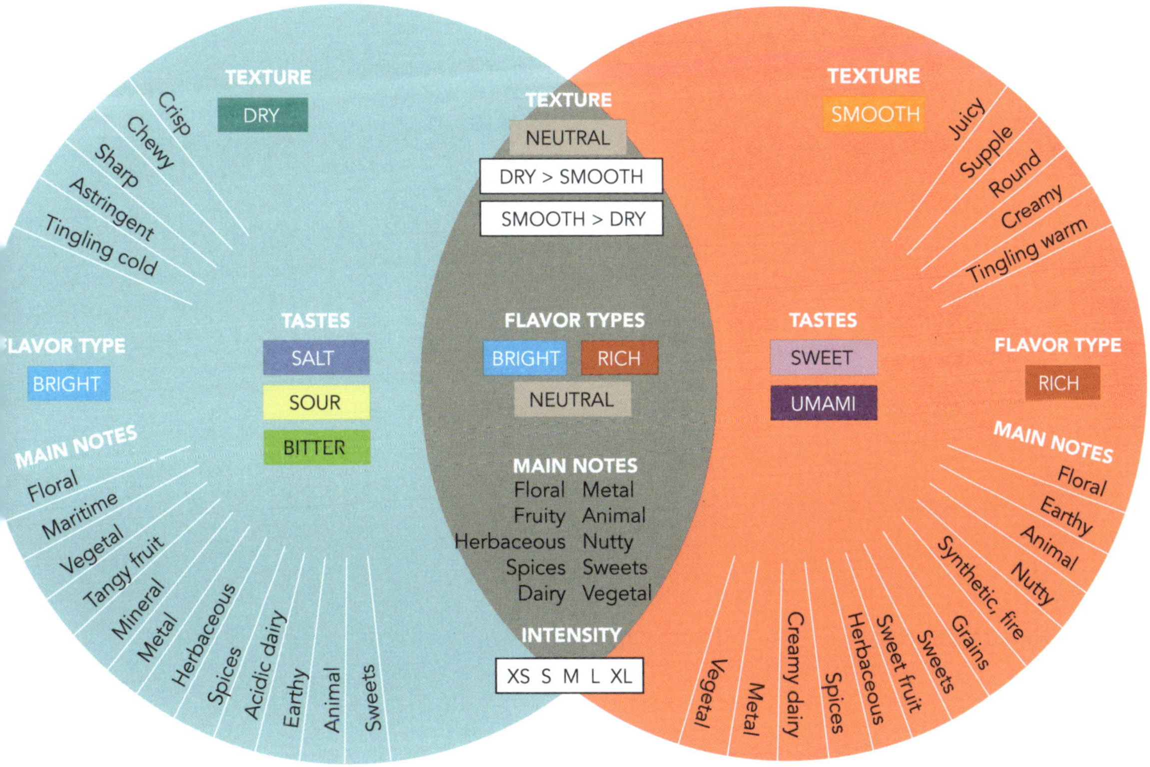

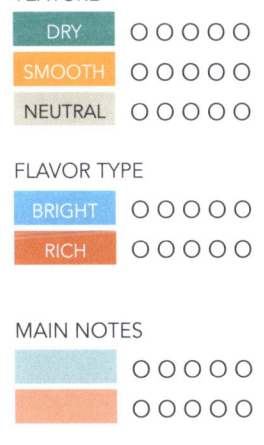

TEXTURE
- DRY ○○○○○
- SMOOTH ○○○○○
- NEUTRAL ○○○○○

FLAVOR TYPE
- BRIGHT ○○○○○
- RICH ○○○○○

MAIN NOTES
- (bright) ○○○○○
- (rich) ○○○○○

TASTES
- SALT ○○○○○
- SOUR ○○○○○
- BITTER ○○○○○
- SWEET ○○○○○
- UMAMI ○○○○○

INTENSITY
XS S M L XL ○○○○○

Tests: the effect food may have on tea and wine and vice versa
(Examples of forms to use for these tests are to be found on page 252)

- Break some crackers into small pieces
- Taste them with whatever you like: peanut butter, cheese, pate, avocado, anything
- Steep the tea of your choice according to the golden rules of tea steeping (see page 40)
- Pour a glass of wine of your choice
- Let the tea cool down first; this way you'll taste it better

First, taste the tea
Take a sip of tea, roll it around in your mouth, close your eyes and register: what do you taste? Write your observations down on the form.
- *Texture*
  What happens in your mouth? Does it feel smooth or dry? Or smooth, round and full at first, but dry in the aftertaste? Or does it feel neutral?
- *Flavor type*
  Does the tea taste rich, deep, or refreshing, bright? Maybe both, or neutral?
- *Taste*
  What is the dominant taste? Sweet? Umami? Bitter? All three?
- *Main notes*
  Do you detect earthy notes, or rather floral? Vegetal? Fruity?
- *Intensity*
  Is it a very subtle tea, in other words, S, or is it robust, mouth filling? L? XL?

Repeat this list with a sip of wine

Then take another sip of tea; this cleanses your mouth. It should now be the case that you can no longer taste the wine. If that is not the case, take another sip of tea, and continue until you no longer taste the wine.

Now, move on to the food.
Take a piece of cracker with the topping of your choice.
- How is the texture?
- What flavor type would you think this is?
- What is the taste like?
- What intensity does it have?
- Swallow and wait a while

What do you perceive now in terms of flavor, texture, intensity, etc? Write it down on the form.

Then take a sip of tea, together with the piece of cracker.
• Chew, mix and let them roll around in your mouth
• What do you perceive now in terms of texture, flavor type, tastes, main notes and intensity?
• Swallow both the tea and the cracker
• Wait a moment and register again:
• Has anything changed? In what way?

Repeat with a sip of wine, together with the piece of cracker.
Note the similarities and differences between the wine and the tea in terms of effects. It is not important what you prefer or like for this test. The idea is for you to learn how to analyse and describe what you taste. You may, of course, write down on the form whether you liked it or not; however, that is not the main objective here.

Repeat the test with a cracker with another topping or just take the same cracker and try it with a different tea and wine. Just play around and discover. You will be amazed by the different effects!

Note:
Always write down your tasting experiences. What are the effects, what did you register? It is not about what you like or not when doing these tests. The purpose is that you register flavors and effects, learn to recognize them. Do write down your personal preferences if you feel like it, but keep in mind that the goal is to learn how to taste in an objective manner.

CHAPTER 4

Tea and food pairing

At the end of the previous chapter you learned about and experienced what effects tea, wine and ingredients have on each other. In this chapter, we are going to take things further. A cracker with peanut butter is great to start with, but what if it concerns a more complicated dish you would like to find the right tea for? Maybe a casserole with fish and vegetables, or a steak with fries and salad? In short, how do you know which tea pairs best with your dish?
Remember that a dish is the sum of different parts. In other words, a certain tea may collide with a raw tomato, but if that tomato is processed in a dish with various other ingredients, the very same tea could suddenly balance nicely with the tomato. That is why you should not only think about the individual ingredients, but consider the sum total. Keep the whole dish in mind with the "hero" as your starting point, whether the hero is tea, meat, fish, sauce or vegetables.
Incidentally, finding the right combination is not something that you can do just on the basis of a list. It is a matter of trying and tasting (with all your senses) as often as possible. Charts and lists will point you in the right direction, and they are helpful as a starting point. Just like the flavor wheels on page 57 and 248 can be useful to determine and describe what it is exactly that you taste in tea, wine, beer, coffee or chocolate.

BUT HOW?
Suppose you are going to make pasta with prawns in garlic-herb and cream sauce and you want to serve wine with that. You might say the following:
- I will drink the wine I already have, whatever it is, and we will see if it matches the food or not
- I think a dry white wine will go well with this food
- Probably a juicy, bright, fruity, slightly dry white wine
- Sauvignon Blanc, perhaps
- I will choose a Sauvignon Blanc by Clos Henri, Petit Clos, Marlborough, New Zealand

That is exactly how you might also choose a tea:
- I will drink the tea that I always drink and we will see if it combines well with the food or not
- I think a green tea might go well with this
- Maybe a Japanese green tea
- In that case, I want a dry, bright, herbaceous and fruity Sencha
- I will choose a Sencha Fukamushi from the Otsuka tea farm in Shizuoka, Japan

BUT WHAT TO DO IF YOU HAVE NO CLUE WHATSOEVER?
A. You could look for a similar recipe in my tasting notes on page 260 at the back of this book to see which tea matches that dish, or comes close to it.
B. You could go to chapter 3 (page 54) to see how you could analyse the dish or tea of your choice, based on the five factors explained there.

My advice? Try option B, as you will learn the most from that. However, if you do not have enough time or feel like taking a chance, then choose option A.
You will find an example of what I mean with option B on the next page.

FOOD ANALYSIS:

Imagine that you intend to make a dish of roasted pumpkin, with mushrooms, gorgonzola and pecans. (recipe on page 92).
Start by analyzing the five factors of this dish:

Main taste(s)
- *The dish is sweet, salty and umami*

What taste in tea might work with that? Combining sweet tastes together is possible and often harmonious, but is also a bit boring. It could make the total effect heavy, rather bland and too sweet altogether.

Sweet and sour often work well together, but there is not much truly sour tea to be found; unless acidic ingredients have been added to it, such as hibiscus or lemon. Or you could go for a splurge and try Goishicha, a bright and acididic post-fermented tea from Japan, which also has quite some umami notes (see page….). For less exotic, more mainstream teas, you could also opt for one with a hint of citrus or red fruit, such as some African and Sri Lankan black teas (see page 280).

Sweetness smoothes out the sharp edges of acidity, but this could also eliminate the zest and liveliness that comes with acidity. So be careful with sweet tea if you want to keep your dish tart and zesty.

Sweet often matches nicely with bitter, salty and umami.

In short, quite a lot of tea could go with this dish.

The main aromas
Which dominant aromas do you perceive? In this case, one could describe them as:
- *quite earthy, cheesy, sweet vegetable and somewhat nutty*

Could that work with maritime notes, like seafood or fish? Mwah, not really. That means that most Japanese and some Chinese and Korean teas with strong maritime notes will not make it to your shortlist. Deduction can often lead to your decision.

The texture
- *The texture is smooth, full*

This is much easier to pair than a dry or astringent dish. A dry or astringent tea with this food means contrast, which could be risky, but also adventurous and might work out exceptionally well. A neutral tea (neither smooth nor astringent) is a safe choice and will result in a harmonious pairing.

The flavor type
- *This dish definitely falls under the flavor type "rich"*

The same goes for most dark oolongs, most black teas, and Shu Pu-Erh. If you choose one of those, you will make a safe choice because they have similar textures and related main flavors. If you want to be bold, you could try some teas from the opposite spectrum: light oolongs with grassy and floral notes or a Darjeeling first flush.

The intensity
- *In this case the intensity is L. (For an explanation about what I mean with this, see page 52).*

Which is also the case with dark oolongs, various black teas, or some Pu-Erh teas.

Summarized:
The **flavor profile** of this dish is
- *sweet, salty and umami, smooth, rich, earthy, nutty, fruity, L.*

Shortlist of teas to choose for this dish:
Harmony: dark oolong, Chinese black tea, Shu Pu-Erh, Hōjicha
Contrast: light oolong, Ceylon, African, Indian or Nepalese tea, Earl Grey

Green, white and yellow teas are probably too light to be able to stand up to it, but might still enhance the food.

COOKING TECHNIQUE AND TEA

The way you prepare a dish or ingredient has a lot of influence on the final flavor of food, as already mentioned in the previous chapter. Different cooking techniques may cause the very same ingredient to either taste more intense or bland or something in between. Keep this in mind when choosing a tea. These changes in perception might occur with texture, flavor type, taste, main flavors, complexity and intensity.

See the table below for cooking techniques and the effect that has on flavor profile.

Cooking techniques and tea

Preparation	Texture	Flavor type	Taste	Intensity
Onion				
Raw	Dry, sharp, astringent	Bright	Bitter	L
Sautéed	Smooth, soft	Rich	Sweet	M
Caramelized	Smooth, soft to crunchy	Rich	Sweet and umami	XL
Fish and seafood				
White fish	Neutral	Neutral	Salt, slightly umami	S-M
Fatty fish	Smooth, oily	Rich	Salt, umami	M-L
Raw	Smooth or neutral	Rich	Umami	S-M
Boiled or steamed	Neutral, soft, a bit dry	Neutral	Salt	S
Sous-vide	Neutral to juicy	Neutral	Salt, slightly umami	S-M
Fried, grilled	Both dry, crispy and smooth, juicy	Rich	Salt, umami	M-XL
Smoked	Smooth, neutral, dry	Rich	Salt, umami	L-XL
Barbecued	Both dry, crispy and smooth, juicy	Rich	Salt, umami	XL

Fruit and vegetables
Can be dry, neutral, or smooth, bright, neutral or rich, bitter, sweet, sour, umami, with an intensity anywhere between XS and XL. There are too many variables to define all possibilities with fruit and vegetables. Keep in mind that bitter, salt and sour often lead to a dry or astringent, bright texture and flavor type, whereas sweet and umami often lead to smooth and rich. Stewed fruit and vegetables are often sweet and rich, raw fruit and vegetables may be dry, neutral, juicy, bright, crunchy and so on.

TIP
Raw onion is difficult to combine with tea, as in most cases, the tea will strongly enhance its sharpness, making the onion much too overpowering. To prevent this, pour boiling water over the sliced raw onion in a bowl and wait a minute. Rinse with cold water and drain well. An alternative is to soak the onion in wine vinegar for a few minutes.

Preparation	Texture	Flavor type	Taste	Intensity
Poultry				
Breast	Neutral to juicy	Neutral	Slightly umami	S
Thigh	Smooth, juicy	Rich	Umami	M-L
Boiled or steamed	Neutral, soft, a bit dry	Neutral	Slightly umami	S-M
Sous-vide	Neutral to juicy	A bit rich	Umami	S-M
Stewed	Neutral to juicy	Rich	Umami	M
Smoked	Smooth, oily, neutral, dry	Rich	Umami	L-XL
Fried, grilled	Both dry, crispy and smooth, juicy	Rich	Umami	L-XL
Barbecue	Both dry, crispy and smooth, juicy	Rich	Umami	XL
Deep fried	Both dry, crispy and smooth, juicy	Rich	Umami	XL
Meat				
Raw	Neutral to juicy	Rich	Umami, sometimes sweet	M-L
Boiled or steamed	Neutral, soft, a bit dry	Rich	Slightly umami	M
Sous-vide	Smooth, juicy, neutral	Rich	Umami	M
Stewed	Neutral to juicy	Rich	Umami	L
Fried, grilled	Both dry, crispy and smooth, juicy	Rich	Umami, sometimes sweet	L-XL
Smoked	Neutral, dry	Rich	Umami	L-XL
Barbecue	Both dry, crispy and smooth, juicy	Rich	Umami, sometimes sweet	XL

HOW DO THE FIVE TASTES REACT TO EACH OTHER?

SALTY
- Enhances sweet and umami
- Suppresses bitter and sour

SOUR
- Acidity breaks down fat, and thus cleanses your palate. Smooth and full becomes dry
- Suppresses the other four flavors
- Softens spicy food and increases astringency

BITTER
- Enhances umami
- Neutralizes fat
- Is softened by fat or cream
- Increases astringency

UMAMI
- Enhances all tastes
- Makes for an interesting combination with sweet

SWEET
- Softens a bright sensation, making it smooth, fuller, and stickier
- Suppresses the other four flavors
- Takes the edge off and reduces the sharpness of spicy foods

To counterbalance a fat or creamy dish, you can serve an astringent tea with it and vice versa. You can smooth out astringent or dry food with a creamy, mellow and smooth tea. If a dish is complex and intense, take this into account when choosing a tea to pair with it. Very light teas will be overshadowed by the food.
A complex tea may lose much of its aromas due to the many flavors in the dish. A complex, powerful dish is best accompanied by a strong tea with rich notes and a smooth finish.

Tea and food pairing summary

It is usually best to drink a tea when it is as fresh as possible or most recently plucked because the aromas and flavors deteriorate over time. However, there are some types of tea that can be stored and aged just like wine. They even improve with age. Examples of teas that are suitable for aging, depending on their quality, are:
- *Post-fermented tea, for example, Pu-Erh*
- *High-quality white tea, loose or pressed*
- *Dark and extra roasted oolongs, such as Rock Oolongs, Dong Ding, Tieguanyin, and Feng Huang Mi Lan Dan Cong*

Storage
It is extremely important that you store the tea correctly. Always store it in a cool, dark place with little to no air. This goes for any tea, not just for the ones you would like to age.

Determining the flavor profile
Analyzing tea is done by means of five factors. These can also be used for wine, beer, chocolate and food.
1. The texture
2. The flavor type
3. The basic taste or tastes
4. The main aromas and sub aromas (also called main and sub notes)
5. The intensity or volume of the flavor(s)

FISH, SEAFOOD, SALTY FOOD
BALANCE: look for tea with main notes that are bitter-sweet, sour, bright, herbaceous, vegetal or maritime. Sub notes could be spinach, seaweed, broth, beans, oyster, herbs, citrus.
CONTRAST: look for tea with main notes that are sweet and umami, rich, earthy, spicy. Sub notes could be forest, clay, hay, soft fruit, nuts, vanilla, mushrooms, butter, cream, caramel, pipe tobacco, cinnamon.
ENHANCEMENT: look for tea with main notes that are sweet, bitter, rich or bright, floral or fruity. Sub notes could be red grapefruit, chicory, jasmine, orchid, tropical fruit.

MEAT, POULTRY, UMAMI FOOD
BALANCE: look for tea with main notes that are sweet, umami, rich, earthy, animal or fruity. Sub notes could be hay, mushrooms, wood, cloves, dried fruit, butter, tobacco, leather, smoke, nuts, honey, minerals.
CONTRAST: look for tea with main notes that are sour, saline, bitter, bright, floral or vegetal. Sub notes could be red fruit, seaweed, asparagus, rose, chicory, honeysuckle, grapefruit.
ENHANCEMENT: look for tea with main notes that are sweet, bitter, saline, bright, spices, vegetal, maritime, herbaceous, floral or fruity. Sub notes could be anise seed, mint, grapefruit, shell fish, nasturtium, licorice.

VEGETABLES
BALANCE: look for tea with main notes that are sweet, saline, umami, rich, nutty, dairy and vegetal. Sub notes could be peas, corn, butter, almonds, peanuts, mushrooms, cream, beans.
CONTRAST: look for tea with main notes that are sour, bright, fruity, floral, or spicy. Sub notes could be citrus, green apple, peach, mint, nasturtium, orange blossom, cinnamon, ginger.
ENHANCEMENT: look for tea with main notes that are umami, rich, floral or animal. Sub notes could be dried fruit, honey, hay, jasmine, rose.

ACIDIC FOOD
BALANCE: look for tea with main notes that are sweet, umami, rich, soft fruit or dairy. Sub notes could be honey, hay, mango, peach, pear, butter, milk, cream.

CONTRAST: look for tea with main notes that are saline, umami, rich, maritime, smoky or animal. Sub notes could be vegetable stock, stable, hay, seaweed, oyster, charcoal, cigar, camp fire, pepper.
ENHANCEMENT: look for tea with main notes that are umami, sour, bright, earthy, floral or fruity. Sub notes could be mushroom, yam, forest floor, gardenia, citrus fruit, red fruit.

SWEET FOOD

BALANCE: look for tea with main notes that are sweet, round, smooth, rich to neutral, floral, soft fruit or dairy. Sub notes could be rose, hyacinth, orchid, mango, peach, pear, dried apricot, butter, caramel, cocoa, cream.
CONTRAST: look for tea with main notes that are sour, bitter, bright, fruity, rich or spicy. Sub notes could be citrus, tropical fruit, red fruit, cinnamon, ginger, pepper, mint.
ENHANCEMENT: look for tea with main notes that are saline, umami, rich, smooth, earthy, mineral or floral. Sub notes could be seaweed, mushroom, hay, rock, chamomile, licorice.

In the appendix on pages 272 - 277 you will find a list with a few examples of every tea type, their specific flavor profile and some potential food pairings. Please bear in mind that the result depends not only on the type of tea but also on the way the food and tea are prepared, which herbs and spices have been used, what were the cooking techniques and what are the the side dishes, as explained earlier, on page 60. In addition, two identical types of teas (or wine) from different origins could have an entirely different effect on food. The list is meant to point you in a plausible direction, but the proof is always in the pudding.

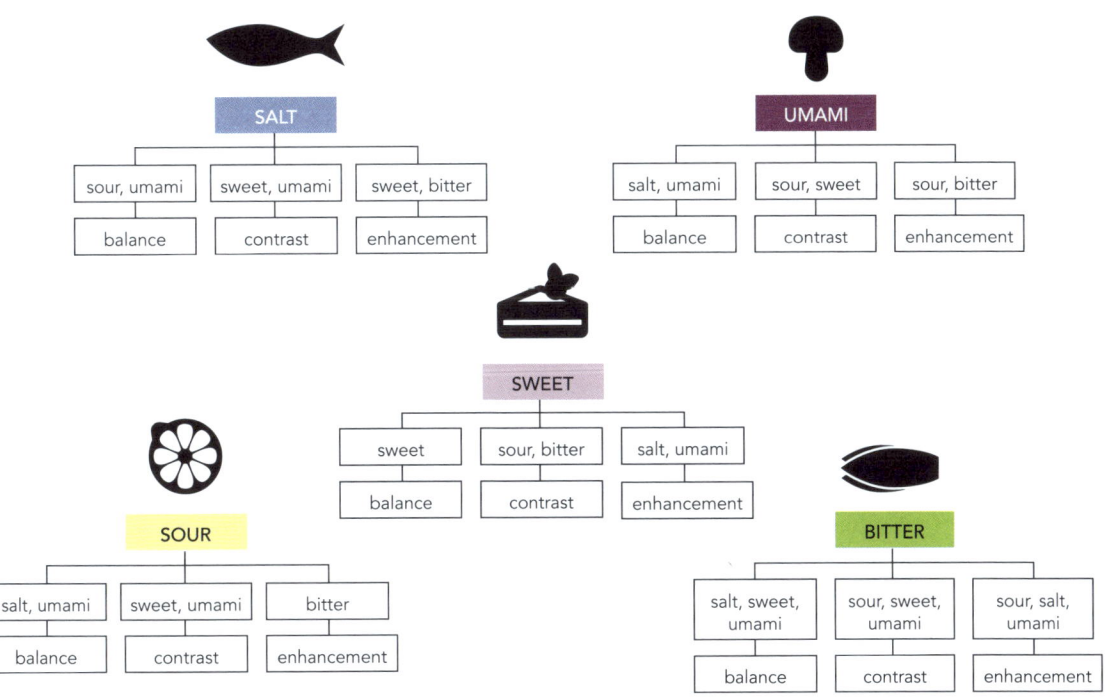

CHAPTER 5

RECIPES WITH THREE TEA SUGGESTIONS

For each recipe:
use the cold brew hot tea method (see page 36 - 37),
or steep the chosen tea 5 minutes before serving
the food and serve the tea straight away.
This way, the tea has time to cool down a bit.

> You will find many more tea suggestions
> for food on pages 256 - 273.

PB Plant based

VG Vegetarian

SF Seafood-Fish

MP Meat-Poultry

S Sweets

Mashed potatoes with purslane, basil and almonds

Serves 2

2 bunches purslane (or endive, if purslane is not available)
500 g (17.6 oz) mashed potatoes
4 tbsp roasted and salted almonds
8 basil leaves
extra virgin olive oil
zest of 1 lemon
½ tbsp lemon juice
salt and pepper

This is a fast and simple summer dish, perfect for hot summer days. Wash the purslane and pat dry, then roughly chop it.
Heat up the mashed potatoes or make it from scratch by bringing plenty of cold water to a boil with 500 g (17.5 oz) of peeled and chopped potatoes of equally sized chunks and a large pinch of salt. Cook for 15 minutes, drain, add some hot milk or hot vegetable stock, a tbsp of butter or olive oil and mashed potatoes until creamy.
Mix in the purslane, the lemon zest, the lemon juice, another splash of olive oil if necessary, salt and pepper.
Place the basil leaves on top of each other, roll them up tightly and cut thin slivers crosswise. Divide them over the mashed potatoes, together with the chopped almonds.

Optional
Replace the almonds with tiny cubes of fried bacon.

* Green tea with lemon
Blend
The tea gets more depth and flavor. Both the purslane and the basil are enhanced, the mashed potatoes become creamier, with more umami.

** Yellow tea
China
The almonds become more intense, the purslane becomes smooth and creamier, the basil becomes stronger and the mashed potatoes sweeter. The tea acquires more umami and becomes sweeter.

*** Anji Bai Cha
green tea, China
The purslane becomes smooth, sweeter. The food acquires more depth and umami, becomes stronger. The potatoes and nuts make the tea sweeter, the zest and basil make it brighter.

Roasted sweet potatoes with broccoli and tahini

Serves 4

1 kg (35 oz) sweet potatoes or yams
1 red onion
8 small shallots
4 cloves garlic
500 g (17.5 oz) broccoli florets
1 liter (34 fl. oz) vegetable stock
50 ml (1.7 fl. oz) olive oil
1 tsp cumin seed (whole or powdered)
1 tsp coriander seed (whole or powdered)
2 cm (0.75 inch) ginger
handful of Italian parsley or coriander
optional: 4 tbsp of pomegranate seeds
salt and pepper

Sauce
150 g (5.25 oz) tahini
1 tbsp sweet soy sauce (Ketjap Manis)
150 ml (5 fl. oz) cooking liquid from the broccoli
1 tbsp pomegranate molasses
1 tbsp wine vinegar

flatbread

Marinade
Preheat the oven to 200°C (400°F) and move oven rack to middle position. Peel and grate the ginger. Roast the seeds in a hot, dry skillet until fragrant. Rub into a powder with the mortar and pestle. This means a little more work, but it has much more flavor. If you do not have a mortar and pestle, then use store-bought powdered spices.

Vegetables
In a large bowl, mix the olive oil and the ginger, cumin, coriander, salt and pepper. Peel the sweet potatoes, cut them into 2½ cm (1-inch) chunks and add to the bowl. Peel the red onion and shallots, cut into wedges and add to the bowl, with the unpeeled cloves of garlic. Mix well until all the ingredients are covered with the mixture. Transfer to a baking sheet lined with parchment paper and place in the middle of the oven until the potatoes are cooked and the onions slightly blackened. This takes about 20 minutes. Bring the vegetable stock to a boil, add the broccoli florets, lower the heat and cook until al dente. Remove the vegetables and drain in a colander. Transfer to the big bowl with the oil-spice mixture. Add some more oil and spices if there is nothing left in the bowl.

Sauce
Stir the tahini well until smooth, transfer to a blender. Add the other ingredients. Pulse and taste. Add more of the ingredients if necessary. Scoop the sauce into a sauce bowl.

Finish
Chop the herbs. Mix the vegetables with the potatoes and onions and place in a shallow serving dish. Remove the skins from the roasted garlic and add to the serving dish. Garnish with the chopped herbs and pomegranate seeds. Serve the sauce on the side, together with flatbread.

Optional
Serve with roasted chicken thighs or roasted merguez sausages.

* Jasmine	** Hōjicha	*** Wen Baozhong
green or white tea, China	roasted green tea, Japan	light oolong tea, Taiwan
The tea acquires more depth, becomes less floral, acquires umami and adds floral notes to the food, which also becomes lighter and fresher, more intense.	The tea acquires notes of aniseed, with a fresh and clean texture, adds nutty notes to the sauce, enhances the food, makes it sweeter and deeper.	The tea makes the sauce and the potatoes lighter, enhances all flavors and brings them together. The umami is emphasized, floral notes are added.

PB

Pulled jackfruit with BBQ sauce and coleslaw

Serves 6 - 8

1 kilo (35.27 oz) jack fruit
6 - 8 buns

Marinade for jackfruit
2 heaped tbsp brown sugar
½ tbsp pimentón (powdered smoked paprika)
½ tsp cayenne pepper or chili pepper
200 ml (6.76 fl. oz) ketchup
3 small shallots
1 clove of garlic
½ tbsp ground cumin
2 tbsp white wine vinegar
1 tbsp vegan umami sauce
sea salt and pepper

Coleslaw
½ cabbage, white or red
2 small carrots
1 stalk of celery
1 small red onion
1 green bell pepper
200 ml (6.76 fl. oz) vegan mayonnaise
zest of 1 lime
juice of 2 limes
1 tbsp caraway seeds
sea salt and pepper

6 hours ahead or overnight
Start by making the pulled jackfruit. Taste the jackfruit. If too acidic for your taste, rinse well with cold water and drain. Remove all seeds and hard pieces. Pull the remaining pieces of jackfruit apart with a fork to make it look like shredded meat. Place all marinade ingredients in a blender or food processor and pulse. Transfer to a bowl, add the jackfruit, mix well. Cover and place in fridge for at least 6 hours or overnight.

Coleslaw
Wash the cabbage, pat dry. Remove the core. Shave or cut the cabbage into very thin strips with a mandoline or food processor.
Chop the onion very finely. Wash and dry the bell pepper, remove seeds, cut into very thin strips.
Peel the carrots, cut into very thin julienne (match sticks) or grate them. Wash and dry the celery stalk, cut crosswise into thin slices.
Mix all vegetables in a large bowl. Mix the vegan mayonnaise in a small bowl with the caraway seeds, the zest and juice of the lime, salt and pepper. Add the sauce to the vegetables. Stir well, cover. Place in fridge. May be made one day ahead.

>>

BBQ sauce
This amount makes 500 ml (16.9 fl oz)

60 ml (2.10 fl oz) white wine vinegar
60 ml (2.10 fl oz) water
200 ml (6.76 fl oz) ketchup
125 g (4.4 oz) brown sugar
Pinch of salt
Pinch of smoked paprika powder (pimentón)
Optional: pinch of ground chili pepper

>>

BBQ sauce
Mix all the ingredients in a blender until the sugar has dissolved. Season to taste. Bring to a boil and cook for 1 minute. Allow it to cool before transferring it to a jar or container. Place in the refrigerator, covered. May be made up to three days in advance.

Finish
Before serving, let sauce warm up to room temperature for at least half an hour. Heat a large pan, add 1 tbsp of oil, add the marinade and jackfruit, lower the heat, simmer for about 10 minutes.
Cut the buns in halves, add coleslaw, jackfruit and a bit of BBQ sauce.

Pairs well with the cocktails Holy Smoky Mary and Bombay Bubble on page 216 - 217. Or choose one of the warm teas recommended below.

Optional
Replace the jackfruit with 600 g (21.30 oz) pig's neck. Use the same marinade. Simmer the meat in the marinade, covered, for at least 5 hours either on the stove or in the slow cooker, or place in the oven at 95°C (203°F). The same teas are applicable.

* Earl grey
black tea, scented, blend
The tea becomes fruitier, makes the food fresher, brighter.

** Assam
black tea, India
The tea tastes a bit citrusy at first, becomes creamy and sweet.
All flavors come together, become deeper, enhanced.

*** Kamairicha
green tea, Japan
The tea acquires nutty notes, becomes sweeter, and very intense, with a full and creamy texture. It brings all flavors together, with a fresh finish.

Crustless pie with broccoli, tomato and Parmesan cheese

Serves 4 - 6

*500 g (17.63 oz) broccoli
1 red onion
1 clove garlic
1 tin of peeled and chopped tomatoes 400 g (14 oz)
2 tbsp chopped basil
4 eggs, lightly beaten
200 ml (6.76 fl oz) crème fraîche
75 g (2.65 oz) grated Parmesan cheese
12 kalamata olives, pitted*

Preheat the oven to 200°C (392°F) and move oven rack to middle position. Wash the broccoli and divide it into florets. Dice the stalks. Cook or steam it to al dente in about 5 minutes, then drain in a colander.
Butter a pie pan or oven dish. Chop the onions and garlic. Heat some oil in a skillet and fry the onion until translucent. Add the garlic. Pass the chopped tomatoes through a strainer into a bowl. Add the chopped tomatoes to the onion. Bring to a slow boil until almost all liquid has evaporated. Add the chopped basil. Slice the olives and add to the mixture. Add salt and pepper to taste. Mix the beaten eggs with the crème fraîche, salt and pepper. Add the broccoli to the oven dish or pie pan, followed by the tomato mixture. Pour the egg mixture onto the tomato layer and cover with grated cheese. Bake in the oven for 25 - 30 minutes.

Optional
Replace the olives with chopped bacon, frying it together with the onions.

* Green tea of your choice
The green tea makes the broccoli sweeter and softer, and the tomato more intense and sweeter. The tea acquires more zest.

** Ceylon Uva
black tea, Sri Lanka
The tea enhances all the flavors and it makes the texture mellow and adds note of cinnamon. The tea itself becomes brighter and cleaner, and the cheese more intense.

*** Dong Fang Mei Ren
dark oolong, Taiwan
Cinnamon appears in this combination as well. The tea adds floral notes to the food, makes it lighter and brighter, enhances the pepper, makes the broccoli sweeter. The tea becomes deeper, less sweet, more umami.

Pea mousse with lemon, mint and cheese wafers

Serves 4

200 g (7.05 oz) frozen peas
12 mint leaves
1 clove garlic
50 ml (1.7 fl. oz) sour cream
zest and juice of ½ lemon
1 courgette
lemon peel and small mint leaves for garnish
salt and white pepper

Cheese wafers
4 tbsp grated Parmesan cheese
parchment paper

Pea mousse
Boil the peas in a few tbsp salted water over low heat. Strain and drain well. Set 5 tbsp of peas aside. Transfer the remaining peas to a blender. Chop the 12 mint leaves and the garlic roughly, add to the peas, with $^{2}/_{3}$ of the sour cream, the lemon zest, 1 tbsp of lemon juice, ¼ of a tsp salt and white pepper. Pulse into a firm purée. If it becomes too thick, add some cream. If too thin, add more peas. Taste the purée, add lemon juice, mint, pepper and salt if necessary.

With a mandoline cut the courgette into very thin lengthwise slices, each about 2 mm (0.01inch) thick. Sprinkle with a pinch of white pepper (not salt, as this will make the slices soggy). Lightly brush 4 small round oven bowls, ø 6 - 7 cm (2 - 2½ inches) with neutral oil, such as soy oil. Stick the slices of courgette to the inside of the bowl, cut away any excess if too long. Scoop the pea purée into the bowls. Cover with clingfilm, place it in the fridge for at least 1 hour.

Cheese wafers
Preheat the oven to 200°C (392°F) and move oven rack to middle position. Line a baking sheet with parchment paper, sprinkle grated Parmesan cheese in the shape of circles of ø 6 - 7 cm (2 - 2½ inches). Place in the oven until the cheese is golden. This happens very quickly, so stay near the oven. Overly baked cheese tastes bitter, so paler wafers are better than darker ones.

Finish
Remove the clingfilm from the bowls, place a serving plate over each bowl and turn it around, shaking them gently until the mousse slips out onto the plate. Garnish with peas, mint and lemon peel and top each plate with a wafer.

Optional
Preheat the oven to 150°C (302°F). Place 4 thin slices of bacon onto the oven rack and bake until golden. Transfer to a stack of kitchen paper to cool and turn crispy. Serve with Hōjicha, roasted Japanese green tea.

* Gunpowder
green tea, China
This tea slightly enhances all the flavors. The tea itself tastes more vegetal and takes on more umami.

** Meng Ding Huang Cha
yellow tea, China
The slightly nutty notes of the tea blend with the food, the tea becomes more intense and deeper, takes on vegetal notes, while the food becomes sweeter and fuller.

*** Zhu Ye Qing (Bamboo Leaf)
green tea, China
The flavors of tea and food compliment each other. Tea and mousse become silkier, thicker. The tea enhances all flavors, and the umami in the tea becomes prominent.

Courgettes stuffed with mushrooms and Camembert cheese

Serves 2

4 round courgettes (round zucchini, or the usual ones if not available)
250 g (8.8 oz) brown mushrooms
2 shallots
1 clove garlic
olive oil or butter
optional: a splash of dry white wine
1 tbsp thyme or lemon thyme leaves
150 g (5.3 oz) Camembert cheese, cold

Preheat the oven to 200°C (400°F) and move oven rack to middle position. Wash and dry the courgettes. Cut off the top part like a lid, set aside and scoop out the flesh of the courgettes with a spoon. Chop the flesh. Chop the shallots and garlic very finely. Chop the thyme leaves. Wipe off any dirt from the mushrooms and slice or chop them.

In a large skillet, heat the butter or oil. Add the shallots, cook until translucent, add the garlic and thyme, cook for 1 minute, add the mushrooms. Turn up the heat, stir while baking the mixture, then add the wine (or water, or black tea extract, e.g., Shu Pu Erh). Allow to evaporate until only 1 tbsp of the liquid is left. Add the chopped courgette flesh. Cover and lower the heat. Cook until the mushrooms are tender. Add salt and pepper to taste.

Fill the courgettes with this mixture. Cut off 8 slices of the cold cheese and place two on top of each stuffed courgette. (Warm cheese is difficult to slice). Put the top of the courgettes on top of the cheese, place them onto a baking sheet lined with parchment paper and place in the middle of the oven. Bake for a few minutes until the cheese turns golden brown, with brown crispy edges here and there.

Optional
Replace the cheese with thin strips of bacon.

* **English breakfast**	** **Dong Ding**	*** **Tamaryokucha**
black tea, blend	*light oolong, Taiwan*	*green tea, Japan*
The tea becomes creamy, sweeter and softer, and makes the food deeper and fuller. The cheese tastes more pronounced.	The food tastes stronger, becomes nutty. The pepper and cheese are enhanced. The tea acquires more umami, with notes of aniseed. Aftertaste is bright.	All flavors become stronger and intertwine, the mushrooms and cheese are enhanced. The tea becomes more herbaceous, less sweet, more umami.

Lentils with aubergine, bell pepper and celery root

Serves 4

2 cans lentils, about 800 g (28.5 oz)
1 celery root
1 aubergine
1 red bell pepper
1 yellow bell pepper
1 red onion
4 cloves garlic
2 tsp Ras el Hanout (available at shops selling Middle Eastern products)
pinch chili powder
4 tbsp olive oil for baking
12 cherry tomatoes
zest and juice of half a lemon
3 tbsp extra virgin olive oil
salt and pepper

Sauce
250 ml (8.8 fl. oz) Greek yoghurt, 10% fat
½ cucumber
handful mint leaves
salt and pepper

Vegetables
Preheat the oven to 275°C (527°F) and move oven rack to middle position. Peel the celery root and cut it into 2½ cm (1 inch) cubes. Place them into a large bowl. Peel the onion and cut it into wedges with the root end intact, so the scales stay attached. Add the wedges to the bowl, together with the unpeeled garlic cloves. Mix the olive oil with the Ras el Hanout, the chili powder and a large pinch of salt. Pour this mixture over the celery root and onion and stir well. Transfer to a baking sheet covered with parchment paper.

Wash and dry the aubergine and the bell peppers. Puncture the aubergine around with the point of a knife. Grease an oven sheet, place the aubergine and bell pepper onto it and place it on a high shelf in the oven. Leave in the oven until they are blackened and blistered. This may take up to 30 minutes. Turn regularly with thongs.
Place the blackened bell peppers in a large bowl and cover. Slit the aubergine and place it upside down in a strainer over a bowl.
Lower the temperature of the oven to 200°C (392°F).
Place the sheet with celery root and onions in the center of the oven for about 20 minutes, until the edges turn golden. Stir regularly.
In the same bowl where the celery root and onions were mixed, place the cherry tomatoes and stir till covered with the oil and spices. If necessary, add more oil and spices.

After 15 minutes of roasting, remove the garlic cloves from the baking sheet and add the tomatoes.

Wash and dry the cucumber, cut it lengthwise into quarters, remove the seeds and finely dice it into cubes.
Peel and mash the roasted garlic cloves and add them to the yoghurt, together with the diced cucumber. Chop the mint leaves and add them to the yoghurt. Season to taste with salt and pepper. Cover and set aside.

>>

\>\>

Remove the skins and seeds from the bell peppers over a strainer on top of a bowl, to catch the juices running from the bell pepper. This way, the seeds and skin do not fall into the juice. Cut the peeled bell peppers into large pieces. Cut open the aubergine and thoroughly scrape out the flesh. Discard the blackened skin.
Scoop the flesh into the bowl with the bell pepper.

Dressing
Mix the extra virgin olive oil in a bowl with the juices of bell peppers and aubergine. Add 1 tbsp lemon juice, salt and pepper. Stir well, adjust to taste.

Finish
Strain the lentils, then heat some olive oil in a pan to heat them. Check if they are cooked. If not, continue to cook until done.
Chop some mint leaves, add the lemon zest, and mix well.
Take the lentils off the heat. Add the dressing and the roasted celery root, onions, bell pepper and aubergine. Mix carefully. Transfer the mixture to a wide serving dish, sprinkle with the mint-lemon zest mixture. Serve.

Tip
Prepare some very strong black tea using 8 g (0.28 oz) tea and 300 ml (10 fl.oz) filtered water at 95°C (203°F). Steep for 2-3 minutes and pass it through a strainer. Add the tea to the lentils 5 minutes before serving. This will make the flavor deeper, warmer and more intense, and the tea will also bring the flavors together.

Optional
Serve with fried merguez lamb sausages.

Optional
Serve with grilled haddock fillet, sprinkled with smoked paprika powder (pimentón).

* English Breakfast
black tea, blend
The tea becomes sweeter and softer, enhances the lentils. The flavors come together, but remain distinctive.

** Keemun
black tea, China
The tea adds a hint of rose to the food. All flavors complement each other.

*** Shu Pu-Erh
(cooked), post-fermented tea, China
The earthy notes of both food and tea are enhanced. All flavors mingle. The tea becomes softer, brighter and sweeter.

Roasted winter vegetables with lemon-yogurt-mayo sauce

Serves 4

50 g (1.76 oz) skinless hazelnuts
500 g (17.6 oz) Jerusalem artichokes
2 yellow beetroots
1 small pumpkin
8 small or 4 large shallots
2 cloves garlic
a handful Italian parsley

Marinade

50 ml (1.7 fl. oz) olive oil
1 tsp cumin seeds
1 tsp fennel seeds
1 tsp caraway seeds
1 tsp of aniseed
½ tsp chili flakes or chili powder
2½ cm (1 inch) ginger root
salt and pepper

Sauce

4 tbsp Greek yoghurt, 10% fat
4 tbsp mayonnaise
1 tbsp lemon zest
1 tbsp lemon juice
1 tsp mustard
sea salt and pepper
optional: bergamot lemon

Vegetables

Turn the oven up to 200°C (392°F).
In a large bowl, mix all the ingredients together for the marinade. Peel the Jerusalem artichokes, cut into 1 cm (½ inch) slices, add them to the bowl with marinade.
Peel the shallots and cut them into quarters. Wash and dry the pumpkin. Remove the seeds and cut it into 2½ cm (1 inch) chunks. Remove the seeds and cut it into 2½ cm (1 inch) chunks.
Peel the beetroots. Cut into 8 wedges. Add all vegetables and the unpeeled cloves of garlic to the bowl.
Stir until they are all well covered with marinade. Divide this mixture over the baking tray with wax paper. Place in the middle of the oven and roast for about 20 minutes, or until the vegetables are roasted and the onions are blackened at the edges.
Remove the cloves of garlic after 10 minutes of roasting and let them cool.

Sauce

Mix all the ingredients for the sauce. Peel the roasted cloves of garlic and rub two of them into a paste with a bit of salt and add this to the sauce.

Finish

Scoop the roasted vegetables into a shallow bowl. Chop the other 2 cloves of garlic and divide them over the bowl. Roughly chop the parsley, mix it with the chopped hazelnuts and some sea salt and sprinkle this over the vegetables. Serve with rustic bread and the sauce.

Optional
Serve with fried chicken thighs.

* **Gunpowder**	** **Hōjicha**	*** **Dong Ding**
green tea, China	roasted green tea, Japan	light oolong, Taiwan
The tea acquires more depth and flavor and becomes sweeter. The food becomes sweeter and deeper. The sauce becomes lighter.	The tea enhances the sauce, adds nuttiness, and softens it. The vegetables are enhanced and they become sweeter as well. The tea becomes brighter.	The tea becomes brighter and more floral. The vegetables and the spices become more prominent. The tea and the food balance each other out.

Roasted cauliflower with almonds and Camembert cheese

Serves 4

1 cauliflower
3 tbsp olive oil
2 tsp ground cumin
½ tsp smoked paprika (mild)
150 g (5.3 oz) Camembert cheese, cold
4 tbsp chopped raw almonds
handful Italian parsley
pepper
sea salt

Almonds
Preheat the oven to 180°C (375°F) and move oven rack to middle position. Line a baking sheet with parchment paper, add the chopped almonds and roast until golden, about 8 - 10 minutes. Transfer to a plate to cool off. Keep the sheet with parchment paper for later use.

Cauliflower
Turn the oven up to 200°C (400°F). Divide the cauliflower into large florets, about 1 - 1½ cm (2½ - 3½ inches) each. Bring plenty of water to a boil, add a large pinch of salt and the florets. Blanch them for 3 minutes, transfer to a colander, drain well and pat dry with paper towels. In a large bowl, mix olive oil with cumin, smoked paprika, salt and pepper, brush the florets with this mixture. Place the florets onto the baking sheet lined with parchment paper and place this in the middle of the oven. Roast until golden for about 15 - 20 minutes.

In the meantime, cut the cold Camembert into long slices, each about 6 mm (¼ inch) thick. Chop the parsley and roasted almonds and mix together with some sea salt. Remove the cauliflower from the oven when cooked and golden, cover with the slices of cheese and return to the oven to melt. This only takes a few minutes.

Finish
Divide the cauliflower over 4 small plates, and sprinkle with the almond-parsley mixture. Delicious with fried potatoes and a green salad.

Optional
Replace the cheese with slices of chorizo, leave out the almonds. Replace the smoked paprika powder with 2 tsp of turmeric.

* English breakfast
black tea, blend
The tea enhances the cumin, becomes fuller, with more umami, the cauliflower becomes sweeter and softer. The cheese acquires the flavor of the tea.

** Ceylon
black tea, Sri Lanka
The tea becomes fuller, sweeter and fruitier, acquires more umami. The food becomes fresher and lighter, is enhanced, acquires more umami. Clean aftertaste.

*** Yue Guang Bai
white tea, China
The tea becomes earthier and creamier, with more umami and depth. The food becomes stronger, with more umami, the cheese less salty, and velvety.

Pasta with tomato, broccoli and Camembert or red flora cheese

Serves 4

500 g (17.5 oz) broccoli
1 liter (34 fl.oz) vegetable stock
300 g (10.5 oz) penne pasta

Sauce
1 red onion
1 clove of garlic
2 handfuls basil leaves
200 ml (6.7 fl oz) crème fraîche
8 sun-dried tomatoes in oil

250 g (8.8 oz) Camembert or Pont-l'Évêque cheese, cold
salt and pepper

Pont-l'Évêque cheese is a pungent, slightly nutty cheese with an orange-brown washed rind and is made in Normandy, just like Camembert. The latter is less pungent, a bit more peppery, both are creamy and smooth.

Broccoli
Wash the broccoli and cut it into chunks. There is no need to do this in a neat way, as the chunks will be puréed later on anyway. Bring the stock to a gentle boil, add the broccoli and cook until al dente. The broccoli should look bright green. Scoop the broccoli out of the stock with a slotted spoon and transfer to a colander over a large bowl. Add the pasta to the stock and cook al dente. Drain and set aside.

Sauce
Preheat the oven to 220°C (428°F) and move oven rack to middle position. Cut the onion and garlic into pieces. Pour 1 tbsp of the oil out of the jar with the sun dried tomatoes into a skillet. Fry the onions over low heat until they turn golden, about 10 minutes. Add the garlic. Fry for one more minute. Scoop the broccoli into a blender or food processor. Add the onions, the basil, the crème fraîche, salt and pepper. Pulse until you get a chunky sauce. Chop the sun-dried tomatoes and add to the sauce. Do not pulse. Season to taste.

Finish
Butter an oven dish. Mix the pasta with the broccoli sauce and transfer to the oven dish.
Take the cheese out of the fridge and cut it into 6 mm (¼ inch) slices. Divide over the broccoli-pasta mixture. Place in the upper part of the oven and let it melt for a few minutes.

This dish may be made one day ahead. Cover the dish with aluminium foil and put it in a preheated oven at 200°C (400°F) for 25 - 30 minutes.

* Gunpowder
green tea, China
The food becomes lighter and fresher. The tea tastes softer, less dry, brighter.

** Dong Fang Mei Ren
dark oolong, Taiwan
The tea becomes fuller, and acquires more umami, adds sweetness, floral notes and nuttiness to the food, which becomes deeper, richer and creamier.

*** Mao Feng
green tea, China
The tea becomes richer, acquires more umami, adds nutty and vegetal notes to the food. The food acquires more depth, all flavors are enhanced, clean palate.

Pumpkin with mushrooms, Gorgonzola and pecans

Serves 2

1 pumpkin
1 small red onion
1 clove garlic
½ tbsp rosemary leaves
½ tbsp thyme leaves
125 g (4.4 oz) mushrooms
½ glass dry white wine
or ½ glass cold black tea
1 tbsp butter
olive oil
100 g (3.5 oz) Gorgonzola piccante cheese
8 salted pecans
handful Italian parsley
salt and pepper

Mushrooms
Preheat the oven to 200°C (400°F) and move oven rack to middle position. Finely chop the onion and garlic. Chop the rosemary and thyme coarsely. Wipe the mushrooms clean and chop them. Heat 1 tbsp of olive oil in a skillet, add the onion and fry until translucent. Add the garlic, and fry for one more minute. Add the chopped rosemary and thyme. Fry for one minute. Add the chopped mushrooms, turn up the heat and fry for 2 minutes. Add the wine or tea and allow to reduce to approximately 1 tbsp of liquid. Season to taste with salt and pepper. Turn off the heat.

Pumpkin
Wash and dry the pumpkin. Cut lengthwise in two and remove the seeds with a spoon. Lightly brush the two halves with olive oil. Sprinkle with salt and pepper, then roast in the middle of the oven for about 30 - 40 minutes or until cooked. Remove from the oven, spoon the mushroom mixture into the hollowed pumpkin halves. Place back into the oven for about 10 minutes. In the meantime, crumble the cheese, chop 6 pecans and a handful of parsley.

Finish
Remove the pumpkin from the oven, divide the nuts and cheese over the two halves and place back into the oven for a few minutes until the cheese has melted. Just before serving, garnish with the two remaining pecans and the chopped parsley.

Optional
Replace the cheese with some minced meat, fried together with the onions.

* English breakfast
black tea, blend
The flavors all blend together nicely and are enhanced by the tea. Initially the flavor of the tea disappears, but after a second sip the tea acquires more umami, is sweeter and brighter.

** Da Hong Pao
dark rock oolong, China
The tea enhances all flavors, brings more depth, connects the flavors, while the tea itself becomes less sweet, acquires more umami, with stronger earthy notes.

*** Shu Pu-Erh (cooked) Third steep
post-fermented tea, China
The tea becomes vivacious, brighter, less sweet. Flavor explosion of the mushrooms. The food becomes deeper and sweeter, with strong, earthy notes. The aftertaste is fresh and clean.

Portobello mushrooms stuffed with spinach, pecans and cheese

Serves 4

8 portobello mushrooms
250 g (8.8 oz) mixed mushrooms

Filling
2 shallots
1 clove garlic
1 tbsp thyme leaves
1 tbsp butter
300 g (10.6 oz) baby spinach
8 tbsp ground cheese (e.g., Parmesan or aged Gouda)
8 roasted salted pecans, walnuts or almonds
Sauce
1 tbsp Balsamic vinegar
1 tbsp light soy sauce

4 handfuls of mesclun lettuce
salt and pepper

Preheat the oven to 200°C (400°F) and move oven rack to middle position.

Mushrooms
Wipe the portobello mushrooms clean and remove the stems. Chop the stems roughly, carefully spoon out the gills. Clean and chop the mixed mushrooms, add to the stems and gills of the portobellos. Pour hot water over the mixed stems, gills and mushrooms. Cover and set aside for at least 30 minutes.

Sauce
Mix vinegar, honey, soy sauce and thyme.

Filling
Chop onion and garlic finely. Chop the thyme leaves. Melt the butter in a skillet, add the onion, fry until translucent. Add the garlic, fry for one more minute. Strain the mushrooms (keep the liquid), add them to the onions. Fry over half heat until the mushrooms are tender. Turn up the heat. Add the vinegar-soy sauce mixture to the pan. Reduce the liquid over high heat until a small amount is left. Add the spinach in parts and stir fry very briefly. Season to taste with salt and pepper, strain.

Butter an oven dish or baking sheet, add the portobellos, upside down. Fill the mushrooms with the drained mushroom-spinach mixture. Sprinkle with grated cheese. Place in the middle of the oven for about 15 - 20 minutes.

Finish
Place some mesclun leaves on 4 plates, place 2 portobellos on each plate, garnish with the nuts.

* **Gunpowder**	** **Dong Ding**	*** **Yue Guang Bai**
green tea, China	*light oolong, Taiwan*	*white tea, China*
The tea acquires more depth and umami, adds floral and vegetal notes to the food.	The tea enhances the nuts and umami, and brings depth to the food, the tea gains more vegetal notes and more umami, becomes less sweet.	The tea acquires more umami, becomes earthier. The food becomes sweeter and lighter, all flavors enhance each other.

Haddock with leek, beetroot and pomegranate

Serves 4

2 leeks
1 chioggia beetroot (bright pink and white on the inside, optional)
1 red beetroot
1 yellow beetroot
4 shallots
100 g rocket (arugola) salad
1 pomegranate
1 tbsp rapeseed oil or other neutral vegetable oil
4 thick fillets of haddock, 150 g (5½ oz) each

Dressing

3 tbsp extra virgin olive oil
½ tbsp balsamic vinegar
pomegranate molasses
½ clove garlic
pinch of sugar
salt and pepper

Beets

Preheat the oven to 200°C (400°F) and move oven rack to middle position. Scrub and dry the red and yellow beetroots and wrap them in aluminium foil. Place in the oven for 1 to 1½ hours.
In a small jar, blend all the ingredients for the dressing. Close the jar firmly and shake well. Set aside.
Cut the pomegranate in half and gently beat the seeds with the back of a spoon over a bowl through your fingers. Remove all the white membranes. Peel the chioggia beetroot and slice paper-thin with a mandoline.
Slice the shallot into thin rings. Heat the oil in a small skillet and fry the shallot rings until golden brown and crispy. Sprinkle with sea salt and drain on paper towels.
Wash the leeks, cut thinly. Cook in plenty salted water al dente (about 5 minutes). Drain and pat dry. Transfer to a buttered oven dish and cover with aluminium foil.

Salad

Remove the red and yellow beetroot from the oven and lower the temperature to 160°C (320°F). When cool enough to handle, remove the skins and cut the beetroots into wedges. Transfer to another buttered oven dish; cover with aluminium foil. Place both oven dishes in the oven for 15 minutes. Wash and dry the rocket leaves, transfer to a large bowl, add the slices of Chioggia beetroot and add some dressing. Carefully mix and transfer to 4 plates.

Fish

Pat the filets of fish dry, brush with rapeseed oil, sprinkle with pepper and salt. Heat a skillet till piping hot, add the fish fillets. Do not move them around. Fry about 3 minutes on each side.

Finish

Remove the vegetables from the oven, divide over the 4 plates. Add the fish filets. Spoon over the remaining dressing, top with the fried shallots and pomegranate seeds.

* Sencha
green tea, Japan
This tea combines well with the food, but it does make the fish a bit dryer. Keep that in mind when frying the fish, you should slightly undercook it. The tea enhances the food, makes the beetroot brighter and lighter.

** Hōjicha
roasted green tea, Japan
The woody and nutty notes combine well with the earthy notes of the vegetables and the fried onion. As this tea is quite smooth, it does not have a drying effect on the fish.

*** Yue Guang Bai
white tea, China
This earthy, sweet tea goes well with the vegetables. The tea becomes lighter and brighter and the fish becomes sweeter, less fishy.

Hake stuffed cabbage

Serves 4

Marinade
4 thick hake fillets, or other firm white fish; skinless
1 tbsp olive oil
zest and juice of 1 lemon

Cabbage rolls
4 large, dark green cabbage leaves
Iced water
2 shallots
1 clove garlic
250 g (8.81 oz) mixed mushrooms
1 leek
150 ml (5 fl. oz) sour cream
1 tbsp unsalted butter
handful tarragon
handful flat parsley
6 anchovy fillets
2 tbsp liquid smoke
olive oil
4 tbsp grated Parmesan cheese
250 g (8.81 oz) orecchiette pasta
pinch chili pepper
splash dry white wine (optional)
ice cubes
white pepper
salt

Marinade
Mix the olive oil with the lemon zest, 1 tsp juice, white pepper and salt and coat the fish with it. Cover and set aside.

Cabbage rolls
Cut the area with the thickest part of the grain away from the cabbage leaves (see photo). Wash the leaves and blanch them for 7 minutes in salted, simmering water. Remove the leaves from the pan and let them cool in plenty of iced water. Then let them drain well on a tea towel. Pat dry gently. Save the blanching liquid for the pasta. Cut the smallest leaves into thin strips.

Filling
Preheat the oven to 180°C (356°F) and move oven rack to middle position. Wipe the mushrooms and put half of them in the food processor with the garlic, parsley, olive oil, chili pepper and salt. Pulse in the food processor. Add the Parmesan cheese and pulse again. Grease an oven dish.
Put the liquid smoke into a bowl. Brush the four cabbage leaves generously with the liquid smoke, using a brush. Place a piece of fish onto each strip of cabbage and spread a layer of the mushroom mixture onto the fish. Roll up the cabbage leaf like a spring roll and place the fish roll onto the baking dish with its seam down. Put it in the oven for 20 minutes. Meanwhile, cook the pasta to al dente in the blanching liquid and prepare the sauce.

>>

\>\>

Sauce
Chop the shallots. Cut the other half of the mushrooms into slices. Wash the leek, drain well, and remove the dark green leaves and the bottom part and cut the light part into thin rings. Melt the butter in a large pan, add the shallots and sauté until translucent. Add the anchovies and stir until slightly melted. Add the mushrooms and fry them gently over a high heat for a few minutes. Deglaze with half a tablespoon of liquid smoke and a splash of water, green tea extract or white wine. Chop the tarragon. Turn the heat to medium-high, then add the leeks, cabbage strips and tarragon. Cover and braise for a few minutes until the leek is still bright green but already soft.

Finish
Off the heat, stir the crème fraîche into the sauce with a dash of pasta cooking liquid. Then mix this with the pasta and transfer to a preheated serving bowl. Place the cabbage rolls on top of the pasta.

Optional
Replace the fish with silken tofu, follow instructions according the recipe.

* Green tea with lemon
The tea enhances the food, the tea becomes slightly drier, but also brighter. The food becomes lighter and brighter, but slightly overrules the tea.

** Mao Feng
green tea, China
The tea acquires more umami, emphasizes the vegetal notes of the food.

*** Dong Ding
light oolong, Taiwan
The tea acquires more umami and depth, emphasizes the tarragon, makes the sauce lighter, the fish creamier.

Fish with cauliflower, tomato, and Angostura sauce

Serves 4

1 cauliflower, washed and divided into florets
2 tbsp olive oil
4 white fish fillets, e.g., cod or haddock
40 g (1.4 oz) of unsalted butter, cold, cut into small cubes
juice of ½ an orange
½ tbsp honey
2 tbsp Balsamic vinegar
½ tbsp mustard, such as Dijon
½ tbsp Angostura bitters
12 cherry tomatoes
1 tbsp capers, rinsed and drained
4 basil leaves
salt and pepper

Vegetables
Preheat the oven to 200°C (400°F) and move oven rack to middle position. In a large bowl, mix the olive oil with the pepper and salt. Add the florets, mix well. Cover an oven tray with parchment paper, add the florets and roast until golden, with blackened edges, for 15 - 20 minutes.
Place the washed and dried cherry tomatoes into the bowl and mix until covered with oil, salt and pepper. Add more oil if necessary. Add them to the florets 5 minutes before those are done.

Sauce
In a small saucepan, heat the orange juice and reduce until about 1 tbsp is left. Add the vinegar, mustard, Angostura bitters and honey. Stir well. Lower the heat. Whisk in the cubes of cold butter until fully incorporated into the sauce. Season to taste.

Fish
Brush the fish fillets lightly with oil and sprinkle with salt and pepper. Heat a dry skillet until very hot. Add the fish, lower the heat a bit, bake for a few minutes without moving the fish in the pan. Flip over the fillets when golden, bake the other side for about 1 minute, until no longer translucent, but just cooked.

Finish
In a small saucepan, heat 1 tbsp of oil and fry the capers for a few seconds. Transfer with a slotted spoon, drain on kitchen paper. Roll up the basil leaves and cut them crosswise into thin slivers.
Divide the vegetables over heated plates, add the fish and some of the warm sauce. Garnish with fried capers and basil strips. Serve with mashed potatoes.

Optional
Replace the fish with fried tofu: pat tofu slices dry, brush lightly with oil, add pepper, salt and the zest of the orange, and fry until golden in hot oil.

* Sencha
green tea, Japan
The tea becomes sweeter when combined with the cauliflower, brighter with the tomato, acquires more umami with the fish. The food becomes brighter and lighter.

** Tieguanyin
light oolong, China, Taiwan or Thailand
The tea takes on more umami. The food acquires floral notes and becomes brighter. There is a general enhancement of flavors and balance.

*** Yue Guang Bai
white tea, China
The flavors of both tea and food intertwine and compliment each other. The result is a fuller and juicier dish, with the tomato and the cauliflower becoming fresher, with a clean aftertaste.

Monkfish with fennel, samphire and feta cheese

Serves 2

1 bulb fennel
2 shallots
50 g (1.76 ounces) samphire
2 tbsp olive oil
pinch chili powder
1 glass Noilly Prat or white wine
100 g (3.5 oz) feta cheese
300 g (10.58 oz) monkfish fillet (or haddock or cod, if monkfish is unavailable)
½ lemon
salt and white pepper

Mashed potatoes
1 liter (34 fl. oz) water
1 stock cube
500 ml (17 fl. oz) water
100 ml (3.4 fl. oz) full milk
30 g (1.58 oz) butter
handful chervil
salt and white pepper

Cut off the stalks of the fennel bulb and keep the green part. Remove the outer skin. Slice it lengthwise, very thin, with a mandoline or a very sharp knife. Chop the shallots into tiny cubes. Wash the samphire, and drain it.

Mashed potatoes
Peel, wash and chop the potatoes roughly and cook until done, about 15 minutes. Warm up the milk. Drain the potatoes, add the hot milk and the butter and mash until silky. Season with salt and pepper to taste. Roughly chop the chervil and mix it into the mashed potatoes.

Vegetables
Heat the olive oil in a large skillet. Add the slices of fennel, chili powder and chopped shallots. Turn down the heat and sauté until translucent. Deglaze with the Noilly Prat or white wine and let it reduce briefly over high heat. Then cover the pan, turn down the heat and simmer the fennel until cooked. Add the samphire and feta cheese. Season to taste. Cover and keep warm.

Fish
Preheat the grill or griddle.
Pat the fish fillets dry, brush some oil onto them and sprinkle them with salt and pepper. Cover an oven sheet with aluminium foil, add the fish and place the sheet under the grill. When the fish is getting brown, after 2 or 3 minutes, remove from the grill and splash with some lemon juice.

Finish
Scoop mashed potatoes and fennel mixture onto preheated plates, place the fish on top and garnish with some of the fennel greens.

Optional
Replace the fish with 100 g (3.5 oz) chopped walnuts, and splash the lemon juice onto the fennel.

* Sencha
green tea, Japan
The tea takes on more umami and depth and brings all flavors together.

** Jangwon
green tea, Korea
The tea adds herbal notes and umami to the dish, enhances the fish and the vegetal notes of the chervil. The tea becomes sweeter, with more umami.

*** Darjeeling
first flush, black tea, India
The tea makes the food softer, sweeter and more intense. The mashed potatoes become creamier and more floral, make the tea sweeter and fuller.

SF

Risotto with spinach, prawn, lemon and basil

Serves 4

300 g (10.5 oz) risotto rice
1500 ml (51 fl.oz) vegetable stock
1 wine glass of Noilly Prat (Vermout)
2 shallots
1 clove garlic
zest and juice of 1 lemon
10 basil leaves
200 g (7 oz) washed spinach
16 - 20 unpeeled prawns
50 g (1.76 oz) butter
olive oil
salt and pepper

Gently heat the stock until it is almost boiling. Keep it like that over a low heat on the back burner.
Peel the prawns. With the point of a small knife, make lengthwise slits in the backs of the prawns and scoop out the black veins with the tip of the knife. Discard the veins.
Finely chop the shallots and the garlic. In a high pan with thick bottom, heat 2 tbsps of olive oil. Add the shallots and sauté until translucent. Add the garlic and sauté for another minute. Add the rice and set the timer to 16 minutes. Sauté for 1 to 2 minutes, until the rice shines and makes a crispy sound: it is calling for the Noilly Prat. Add that to the rice, and stir until almost all the Vermout has evaporated, then add the stock until all the rice is just covered. Stir a little and wait until almost all the stock has been absorbed by the rice. Then repeat: add some stock, stir a little and allow the rice to absorb the stock. The rice will become mushy if stirred too much. Repeat until the rice is al dente. The rice will continue to cook even when off the heat.

Finish

Three minutes before the rice is done add the prawns to the stock. Scoop out after 2 - 3 minutes, as soon as they are not translucent anymore. Do not overcook them. Keep warm under a sheet of aluminium foil. Roll up the basil leaves and slice crosswise into thin slivers. Turn off the heat when the risotto is done, add a splash of olive oil or all the butter to the rice. Add a spoonful of stock, stir, cover and set aside. Add the spinach in parts to the rice, stir. Add the lemon juice, pepper, salt and half the basil and lemon zest to the rice. Stir. Adjust to taste. Add half the prawns, stir very carefully. The rice should not hold its shape, it should still be quite moist. Add more stock if necessary.
Divide over 4 warm bowls or plates. Garnish with the remaining prawns, basil and zest. Serve immediately.

* Sencha
green tea, Japan
The prawns become sweeter, and both the food and the tea acquire more flavor.

** Huang Da Cha
yellow tea, China
The tea adds nutty notes to the food, adds umami. It brings all flavors together, softens the spinach. The food makes the tea brighter, gives it depth.

*** Tamaryokucha
green tea, Japan
The tea is enhanced, and it brings all flavors together. The prawns become sweeter, the rice and spinach become deeper, intense, with the flavor of the tea added to it.

Bresaola with Parmesan cheese and lemon

Serves 2

100 g (3.5 oz) Bresaola (or raw ham, carpaccio, if not available)
1 piece good quality Parmesan cheese
1 lemon
extra virgin olive oil, preferably a grassy kind, like Sicilian
sourdough bread
pepper and sea salt

Divide the thinly sliced Bresaola over two plates. Shave almost transparent slices of the cheese over the meat. Cut the lemon into wedges and place 1 or 2 wedges on each plate.
Serve with the olive oil and the bread.

Bresaola is beef, marinated in a mixture of cinnamon, pepper, bay leaf and clove. It is air-dried for at least two weeks and ripens in the process. This is a protected product: only the meat produced this way in the Valtellina region in Lombardy, Italy, may be called Bresaola. If you cannot find it, replace it with either carpaccio or raw ham. Although the flavor is completely different, the recommended teas for this recipe also go well with ham or carpaccio, as long as they are of good quality.

Optional
Replace the meat with very thin, almost translucent, slices of raw beetroot. Marinate the slices for at least an hour in the following marinade: rub in a mortar and pestle a bay leaf broken into pieces, 4 or 5 peppercorns, a pinch of cinnamon, a pinch of coarse sea salt and 3 cloves. In a bowl, add the spices to 3 tbsp of high-quality olive oil and drizzle over the slices of beetroot. Cover and set aside for at least an hour.
Drain the slices and place them in a microwave, position defrost, for 3 minutes or longer if still too wet. In a conventional oven: switch the oven to 65°C (149°F). Divide the slices over an oven rack, place in the middle of the oven and place a baking sheet under the rack, to catch the dripping juices. Leave in the oven for at least 6 hours, until the pieces are dry. Turn the slices now and then.
Serve with the same tea as recommended below.

* Earl Grey
black tea, scented, blend
The spices become more prominent, the meat fruitier, softer, and fresher. The tea acquires a lot of umami, more depth, and notes of spices.

** Yue Guang Bai
white tea, China
The meat becomes sweeter, the spices more pronounced, the cheese sweeter and softer, the sharpness is gone. The tea acquires more umami and melts together with the food.

*** Shu Pu-Erh
post-fermented tea, China
The meat becomes fuller, deeper and sweeter, and the spices more prominent. The cheese becomes softer, deeper, more intense. The tea aquires more umami. Clean and fresh palate.

MP

Satay with vegetables and noodles

Serves 2

300 g (10.6 oz) chicken thighs, preferably organic
or
400 g (14.1 oz) Brussels sprouts
8 cherry tomatoes

Marinade
1 shallot
1 clove garlic
3 tbsp olive oil
½ tsp grated ginger
2 tsp tamarind paste
1 tbsp Indonesian sweet soy sauce (Ketjap Manis)
salt and pepper

Vegetables
3 tbsp of chopped onion
2 cloves of garlic
1 tsp grated ginger
1 tsp Indonesian chili paste (sambal oelek)
1 stalk lemongrass
1/4 white cabbage
½ courgette (zucchini)
1 red or yellow bell pepper
1 spring onion
1 leek
1 stalk celery
1 tsp palm sugar, or brown sugar
juice of ½ a lime
handful fresh coriander, washed and dried
1 tbsp roasted sesame seeds
rapeseed oil or peanut oil
150 g (5.3 oz) noodles

satay sauce, store bought or homemade

Skewers
Clean the Brussels sprouts or, if using chicken, cut the chicken meat into bite sized chunks.
Mix all the marinade ingredients together. Add the sprouts and the cherry tomatoes or chicken chunks. Stir until fully covered with the marinade. Cover and place in the fridge for at least 1 hour. Thread the pieces onto wooden sskewers that have soaked in cold water.

Vegetables
Wash, dry and cut all the vegetables, cut the cabbage into paper thin slivers, the other vegetables however you like. Discard the outer leaves of the lemon grass and crush the lemongrass with the back of a large chef's knife. Mix together the chopped onion, chopped garlic, grated ginger, chili paste and lemon grass. Heat 1 tbsp of oil in a wok, add the onion mixture, fry for a few minutes. Add all the vegetables except for the spring onion and fry for another few minutes over a high heat. Add the spring onion, the sugar and 3 tbsp of water. Stir well over high heat. Add the lemon juice. Stir well, turn off the heat.

Noodles
Prepare the noodles and satay sauce according instructions on the package.

Finish
Heat a grill pan or BBQ, grill the skewers until the chicken or sprouts are done. Heat up the satay sauce. Sprinkle the sesame seeds over the vegetables. Roughly chop the coriander leaves, sprinkle over the vegetables.

Note: You will find the recommended teas and a recipe for homemade satay sauce on the next page.

>>

Homemade satay sauce

3 tbsp chopped onion
2 cloves garlic
1 tsp ground cumin
1 tsp ground coriander seed
1 tsp ground ginger
1 tsp ground galangal
2 tsp chili paste (sambal oelek)
1 bay leaf
1 kaffir lime leaf
3 tbsp Indonesian sweet soy sauce (Ketjap Manis)
juice of ½ a lime
200 gram (7 oz) peanut butter
400 ml (13.52 fl. oz) full-fat coconut milk

\>\>

Blend the first seven ingredients in a blender. Heat 1 tbsp of oil in a saucepan, add the mixture, fry for a few minutes. Add the Indonesian sweet soy sauce, the peanut butter and a splash of coconut milk. Lower the heat, stir until combined. Gradually add more of the coconut milk, stirring until well blended. Add bay leaf and kaffir lime leaf. Simmer for 20 minutes, stirring often. Turn off the heat, add the lime juice, stir well. Add more coconut milk if the sauce is too thick, or more peanut butter if the sauce is too thin. Season to taste with sweet soy sauce, lime juice and chili paste.

* Gunpowder
green tea, China
The tea acquires more depth and becomes fuller. The sauce becomes lighter and brighter, the Brussels sprouts become sweeter.

** Hōjicha
roasted green tea, Japan
The tea blends well with the sauce and acquires more umami. The flavor of the food intensifies, becomes richer and fuller.

*** Dong Ding oolong
light oolong, Taiwan
The tea acquires more umami, enhances the peanut sauce, makes it lighter and brighter at the same time, while the vegetables gain roasting notes.

Fatteh chicken

Serves 4

500 g (17.5 oz) chicken thighs, preferably organic
1 can of chickpeas (around 400 g (14.10 oz)
1 tsp cumin seed
12 cherry tomatoes
1 red bell pepper
flat bread or pitta bread
4 tbsp chopped almonds
handful Italian parsley
handful mint leaves
olive oil

Marinade
4 tbsp neutral oil (e.g., rapeseed or sunflower)
zest and juice of ½ a lemon
1 clove garlic
4 tsp Ras el Hanout (Moroccan mixture of spices)
handful coriander leaves

Yoghurt sauce
250 g (8.75 oz) Turkish or Greek yoghurt, 10% fat
3 cloves garlic
1 tbsp extra virgin olive oil
handful mint leaves
¼ cucumber (or 1 Lebanese cucumber)
white pepper and salt

Marinade
Preheat the oven to 180°C (375°F) and move oven rack to middle position. Cut the chicken into 2½ cm (1 inch) pieces. Mix all of the marinade ingredients in a large bowl. Add the chicken, and mix well. Cover and place in fridge.

Almonds
Line a baking sheet with parchment paper, add the almonds and roast until golden, about 8 - 10 minutes. Transfer to a plate to cool off, chop roughly.

Vegetables
At the same time, rub the unpeeled cloves of garlic and the cherry tomatoes with some olive oil in a small oven dish. Place in the oven for about 8 - 10 minutes until the skin of the tomatoes bursts and the cloves are soft and golden. Remove from the oven. Set aside.
Turn the oven up to 250°C (482°F). Place the bell pepper on a baking sheet, high in the oven and roast until it is blackened all over. Remove from the oven, place in a bowl and cover. Set aside for 15 minutes. Switch off the oven. When cool enough to handle, remove the skin from the cloves of garlic.
Remove the skin from the bell pepper in a strainer placed over a bowl. Save the juices in the bowl and leave the skin and seeds in the strainer. Cut the peeled and seedless bell pepper into strips. Set aside.
Add a splash of olive oil, pepper and salt to the juices in the bowl. Mix well. Remove the skin and crown from the tomatoes.

Flatbread toast
Cut the flatbread into triangles and transfer it to a baking sheet covered with parchment paper. Place the sheet into the still hot oven for 4 - 6 minutes, until the triangles are golden and crispy.

Sauce
Roughly chop the mint leaves. Mash three of the roasted garlic cloves and mix them with the mint. Peel the cucumber and cut it into quarters lengthwise, removing the seeds. Thinly slice the quarters crosswise. Add these pieces to the yoghurt, and mix in the mint-garlic paste, 1 tbsp of extra virgin olive oil, salt and pepper. Stir well. Season to taste. Cover and set aside.

>>

\>\>

Chickpeas
Heat a large, dry skillet, add the cumin seeds, and cook until fragrant, then remove from the heat and leave to cool on a plate. Grind finely with a mortar and pestle (or use ground cumin if you do not have a mortar and pestle). Drain and rinse the chickpeas, cook them with a dash of olive oil and the ground cumin seeds.

Chicken
Heat the skillet again, this time with 1 tbsp of olive oil. When hot, add the piece of chicken. Fry until done, about 10 minutes.

Finish
Scoop the hot chickpeas into the middle of a large, shallow serving dish. Place the chicken on top. Spoon some of the yoghurt sauce over and around the chicken. Serve the rest of the sauce in a separate bowl. Drizzle the bell pepper oil over the sauce. Divide the bell pepper strips over the bowl. Place some of the crispy bread triangles around the edges, and serve the rest in a separate bowl. Garnish the dish with the roasted chopped almonds, chopped parsley and chopped mint.

Optional
Replace the chicken with an extra bell pepper, and add twice the amount of almonds. Replace the yoghurt sauce with vegan mayonnaise, mixed with roasted garlic, cucumber, parsley, pepper and salt.

* Earl Grey
black tea, scented, blend
The tea becomes softer, creamier and deeper. The food becomes lighter and fresher.

** Honey Black
black tea, Taiwan
The tea becomes less sweet, acquires umami and a hint of cinnamon. The food acquires more depth, becomes sweeter, while the tea adds a subtle honey aroma.

*** Darjeeling
first flush, black tea, India
The tea becomes fruitier, more floral, brighter and adds its flavor to the chicken. The food becomes enhanced and lighter.

Chicken with leek in Noilly Prat cream sauce

Serves 4

4 chicken thighs, preferably organic
2 leeks
2 stalks of celery
1 carrot
2 small onions
1 fennel bulb
50 ml (1.7 fl. oz) Noilly Prat Vermout
100 ml (3.4 fl. oz). chicken stock
1 bouquet garni (a bunch of thyme, bay leaf, parsley)
1 tbsp chopped tarragon
1 tbsp lemon zest
2 tbsp butter or olive oil
125 ml (4.22 fl. oz) crème fraîche
salt and pepper

Vegetables preparation
Wash, dry and clean the leeks, the celery stalks, the carrot, cut all crosswise into thin slices. Wash, dry and clean the fennel and remove the stalks, keeping the green leaves. Cut the fennel into thin slices and then crosswise into strips. Chop the onions.

Chicken
Wash and dry the chicken thighs. Season with salt and pepper to taste. Heat the oil or butter in a large frying pan. Add the chicken thighs and brown. Remove from the pan and set aside. Cover with aluminium foil.

Vegetables cooking
In the same pan, sauté the onion, add the carrot, fennel, celery, bouquet garni and half of the leek. Fry for a minute over high heat. Add the Noilly Prat, reduce until about 1 tbsp of liquid is left. Add the chicken stock, bring to a simmer. Add the chicken, cover. Let simmer for about 15 - 20 minutes or until the chicken is almost done. Add the other half of the leek, simmer for another 5 minutes. This brings color and bite to the sauce.

Finish
Just before serving, add the crème fraîche, stir, but do not boil. Season to taste. Add some lemon juice if the sauce needs more kick.
On a preheated platter, arrange the chicken thighs and pour the sauce over them. Decorate with chopped tarragon, lemon zest and fennel greens. Serve with fried or mashed potatoes.

* Green tea, blend
The tea becomes brighter, softer, makes the sauce lighter. Brings all flavors together and prolongs them.

** Hōjicha
roasted green tea, Japan
The tea acquires more umami and becomes deeper and fuller, enhances the aniseed notes of the sauce. The chicken becomes juicier and more spiced up.

*** Zhu Ye Qing
green tea, China
The tea becomes softer, deeper, creamier, enhances the aniseed notes of the sauce. The food, the sauce and the tea become brighter, lighter and sweeter.

Lamb shank stew with celery root and bell pepper

Serves 4 - 6

2 large or 3 small lamb shanks
olive oil for cooking
1 large red onion
6 cloves garlic
1 tbsp tomato paste
3 carrots
1 stalk celery
2 bay leaves
1 tbsp chopped rosemary
1 tbsp chopped thyme
1 tbsp Balsamic vinegar
1 tin (400 g or14.10 oz) peeled tomatoes, chopped
500 ml (17 fl. oz) vegetable stock
1 large celery root
10 yellow potatoes
8 shallots
3 red bell peppers
1 handful of Italian parley
salt and pepper

Meat
Pat the shanks dry, rub with salt and pepper. Heat 4 tbsp of oil in a heavy pan, add the shanks and brown on all sides. Chop the onion and 2 cloves of garlic. Clean the carrots and the celery stalk, cut them into 2½ cm (1 inch) pieces. Bring the stock to a boil, lower the heat. Remove the browned shanks from the pan and set aside.

Stew
Fry the tomato paste in the hot oil for about 1 minute, then add the chopped onion. When translucent, add the garlic, chopped carrot and celery. Sauté for 1 minute, add the herbs, deglaze with the vinegar. Put the shanks back into the pan, add the chopped tomatoes and the hot stock, bring to a boil. Lower the heat. Cover and simmer until done, about 2 hours. Do not allow to boil.
Remove the shanks from the pan to cool. Discard the bay leaves. Peel the meat off the bones, chop the meat roughly. Pulse the cooking liquid into a chunky sauce. Add the chopped meat and cover the pan.

Vegetables
Preheat the oven to 200°C (400°C). Line a baking sheet with parchment paper. Peel the celery root, cut into 2 cm (0.8 inch) square cubes. Wash and dry the potatoes, peel the shallots and the remaining 4 garlic cloves and cut all into wedges. Mix 2 tbsp of olive oil with salt and pepper in a large bow and add all wedges. Stir until all are covered with oil. Divide them over the baking sheet. Roast in the middle of the oven for about 20 - 30 minutes or until all are done. Stir once in a while. Wash and dry the bell peppers, remove the seeds, cut into strips, add to the oily bowl and stir. Add some more oil if necessary. Add to the baking sheet with the potatoes and shallots and bake for 10 more minutes.

Optional
Replace the meat with 600 g (21.30 oz) jackfruit (see page 74 for instructions for the jackfruit). Add to the sauce and simmer for about 10 minutes.

* English breakfast
black tea, blend
The tea becomes fruitier, fresher and brings all flavors together. The stew becomes lighter, brighter.

** Shu Pu-Erh (cooked)
post-fermented tea, China
The tea acquires more umami, becomes brighter, makes the food fuller, sweeter, deeper, earthier. Mutual enhancement.

*** Ruby #18
black tea, Taiwan
The tea becomes richer and sweeter, and makes the food brighter, fruitier and deeper at the same time.

Mariëlla's brownies

Serves 12

250 g (8.81 oz) dark chocolate, good quality, at least 70% cocoa solids
250 g (8.81 oz) granulated sugar
250 g (8.81 oz) soft unsalted butter
3 large eggs and 1 yolk
70 g (2.46 oz) all-purpose flour
70 g (2.46 oz) cocoa powder
pinch salt
2 tsp ground cinnamon
2 tsp ground cardamom
1 tsp ground ginger
pinch ground cloves
optional: 20 walnuts or pecans, roughly chopped

Preheat the oven to 175°C (347°F) and move oven rack to middle position.
Grease a rectangular baking pan of about 28 x 18 cm (11 x 7 inch) with butter.
Cut a strip of parchment paper a bit longer than the length of the baking pan, place on the bottom, with the ends of the paper sticking out. This way the brownies will be easier to remove from the pan once they are done and cooled off.
Melt the butter in an oven dish while the oven is heating up. The butter should not turn brown, so keep an eye on it. Chop the chocolate into uniform tiny pieces. Melt it using a bain-marie or double boiler while stirring regularly The bottom of the bowl with the chocolate should not touch the boiling water, to prevent the chocolate from burning. It is the steam that does the trick.
Once the chocolate is almost melted, take it off the heat, allow it to cool off a bit.
In a large bowl, mix the sugar with the melted butter. With an electric hand mixer beat until smooth. Add the melted chocolate, beat until well incorporated.
In another large bowl, sift the cocoa powder, the flour, the spices and the salt. Mix them well. Add the eggs and yolk one by one, stirring after each egg is added. Add the flour mix and carefully spoon this through the mixture until well blended. If you are using nuts, add them now, stir well.
Pour the dough into the baking pan. Shake the pan a little to divide the mixture equally over the area.
Place it in the middle of the oven. After 15 minutes, give the baking tin half a turn and let bake for another 15 minutes or until a wooden pin comes out clean when stuck in the middle.
Let the brownies cool inside the tin, then release by lifting the cake out of the tin with the help of the parchment paper sticking out. Cut into squares. The brownies taste quite good frozen, especially on a hot day.

* Earl grey	** Si Ji Chun	*** Ruby #18
black tea, scented, blend	*light oolong, Taiwan*	*black tea, Taiwan*
The tea becomes fuller, creamy, with more flavor. The brownies become lighter and brighter.	The tea becomes fuller, softer, sweeter, and acquires notes of chocolate. The brownies become lighter, fresher, and acquire floral notes.	The brownies and the tea become deeper, more intense, sweeter. The honey notes of the tea are enhanced, the chocolate becomes more chocolatey.

S

Orange almond cake with cacao nibs

Serves 12

2 oranges
250 g (8.81 oz) granulated sugar
250 g (8.81 oz) finely ground almonds, or almond meal
6 free range eggs
3 tbsp liqueur (e.g., tea liqueur, recipe on page 136)
1 tsp baking powder
2 tbsp cacao nibs
pinch salt

Claudia Roden's original recipe also includes orange blossom water. In this version I have replaced it with homemade tea liqueur made with dark oolong.
The liqueur adds depth to the cake. I also add cacao nibs, for a nice crunch and some contrast. For an extra treat, serve warm salted caramel sauce on the side, for recipe, see page 179.

Preheat the oven to 180°C (356°F) and move oven rack to middle position. Wash the oranges and cook them whole for about 90 minutes in water, until they are soft.
Beat the eggs with the sugar. Add ground almonds, baking powder, cacao nibs, salt and liqueur. Mix well.
Drain the orange over a sieve and allow to fully drain; wait till they are cool enough to handle. Cut them open, remove the seeds and blend into a purée, skin and all, in a food processor or blender.
Add to the batter and mix until thoroughly combined.
Grease a baking tin of about 22 cm (8.66 inch) diameter and lightly dust it with some ground breadcrumbs. If you would rather make this cake gluten free, then use cacao powder instead of the breadcrumbs.
Pour the batter into the baking tin and place it in the middle of the oven for about 60 minutes. Rotate pan during baking to ensure an even bake.
Let it cool in the baking pan. Remove and slide onto a flat dish.

* Earl Grey
black tea, scented, blend
The tea enhances the orange, the flavor in general becomes very refreshing. The sauce gains citrus notes and becomes lighter and brighter.

** Tieguanyin, extra roasted
oolong tea, China
The tea becomes fruity and brighter, makes the orange stronger, the sauce lighter and brighter, the cake deeper and more intense.

*** Darjeeling
first flush, black tea, India
The tea becomes sweeter and rounder, makes the cake lighter, fruitier, with stronger orange notes and some floral notes in the aftertaste.

s

Frisian thumbprint cookies

Makes about 25 cookies

250 g (8.81 oz) flour
100 g (3.52 oz) roasted and ground hazelnuts or almonds, or meal
100 g (3.52 oz) soft unsalted butter
150 g (5.29) light brown sugar
1 large egg
1 tsp cinnamon powder
1 tsp ground ginger
1 tsp ground anise powder
pinch ground clove
pinch ground cardamom
pinch ground black pepper
pinch salt

Preheat the oven to 160ºC (320ºCF), and move oven rack to middle position.
Beat the butter with the sugar until creamy. Add the egg and beat until fully combined.
Sift the flour over the butter, stir until combined. In a small bowl, mix all spices, salt and pepper. Add to the dough.
Roll out the dough on parchment paper until about 1 cm (0.4 inch).
Cover and place in fridge for about 30 minutes.

Remove from fridge, cut the dough into strips of 2 x 4 cm (0.78 x 1.57 inch). Transfer the strips to a baking sheet lined with parchment paper and with your thumb make an imprint into each strip of dough. Place the baking sheet for about 20 minutes until done and the edges are golden.

Goes very well with the peach-oolong tea sorbet on page 176.

* Earl grey
black tea, scented, blend
The tea becomes sweeter, acquires more flavor. The cookies become brighter, the nuts are enhanced.

** Feng Huang Mi Lan Dan Cong
dark oolong, China
The cookies and tea become one, both become sweeter and more enhanced, especially the spices.

*** Dong Fang Mei Ren
dark oolong, Taiwan
The tea becomes brighter and fruitier. The cookies become sweeter, the spices and nuts enhanced.

S

Roasted summer fruit with mascarpone

Serves 4

4 ripe peaches
4 ripe apricots
4 tbsp mascarpone
1 tbsp granulated sugar
½ tsp ground cinnamon
zest 1 lemon
1 tbsp lemon juice
50 gram (1.76 oz) peeled pistachios, unsalted
½ tbsp unsalted butter
8 mint leaves
pinch black pepper
pinch salt
ice cream of your choice

Preheat the oven to 225°C (437°F) and move oven rack to middle position. Beat the mascarpone and the sugar together. Add salt, pepper, ground cinnamon and lemon juice. Adjust to your liking.
Roughly chop the pistachio nuts.
Wash and dry the fruit, cut into halves, remove the pits.
Grease an oven dish with butter, place the fruit halves in it, hollow side up. Put flakes of butter in each of the hollow parts of the fruit. Place the dish in the middle of the oven and roast for about 6 - 8 minutes, until the edges blacken slightly. Allow to cool.

Place one peach half and one apricot half on each plate. Place a spoonful of the mascarpone mixture in the hollow parts of the fruit. Divide the zest, chopped nuts and mint over the plates. Place a scoop of ice cream on the side of each plate, and serve. A nice option is Chai ice cream (see the recipe on page 178).

* Earl grey
black tea, scented, blend
The dessert acquires floral notes, becomes lighter and brighter. The tea acquires depth and creaminess.

** Bai Mudan
white tea, China
The tea acquires fruity notes and becomes sweeter. All flavors intertwine, the food becomes lighter, brighter.

*** Da Hong Pao
dark rock oolong tea, China
The tea becomes fruitier and sweeter, makes the food deeper, richer.

S

Lime meringue pie

Serves 8 - 12

250 g (8.81 oz) flour
1 tbsp granulated sugar
125 g (4.4 oz) unsalted butter, cold, cubed
3 tbsp lime juice
1 small free range egg
pinch salt

Filling
6 large eggs
1 can of condensed milk 375 g (13.22 fl. oz)
zest of 1 lime
100 ml (3.4 fl. oz) lime juice
4 tbsp granulated sugar

Lime
Wash, dry and zest the lime.
Squeeze limes out completely and reserve juice.

Dough
Over a large bowl, sift the flour and salt. Add the sugar, mix well. Add the cubes of butter and cut until crumbly with two knives or in a food processor. Add the lime juice. With a cool, dry hand quickly knead until a ball forms. Wrap in cling film and put in fridge for at least 30 minutes. Dust a large surface with flour and roll out the dough until you have a circle of about 25 cm (9.84 inch).
Grease a pie tin with butter, dust it with some flour, line it with the dough. Place the tin into the freezer for an hour.

Pie baking
Preheat the oven to 250°C (482°F) and move oven rack to middle position. Crumple a sheet of parchment paper into a ball, unfold and place in the tin, on top of the dough. Fill with baking beans or dry rice, place in the middle of the oven for about 10 minutes.
Rotate after 5 minutes for even baking.
Remove, switch the oven to 200°C (392°F). Carefully pinch the corners of the parchment paper together and lift the filling out of the tin. Transfer to a large bowl to cool off. Place the tin back into the oven and bake the crust golden, for about 12 - 14 minutes.
Remove from the oven and turn the oven temperature to 175°C (347°F).

Filling
Separate the eggs into yolks and whites. Make sure that no yolk gets into the whites. Beat in the yolks one by one and alternately the condensed milk. Gradually add the lime juice and zest.

Clean a bowl with some lime juice, beat the egg whites with a few drops of lime juice. When they start to turn white, add the sugar in parts during beating. The result should be firm, shiny and fluffy.
Pour the yolk mixture into the pie crust. Divide the fluffy egg whites evenly over the filling. Place in the middle of the oven, bake until golden, for about 25 - 30 minutes. Remove from the oven and let cool in the tin. Place in the fridge for at least 8 hours. Serve cold.

* Earl grey
black tea, scented, blend
The tea becomes creamier and fuller, acquires more flavor, makes the pie lighter, enhances the lime.

** Ceylon
black tea, Sri Lanka
The tea becomes softer, rounder, creamier and fruitier. The pie becomes fruitier, brighter.

*** Darjeeling
first flush, black tea, India
The tea adds floral and fruity notes to the pie, while both become sweeter, fruitier and more intense.

CHAPTER 6

Cooking with tea: theory and recipes

Why cook with tea? What is the added value? Tea contains certain amino acids that have the same flavor-enhancing effect on food as Vet-sin, MSG, or E621. Therefore, tea potentially adds an extra dimension and layer of flavor to food. Tea can deepen the taste of the food.

CATCHING VOLATILES
The flavors of a tea are typically represented as volatile aromas. This means that once a tea comes in contact with oxygen or water, the flavors evaporate. Ideally, the aromas would be captured within a tea and released when needed.

There are four methods to capture aromas:

1. Use a tea extract
When steeped tea is added to a dish, the flavor of the tea often disappears, sometimes even completely. However, the tea still has an effect on the food, and it can enhance and/or balance flavors. A tea extract should not be prepare too far in advance. If you want to have it ready ahead of time, make a cold brew. Also, it should be kept sealed otherwise the aromas will evaporate. See pages 36 - 37.

TEA EXTRACT MADE WITH ICE
The ice cube method is useful for making an extract with a bright, complex and very intense flavor. It is important to make the ice cubes from soft, fresh water with a neutral pH value. If not, the extract will turn murky. Place 10 g (0.35 oz) of tea leaves in a small teapot (e.g., a Kyusu or a small bowl). Cover the tea leaves with ice cubes or crushed ice until the pot or bowl is filled to the brim. Cover and allow to melt slowly. This will take at least three to four hours. The result will be a syrupy extract with a very strong flavor. As soon as the ice has melted, you should use the extract immediately. If you do not, it will turn brown, and - worse - the aromas will evaporate.

Test
Prepare a dish to your liking, for example the vegan tajine on page 164. Then, ten minutes before the food is ready, divide the stew between two pans. Now steep a strong cup of tea, for example English Breakfast, with 150 ml of soft, fresh water and two tea bags, with a steeping time of two minutes. Add the tea to the stew in one of the pans, stir well, and cover both pans. Allow to simmer for another five minutes. Taste the difference between the two. Invite someone else to taste the two dishes with you, preferably without them knowing what you added. Ask the person if they taste anything different and, if so, what the difference is. The tea-infused stew will taste deeper, richer and fuller, although you may hardly taste the tea in it anymore, if at all.

2. Capture tea in fat
Aromas are retained in fat much longer than in water. The problem with fat is that tea has more difficulty dissolving in fat than in water, as tea is water-soluble, not fat-soluble. Also, once the tea is dissolved in fat, it will have the same difficulty escaping, in other words, evaporating. So once it is in, it stays in. In this method, the particles of the tea leaf should be as small as possible in order to speed up the release of

aromas into the fat. You should grind the dry tea with an electric coffee grinder or mortar and pestle, for example. (If you are using a coffee grinder, it must be one that has never been used to grind coffee to avoid making the tea taste like coffee. Remember that tea easily takes on other odors. See page 42).

Dry tea leaves absorb moisture and do the same thing with fat. Therefore, keep in mind that the amount of fat you start with will weigh less after steeping because a part of it is absorbed by the tea leaves. For example, in an infusion of hot cream with tea, the tea leaves absorb part of the cream. When strained and weighed after steeping and after discarding the tea leaves, the weight of the cream will be lower. Even if the wet leaves get pressed firmly to get as much cream out as possible, the exact initial weight of the cream will not be recovered. So, if 200 g (7 oz) of cream is needed for a tea infusion, weigh the cream before and after steeping and add more cold cream until it weighs 200 g (7 oz) again.

Tips
- The tea absorbs less fat if you let it soak for a few seconds in filtered water at the right temperature. Then strain it quickly and let it drain well before adding the amount of fat in which you want to steep the tea.
- If you want to infuse green tea, keep in mind that the tea may become bitter and astringent from too high a temperature. Do not cook the liquid, but as soon as it comes to a simmer, turn off the heat and let it cool to approx. 80°C (158°F) before infusing it with green tea, or let the tea steep in the cold liquid, for at least 8 hours.
- When cooking with tea, use 20 to 30% more tea leaves than you would use if you were going to drink it. The reason for this is that the tea will have to compete with (many) more ingredients.

3. Capture tea in jelly
The aromas in tea can be saved by encapsulating the tea extract with gelatine or agar-agar. This is a solidifying agent obtained from seaweed. It is a gelatinous substance that melts at 100°C (212°F) and doesn't solidify until reaching 49°C (120°F). It is the perfect vegan substitute for gelatine, which is made from animal collagen.

RECIPE FOR GREEN TEA PEARLS
6 g (0.21 oz) Sencha tea
200 ml (6.76 fl. oz) soft, fresh water at 70°C (158°F)
300 ml (10 fl.oz) neutral oil, such as sunflower or rapeseed oil
1.5 g (0.05 oz) agar-agar
50 ml (1.7 fl. oz) of filtered water at 100°C (212°F)
1 pipette

Pour the oil into a tall glass, place this in the freezer for 30 minutes. Prepare the tea with the hot water, steep for two minutes. Strain, set the extract aside, covered.

Dissolve the agar-agar in the boiling water. Stir for 2 minutes over low heat. Transfer to a cold bowl, cool till 70 - 80°C (158 - 176°F). Add the tea extract, stir well. Using a pipette, suck up a portion of the mixture and drop small amounts into the glass with the ice-cold oil. The mixture will form pearls. Place the pearls in a sieve, rinse carefully with cold water. Transfer the pearls to a sterilized jar, close the jar, place in the fridge.

May be made one day in advance. Another jellied tea recipe can be found on page 144 in the recipe for vegan tea oysters.

4. Capture tea in alcohol
Another option is to make a cold brew of tea in alcohol. An average ratio of tea and alcohol is 40 g (1.4 oz) of tea leaves to 1 liter (34 fl. oz) of alcohol. You can use vodka or gin for this method. A tea liqueur recipe can be found on page 122.

TEA LEAVES AS A TOPPING

Recently produced green tea leaves taste particularly bright and vivid and make for a great flavor and texture addition to salads, rice, or pasta dishes. Be sure to use a tea with small fine leaves. Larger leaves can be unpleasant to chew.

SMOKING WITH TEA

Dry tea leaves are also good to use for smoking food. For this, you can use either tea leaves or a mixture of tea leaves and wood chips and/or with other ingredients such as spices, sugar, nuts etc. To prevent the tea leaves from burning, blend the leaves with uncooked rice (any type of rice will do). Do not use your more expensive teas for smoking, as the more refined aromas will inevitably get lost.

RECIPE FOR SMOKING WITH TEA

10 - 15 g loose leaf tea, preferably large leaf tea (e.g., Earl Grey or Jasmine tea)
2 - 3 tbsp wood chips
75 - 100 g (2.64 - 3.52 oz) uncooked rice

Cover a wok with 2 layers of aluminium foil. Mix the ingredients together at the bottom of the wok. Place a round wok rack or microwave rack over the mixture in the wok and cover the rack with two more layers of foil. Fold the edges slightly upwards so that the foil looks like a tray. Arrange the food you would like to smoke, e.g., fish, cheese, chicken, vegetables, in the foil tray on the rack. The smoke must be able to circulate around the tray.
Heat the wok over high heat until smoke starts to appear. Lower the heat. Wait until there is a fair amount smoke and cover firmly with a lid. If the lid does not close off the pan properly, put another layer of foil between the wok and the lid. Allow to smoke for about 10 - 15 minutes and taste regularly to check if it has smoked enough to your liking. If not, continue to smoke it for a little longer.

ADVANTAGES OF COOKING WITH TEA

- Extra (additional) flavor
- Flavor enhancement
- The food becomes brighter or smoother

DISADVANTAGES OF COOKING WITH TEA

- A lot of tea is needed when cooking with tea, which makes it rather expensive.
- Some planning is needed. It is more efficient to have the tea extract, prepared as a cold brew, ready in the fridge ahead of time.
- A hot brew tea can become bitter when prepared too far in advance.

Tips
- Tea changes color when used in cooking. To avoid discoloring the tea, add the tea extract immediately before serving the dish, and mix well.
- Steaming over green tea brings no difference in flavor, as all aromas will evaporate due to the steam. Avoid steaming over tea so as not to waste the tea.
- The following tip applies to all the tea and food pairings in this book. Prepare and serve the tea five minutes prior to serving the food. The tea will be able to cool down.

For easier tea steeping while cooking, use my stress-free method of cold brew tea extract topped with boiling water. See page 36 - 37.

CHAPTER 7

RECIPES WITH TEA AS AN INGREDIENT

For each recipe:
use the cold brew hot tea method (see page 36 - 37),
or steep the chosen tea 5 minutes before serving
the food and serve the tea straight away.
This way, the tea has time to cool down a bit.

You will find many more tea suggestions
for food on pages 256 - 272.

PB Plant based

VG Vegetarian

SF Seafood-Fish

MP Meat-Poultry

S Sweets

Beetroot, avocado and Parma ham with tea liqueur

Serves 4

1 beetroot, raw
1 avocado
coarse sea salt
or salt flakes
ground white pepper
tea liqueur

Tea liqueur
Makes about 250 ml (8.45 fl. oz)

250 ml (8.45 fl. oz) filtered water
80 g (2.8 oz) granulated sugar
10 g (0.35 oz) Da Hong Pao oolong tea (or another dark tea of your choice)
250 ml (8.45 fl.oz) brandy or vodka

Note: *The tea liqueur should be made at least 3 days ahead of time; the longer ahead of time, the better.*

Tea liqueur
Bring the water with the sugar gently to a boil, stirring constantly, until all sugar has dissolved. Stop stirring and turn the heat to low and simmer for 5 minutes, uncovered. Pour into a bowl, cool to room temperature.
Pour some boiling water over the tea until the leaves are submerged. Leave for 10 seconds and strain. Discard the liquid and keep the leaves. Place the rinsed tea leaves into a sterilized jar with a lid. Pour the vodka or brandy onto the tea leaves in the jar. Firmly close the lid and store in a cool, dark place for 24 hours. Then add the sugar syrup, preferably up to the brim of the jar. Make sure to keep as little oxygen as possible between the liquid and the lid; this way the aromas stay inside. A lid that closes well is a must. Close firmly and shake a few times. Put back in a cool, dark place. Wait at least 24 hours before straining the leaves. You may leave them inside the bottle as well. This liqueur keeps for a very long time, years even.

Beetroot, avocado and Parma ham
Preheat the oven to 200ºC (392ºF).
Line a baking sheet with parchment paper. Wrap the beetroot in aluminium foil and place the tray on a rack in the middle of the oven. Bake for 45 minutes to an hour, depending on the size. Remove from the oven, carefully open up the foil (hot!!). Let the beetroot cool enough to handle. Remove the skin and cut into slices of ½ cm (0.2 inch).
(Not enough time? Use pre-boiled beetroot, pat thoroughly dry before slicing. Cooked beetroots have less flavor, though.)
Peel the avocado and cut into slices of 1 cm (0.4 inch).
Sprinkle the beetroot and avocado with white pepper and coarse sea salt. With a round cookie cutter size: 2½ cm (1 inch), cut circles out of avocado and beetroot.
Fold the slices of coppa di parma into roughly the size of the beetroot and avocado. On each slice of coppa, place a slice of beet, cover with another folded slice of coppa and place a slice of avocado on top.
Carefully thread on mini skewers or mini forks.
Pour a splash of the liqueur over the starter.
Pour some more liqueur into tiny glasses on a mini saucer.
Place the skewers with the starter horizontally on top of the glass and serve immediately.

I served this to the jury of the 2013 Dutch Tea Championships. I won, but that was not only thanks to this combination. Or so I hope.

Asparagus with tea butter

Serves 4

Tea butter
100g (3.5 oz) soft butter
1 tsp Matcha
pinch sea salt

Asparagus
16 - 20 asparagus (white if available, otherwise green)
8 new potatoes
4 eggs
pinch mace, or a small piece
pinch granulated sugar
1 tbsp butter
handful Italian parsley
salt and pepper

Tea butter
Place the soft butter in a bowl. Sift the Matcha over the butter. Mix until well blended and bright green. Add salt to taste. Scoop onto a sheet of plastic wrap, roll up like a sausage, firmly twist both ends. Store in fridge or freezer until solid.

Vegetables
Peel the asparagus twice round if you have white ones, from just under the head all the way down to the bottom. Cut off the bottom, about 2½ cm (1 inch). Keep them wrapped up in a moist towel until you are going to cook them. Green asparagus do not need to be peeled, just washed. Wash and scrub the potatoes, place in a pan with plenty water, add a large pinch of salt. Bring to a boil, simmer until done, about 15 minutes. Drain, add some butter, shake and set aside, covered. Simultaneously with the potatoes place the asparagus in another large pan, add mace, sugar, butter, salt and pepper and place a smaller lid or plate on top, to keep the asparagus submerged. Bring the water to a boil, simmer for 5 minutes, turn off the heat and keep covered.

Eggs
Boil the eggs for 5 minutes. Drain, and run cold cold water over them. Peel when cooled enough to handle. Wash and dry the parsley and chop roughly. With a fork, break up the eggs and mix with the parsley. Season to taste.

Finish
Remove the tea butter from the fridge, unwrap, slice off 4 slices of about 1 cm (½ inch) thick. Preheat the plates. Remove the asparagus with a slotted spoon from the pan and transfer them first to a large plate covered with kitchen paper or a clean towel, to drain, and then onto the preheated plates. Place a slice of tea butter on top. Add some potatoes, garnish with the parsley-egg mixture, sprinkle with pepper and salt.

Optional
Serve with ham instead of eggs. The same teas apply.

* **Nepalese Black**
black tea, Nepal
This tea adds freshness to the food, cuts through the fat, while the tea becomes sweeter and more complex.

** **Hōjicha**
roasted green tea, Japan
The tea becomes fruitier and deeper, adds nutty notes to the food, which becomes lighter, fresher.

*** **Darjeeling**
first flush, black tea, India
This is my favourite tea for white asparagus. The tea gains the flavor of asparagus. the asparagus taste fuller, sweeter, acquire floral notes.

Caramelized chicory, Pu-Erh, mushroom gravy, mashed potatoes

Serves 4

Mashed potatoes
500 g (17.63 oz) floury potatoes
2 tbsp butter or olive oil
2 tbsp mushroom broth

Mushroom gravy
3 tbsp dried mushrooms
3 shallots
1 clove garlic
5 g (0.17 oz) Shu Pu-Erh (cooked) post-fermented tea
3 dl (10.14 fl. oz) filtered water

Caramelized chicory
3 large chicory bulbs
1l (33.81 fl. oz) mushroom broth
2 tbsp butter (if unsalted: add a pinch of salt)
1 tbsp olive oil
1 tbsp sugar

Parmesan wafers
3 tbsp grated Parmesan cheese

Heat the broth and keep it warm.
Soak the mushrooms for 30 minutes in boiling water.
Peel, wash and cut the potatoes into large pieces. Cook them in plenty of salted water. Drain, add 2 tbsp stock, the butter or olive oil. Mash the potatoes till creamy. Season with salt and pepper.
Set aside, covered, for example in a warm oven at 65°C (150°F).

Tea extract
Pour 100 ml (3.4 fl. oz) filtered water at 100°C (212°F) over the tea leaves. Steep for 15 seconds. Drain. Discard the liquid.
Pour 200 ml (6.76 fl. oz) filtered water at 100°C (212°F) over the wet tea leaves. Steep for 3 minutes. Strain the tea leaves, reserve the steeped liquid. Set aside and cover. Save the wet tea leaves, covered; you can use them for another steep.

Gravy
Cut the shallots into half rings and finely chop the garlic.
Heat a dash of oil in a pan and fry the onion rings over low heat for 20 - 30 minutes until they turn brown. Halfway through add the chopped garlic.
Sift the soaked mushrooms. Save the soaking liquid. Rinse and chop the mushrooms roughly.
Once the onions are brown, turn up the heat. Add the tea and a generous splash of the mushroom soaking liquid.
Reduce the liquid until it becomes the consistency of gravy, do this over high heat. Season with salt and pepper. Turn off the heat and cover the pan.

Caramelize the chicory
Bring the mushroom broth to a gentle boil.
Cut the ends off the chicory bulbs, remove the outer leaves and add the whole bulbs to the broth.
Allow to simmer for 5 minutes. Drain well and pat dry.
Heat the butter and oil in a large frying pan until the butter no longer foams. Add the sugar and stir until dissolved.
Turn up the heat a little, add the chicory halves with the cut edge down. Let sit in the pan until they turn brown. Do not move them around.

>>

>>

Finish

Remove the mashed potatoes from the oven and turn the oven to 180°C (350°F). Line a baking sheet with parchment paper. Sprinkle all Parmesan cheese on the paper in 2 circles of about ø10 cm (4 inches).
Let the cheese melt in the hot oven until it turns pale yellow. Beware, this goes very fast!
Remove from the oven, let the cheese cool and set.

Spoon the mashed potatoes on preheated plates. On top, arrange three chicory halves. Pour the mushroom gravy around the potatoes and over the chicory, decorate with a Parmesan cheese wafer.

Tip

If you do not have Shu Pu-Erh tea, you can substitute it for English Breakfast black tea. In this case, steep it for 2 minutes, otherwise the recipe is the same as above.

Optional
Replace the cheese wafers with crispy strips of bacon.

Optional
Replace the cheese wafers with coarsely chopped roasted hazelnuts and some orange zest and the butter with plant based margarine.

* **Earl grey**
black tea, scented, blend
The tea becomes fruity, the food becomes lighter, brighter, sweeter and less bitter. Clean palate.

** **Yue Guang Bai**
white tea, China
The tea becomes slightly bitter in a refreshing way, deeper, takes on more umami. And makes the dish lighter, sweeter and milder.

*** **Shu Pu-Erh**
post-fermented tea, China
Use the second steep of the same tea you used for the gravy. The tea becomes fresher, herbaceous, makes the chicory more pronounced, deeper. The mashed potatoes become sweeter and deeper.

Vegan oysters

Makes about 12 oysters

1 aubergine
neutral oil, like sunflower, or rapeseed
3g (0.10 oz) Japanese or Korean green tea
100g (3.52 oz) silken tofu, drained
sea lettuce or 1dl (3.38 fl oz) water with 2½ g (0.08 oz) sea salt dissolved in it
2 x 1g (0.03 oz) of agar
fine sea salt
oyster leaf (indispensable for the right taste)
optional: gills of a portobello mushroom, cooked in very salty water (like sea water)
decoration: oyster leaf blossom, Blinq cress, borage cress, sea lettuce, dulce seaweed

Aubergines
Preheat the oven to 250°C (480°F).
Pierce the aubergine several times and roast it in the oven until blackened and wrinkled, for at least 30 - 45 minutes. Let cool. Scoop out the flesh with a spoon and drain over a bowl. Squeeze out the excess liquid and set bowl aside.
Season the flesh with salt and pepper, pull apart with two forks.
It is okay if the black skin sticks to the flesh. It makes it more authentic and brings a nice contrast of color.
Stir in a splash of oil. Cover and set aside.

Tea
Heat 1dl (3.38 fl.oz) filtered water to 80°C (176°F), pour over the green tea. Steep for 2 minutes. Strain the tea over the tofu. Cover, save the wet tea leaves.

Tofu purée
Soak the sea lettuce in 1dl (3.38 fl.oz) warm water. If you do not have sea lettuce, make salt water.
Purée the tofu with this water. Season to taste. It should taste saltier than sea water.
Cut 4 oyster leaves into small pieces, place in a small pan with the tofu purée and 1g (0.03 oz) of agar.
Bring to the boil, simmer for 3 minutes.
Brush a baking dish of approximately 25 x 25 cm (10 x 10 inches) with neutral vegetable oil.
Pass the tofu purée through a sieve into the baking dish, spread the purée evenly. Cover, place in the fridge for at least 15 minutes until it solidifies.

>>

\>\>

Tea jelly
Pour 3dl (10.14 fl.oz) filtered water of 80°C (176°F) over the saved tea leaves. Steep for 2 minutes, strain the tea over a small saucepan.
Add 1g (0.03 oz) of agar. Bring to the boil and simmer for 3 minutes. Brush a baking sheet or a large flat dish or tray with oil, and pour in the agar mixture. Spread evenly. It should be about 2 mm (0.1 inch) thick. It will become flexible after it sets. Put it in the fridge for 15 minutes to set.

Finish
Divide the 12 oyster leaves over the shells or dishes. If you are using shells, add a splash of salt water to each shell.
Scoop some tofu mixture out of the bowl with a teaspoon and place one scoop onto each oyster leaf. Mould it with the spoon into a natural oblong shape.
Drape the aubergine strings around the mounds of tofu. Press the aubergine flat here and there for a nice oyster effect. If you have mushroom gills, flatten those and skirt them around the tofu as well.
Use a wide palette knife or spatula to create whimsical pieces of jelly, slightly larger than the vegan oysters, and drape these over the oysters. Cut away any overhanging pieces of jelly.
Sprinkle with salt and a little pepper, decorate as desired and serve.
This dish can be prepared 6 hours in advance. If you do the preparation beforehand, simply cover everything and store it in the fridge.

Optional
Use real oysters.

* **Gunpowder**	** **Jin Xuan #12**	*** **Gyokuro**
green tea China	*light oolong*, Taiwan	*green tea*, Japan
The tea becomes both bright and a bit dryer and makes the oyster more salty. The tea's smoky notes are enhanced.	Tea and oyster enhance each other, the flavors merge, while both elements remain equally present.	The tea becomes slightly brighter, adds marine notes and umami to the oyster, enhancement of all flavors.

Cod with beetroot, tarragon and Matcha

Serves 4

650 g (23 oz) cod fillets
neutral oil (rapeseed, sunflower oil)
1 tbsp of butter
500 g (17.63 oz) beetroots
salt and pepper

Sauce
4 tbsp crème fraîche
4 tbsp mayonnaise
1 tbsp chopped tarragon
zest of ½ orange
salt and white pepper

Dressing for salad
3 tbsp good quality oil
1 tbsp white wine vinegar
1 tsp mustard
salt and pepper

Salad
1 tsp sieved Matcha
½ cucumber
mezclun lettuce
samphire
some very thin strips of orange rind

Note: If there is no Matcha tea available: grind a tbsp of high quality Sencha or other green tea as finely as possible in a mortar and pestle.

Beetroots
Preheat the oven to 200ºC (392ºF). In a large bowl mix 3 tbsp of oil with salt and pepper. Peel the beetroots, cut into wedges and add to the bowl. Stir well. Transfer to a baking sheet covered with wax paper. Roast the wedges in the middle of the oven till done, about 45 minutes. Stir twice.

Sauce
In a bowl, mix all ingredients for the sauce and season to taste.

Dressing
Place all ingredients for the dressing into a small jar, close tightly and shake.

Fish
Pat the fish dry with kitchen paper. Sprinkle with salt and pepper. Cover.

Salad
Wash and dry the cucumber. With a mandolin or slicer, cut paper thin slices lengthwise. Drizzle with 1 tbsp of dressing and set aside to marinate for 10 minutes. Wash the samphire. Pour over some boiling water, wait 30 seconds, drain well. In a large bowl, drizzle the lettuce leaves with some dressing and divide over 4 plates. Place wedges of beetroot, cucumber ribbons, samphire and some dabs of sauce on the plates. Garnish with slivers or orange rind.

Finish
In a heavy duty skillet, heat 2 tbsp of oil and 1 tbsp of butter, add the fillets of fish and fry without moving them around for 2-3 minutes. Flip over and bake for another 30 seconds or so, until the fish is still slightly translucent in the middle. Place the fish onto the plates, sprinkle with some Matcha through a fine meshed sieve.

* **Sencha**
green tea, Japan
The tea becomes fruity, acquires more flavor. The tea enhances the food, softens the beetroots, adds nutty notes to the lettuce.

** **Hōjicha**
roasted green tea, Japan
The tea becomes fruity and acquires more umami and depth. It softens both fish and beetroots, adds nutty notes to the entire dish.

*** **Jin Xuan #12**
light oolong, Taiwan
The tea acquires more umami and depth, adds floral notes to the food.
All flavors are enhanced, blend together, while maintaining their own character.

Indian pumpkin curry with tomatoes and (dirty) chai

Serves 4 - 6

1 orange pumpkin
1 red bell pepper
2 medium onions
2 cloves garlic
2½ cm (1 inch) ginger, peeled
1 tbsp garam masala
1 tbsp turmeric
¼ tsp powdered red chili pepper
5 tbsp ghee
1 can full-fat coconut milk 400 ml (13.52 fl. oz)
1 bay leaf
1 can peeled and cubed tomatoes 400 g (14 oz)
12g (0.42 oz) (dirty) chai tea leaves
300 ml (10.14 fl. oz) filtered water
juice of 1 lime
2 tbsp roughly chopped coriander
1 tbsp roughly chopped mint

4 - 6 papadums
white rice

Note: *Dirty Chai is sold in tea bags, but it is just as easy to make it yourself. Just add 12 g (0.42 oz) chai mixture with 1½ tbsp of ground coffee.*

Ghee is clarified butter and is used a lot in the Indian cuisine. You can replace it with vegetable oil that endures high temperature.

Vegetables
Wash and dry the pumpkin. The skin is also edible. Chop the pumpkin into chunks, remove all seeds and membranes. Chop into small cubes, about 2½ cm (1 inch) square. Sprinkle with salt and pepper.
Wash and dry the bell pepper, remove all seeds and membranes and cut into 1½ cm (½ inch) squares.
Chop the onions, the garlic, grate the ginger, transfer all to a mortar and pestle. Add the garam massala, turmeric and chili powder. Grind into a fine paste. (or use a blender or food processor.)
In a large heavy duty pan, heat the ghee and fry the onion-and-spice mixture over medium heat until fragrant and soft. Add pumpkin and bell pepper, fry for 3 more minutes. Add the coconut milk, the bay leaf and the tomatoes, cover, lower the heat and simmer for 25 minutes.

(Dirty) chai
About 10 minutes before the curry is ready, bring the filtered water to a boil and pour it over the (dirty) chai tea leaves, steep them for 5 minutes, pass through a sieve over the curry. Mix it well into the curry, cover and let simmer for another 2 minutes.

Finish
Turn off the heat, add lime juice and half of the chopped herbs, stir well, transfer to a bowl, sprinkle with the other half of chopped herbs.
Serve with rice and papadums.

Optional
Fry 500g (17.63 oz) organic chicken thighs in ghee (or oil) and add to the pan at the same time as the coconut milk.

Optional
Add about 500g (17.63 oz) peeled and deveined prawns 5 minutes before the curry is ready.

* Prince of Whales, English Breakfast
black tea, blend
The tea becomes fresher, fruitier. The curry and the tomato become fuller and sweeter.

** Yue Guang Bai
white tea, China
The tea enhances the spices and umami, disappears at first, but makes a comeback, tasting fresh and sweet.

*** Shu Pu-Erh
(cooked), post-fermented tea, China
The tea becomes fresher, fruitier, with citrus notes, enhances umami, acidity and sweetness of the food.

Razor clams with snow peas and tarragon butter

Serves 4

1 kg (35 oz) razor clams
100g (3.5 oz) soft butter
handful of tarragon
1 lemon
250g (8.75 oz) snow peas
very fresh, recently plucked green tea, e.g., Tai Ping Hou Kui, or use Matcha if very fresh green tea is not available
black pepper and coarse sea salt, e.g., Maldon flakes

Clams
Wash the clams several times in cold, salted water in order to get rid of most of the sand that is inside the clams. Drain well, pat dry.

Tarragon butter
Finely chop the tarragon, add to the soft butter and stir until well combined. Season to taste.

Snow peas
Wash the snow peas, cut off the ends if brown.
Bring salted water to a boil, add the snow peas, and cook until al dente for about 1 - 2 minutes.
Drain well. Add a tbsp of tarragon butter and shake until all snow peas are covered with melted butter.
Season to taste.

Finish
Lightly grease a heavy skillet with some oil, place over high heat. When the pan is piping hot, add the clams.
They are done as soon as they open up. They will still be slightly translucent and continue to cook when out of the pan.
Transfer the clams to a heated platter. Drizzle 1 tbsp of melted tarragon butter over the clams. Season to taste.
Place a few leaves of very fresh tea on each clam, or sprinkle some Matcha over the clams. It is important that the tea be very fresh, one month old at the most, if you use the entire leaf. If older than one month, do grind the tea very finely, or use Matcha.

* Green tea
of your choice
The tea acquires more flavor, becomes sweeter, will make the clams softer, more intense, enhancement of the tarragon.

** Long Jing
green tea, China
The tea becomes sweeter, takes on more umami, adds roasting notes to the dish, enhances all flavors.

*** Gyokuro
green tea, Japan
The tea becomes fresher, sweeter and very herbal, makes all flavors come together, deeper and umami is enhanced.

Strawberry and asparagus salad with Matcha tea butter

Serves 4

Matcha tea butter
5g (0.17 oz) Matcha
100g (3.5 oz) soft, unsalted butter
pinch salt

Dressing
3 tbsp extra virgin olive oil
1 tbsp white wine vinegar
1 tsp Dijon mustard
1 tsp honey
salt and black pepper

Salad
250g (8.75 oz) strawberries
300g (10.5 oz) thin asparagus tips, preferably white, or else green
½ a tbsp of neutral oil, like rapeseed or sunflower oil
12g (0.42 oz) whole unsalted hazelnuts
150g (5.25 oz) baby leaf spinach
75g (2.64 oz) rocket (arugula) leaves
75g (2.64 oz) lamb's lettuce
handful of tarragon
sea salt flakes

Hazelnuts
Preheat the oven to 180°C (356°F).
Line a baking sheet with parchment paper, spread out the hazelnuts. Roast until golden, shaking regularly for even roasting. Transfer to a plate to cool off. Once cool, roughly chop them.

Tea butter
Sift the tea through a very finely meshed sieve over the soft butter and stir till well blended. Season to taste.

Dressing
In a jar, add all ingredients for the dressing, firmly close with a lid and shake until evenly mixed.
Wash the strawberries, drain well, pat dry, remove the crowns, cut into halves. Sprinkle with a bit of black pepper, as this enhances the flavor of the strawberries, but do not overdo it.

Asparagus
Wash and dry the asparagus tips. Peel only if they are white. Cut off part of the bottom, around 2½ cm (1 inch).
In a wok, melt 2 tbsp of tea butter with the neutral oil over medium heat. Add the asparagus tips and fry until done in a few minutes, how long depends on the size of the stalks. The thicker they are, the longer you will need to fry them.

Finish
Roughly chop the tarragon and mix with the chopped hazelnuts. With a slotted spoon, transfer the asparagus tips onto kitchen paper to drain. Allow them to cool off until safe to touch.
In a large bowl, carefully mix the greens together with a tbsp of the dressing. Divide the leaves over 4 plates. Add the asparagus and strawberries, drizzle with a bit of dressing. Sprinkle the hazelnut-tarragon mixture and some sea salt flakes over the plates.

* Earl grey
black tea, scented, blend, cold brew (see page 212).
The tea makes the salad fresher, summer-like, lighter, a bit floral.

** Shu Pu-Erh
(cooked), post-fermented tea, China
The tea becomes lighter, brighter, adds sweetness and earthy notes to the salad, enhances the flavors.

*** Jin Xuan #12
light oolong, Taiwan
The tea becomes fruity and bright, adds floral notes and a creamy texture to the salad, enhances the vegetal notes of the leaves.

Fish burger with Matcha-tarragon mayonnaise

Serves 2

250 g (8.7 oz) skinless firm, white fish fillets, like cod, or haddock
½ tbsp olive oil
2 tbsp bread crumbs, like Panko
1 tbsp toasted sunflower seeds
2 tbsp roughly chopped flat-leaf parsley
salt and white pepper
1 fennel bulb
2 hamburger buns
rocket (arugula) leaves

Dressing
1 tbsp each of orange zest and juice
1 tsp Dijon mustard
3 tbsp extra virgin olive oil
½ tbsp tarragon, finely chopped
1 tsp honey
salt and white pepper

Mayonnaise
4 tbsp mayonnaise
½ tsp Matcha
1 tsp tarragon, finely chopped
1 tsp orange juice
salt and white pepper

Dressing
Add all ingredients to a jar, close firmly and shake vigorously.

Mayonnaise
Blend all ingredients except for the Matcha.
Sift the Matcha over the mayonnaise. Stir well until evenly bright green. Season to taste.

Fish burgers
Chop the fish fillets very finely, transfer to a large bowl, add a splash of olive oil, the bread crumbs, the sunflower seeds, the parsley and salt and pepper. Mix well, divide in two portions, knead into patties. Cover and place in the fridge for at least 30 minutes.

Fennel
Preheat the oven to 200°C (392°F).
Remove the thick outer skin of the fennel, cut off the stalks and remove the leaves; keep those for decoration if needed. With a mandoline shave fennel bulb lengthwise into very thin slices.
Place the slices on a baking sheet lined with parchment paper, drizzle lightly with olive oil, salt and pepper and roast until soft, with golden crispy edges. Transfer to a plate.

Finish
Cut the buns horizontally in two, place in the oven until slightly toasted. At the same time, heat a lightly greased heavy skillet or grill pan until piping hot, add the fish patties and fry until golden on both sides.
Drizzle some of the dressing over fennel slices and rucola.
Spread Matcha mayonnaise onto the buns, place some rucola and fennel slices on top. Add the patties, top off with a dab of Matcha mayonnaise, place the top part of the bun on top or sideways.
Serve with some extra Matcha mayonnaise in a separate little bowl.

Optional
Replace the fish with turkey or chicken thighs.

* **Sencha**
green tea, Japan
The tea enhances the food, but itself needs a few more sips to recover. It then tastes deeper, softer and sweeter.

** **Tieguanyin**
oolong, China, Taiwan or Thailand
The tea becomes sweeter, smooth, takes on more umami, adds floral notes to the food, makes it lighter, brighter.

*** **Long Jing**
green tea, China
The tea acquires more umami and becomes sweeter, enhances all flavors, prolongs the aftertaste.

Fennel salad with orange, hazelnuts and tea dressing

Serves 4 - 6

2 fennel bulbs
3 oranges
1 red onion
½ tbsp olive oil
5 g (0.17 oz) granulated sugar
1 tbsp apple cider vinegar
75 g (2.64 oz) unsalted, peeled hazelnuts
18 kalamata olives, pitted
salt and black pepper

Tea dressing
3 g (0.10 oz) Dong Fang Mei Ren dark oolong
1 tbsp each orange zest and juice
1 tsp Dijon mustard
3 tbsp extra virgin olive oil
½ tbsp apple cider vinegar
½ tsp honey
salt and white pepper

Tea dressing
Place the tea in a small bowl. Pour over 100 ml (3.4 fl. oz) filtered water at 95°C (203°F). Cover and steep for 1½ minutes. Strain over a small jar. Add the honey, cover and cool. Add remaining ingredients, close firmly and shake vigorously. Cover and set aside.

Hazelnuts
Preheat the oven to 175°C (347°F). Line a baking sheet with parchment paper, add the hazelnuts and roast until golden. Cool, then chop roughly.

Fennel
Wash and dry the fennel, remove the thick outer skin, cut off the stalks and remove the leaves; keep those for decoration. Cut the bulb into 4 wedges. With a mandoline, shave the wedges lengthwise into very thin slices. Add dressing to taste, mix in carefully, cover and marinate for at least 1 hour.

Onion
Peel the onion and cut horizontally in two. With a mandoline or shaving tool, shave the halves into very thin rings. In a heavy skillet, heat 1 tbsp of olive oil, lower the heat, add the onion rings and fry until caramelized. Add sugar and vinegar and reduce over high heat till the vinegar has almost evaporated.

Orange segments
With a very sharp knife, cut off the ends and skin of the orange, including the white pith. Cut the wedges loose from the membranes over a bowl, catch the juice. Keep the wedges in the juice.

Finish
Drain the fennel and transfer to a large bowl. Add the wedges of orange, the olives and half of the onion rings. Mix carefully and divide over 4 plates. Sprinkle with chopped hazelnuts, the rest of the onion rings and the fennel greens.

* **Earl grey**,
black tea, scented, blend
The tea becomes sweeter, deeper, enhances the flavors and the freshness of the salad, adds floral notes to it.

** **Dong Fang Mei Ren**
dark oolong, Taiwan
The tea becomes brighter, lighter, its honey notes stronger. All flavors of the food are enhanced and intertwine, the salad becomes softer, sweeter.

*** **Ruby #18**
black tea, Taiwan
The tea acquires umami, depth, flavor, makes the food deeper, more intense, sweeter, smooth. All flavors are enhanced, intertwine. The salad becomes sweeter, deeper.

Vegan sashimi

PB

Serves 4

350g (12.34 oz) watermelon, pitted
2 sheets nori (dried seaweed to make sushi with)

Marinade
5 g (0.17 oz) Shu Pu-Erh (cooked)
500 ml (17 fl. oz) filtered water
2 tbsp light soy sauce
1½ tbsp vegan umami from a bottle or tube
1 tbsp white miso paste
½ tbsp sushi vinegar (or white wine vinegar)
100 ml (3.4 fl. oz) salt water, made with 12 g (0.42 oz) of salt diluted in 500 ml (17 fl. oz) hot water

Note: *Preparation time is at least 6 hours, or overnight.*

Marinade
Bring the filtered water to a boil and pour half of the water over the Pu-Erh tea. Steep for 15 seconds, strain, throw the liquid away. Now add the other half of the hot water to the tea and steep for 5 minutes. Strain into a bowl. Add the soy sauce, vegan umami, miso paste, salt water and vinegar. Mix well. Taste and add salted water if necessary. It needs to taste saltier than sea water, as the sugars in the melon will tone down the saltiness of the marinade.

Watermelon
Cut the watermelon into 1½ cm (ø inch) rectangles. Remove the rind. Cover the bottom of a rectangular oven dish with a sheet of nori. Place the watermelon on top, in one layer, snuggly. Add the marinade, the watermelon should be quite submersed in it. Then place the other sheet of nori on top of the watermelon, cover and place in the fridge for at least 6 hours, or overnight.

Allow the watermelon to warm up to room temperature, remove the nori, transfer the watermelon pieces to a colander. Drain very well, pat dry with kitchen towel, until no longer soggy.
Dehydrate them to change the texture, preferably in an electric dehydrator, or else a microwave oven. If not available use a conventional oven.

>>

\>\>

Dehydration

In an electric dehydrator: follow the instructions of the manufacturer.
In a microwave oven: divide the watermelon pieces over the disc of the oven. The disc should be very clean and dry. Keep the rectangles 1 cm (ø inch) apart. Switch the microwave oven to defrost, 30 min. Turn the rectangles now and then. If they are still wet after 30 minutes, switch to an extra 5 minutes, or more if needed, until the pieces are dry. They should have the firm texture of tuna.

In a conventional oven: switch the oven to 65°C(149°F). Divide the rectangles over an oven rack, place in the middle of the oven and place a baking sheet under the rack, to catch the dripping juices. Leave in the oven for at least 6 hours, until the pieces are dry. Turn the rectangles now and then.

Finish

Cut the dried rectangles into small strips and place on top of lightly kneaded sushi rice, like sashimi.
Or serve as a salad: sprinkle with very thin slivers of nori and toasted sesame seeds.
Or roll the sides of the dried rectangles into a mixture of toasted golden and black sesame seeds.
You may also grill the slices, like you would tuna or steak. Lightly brush some neutral oil, e.g., rapeseed or sun flower oil, on both sides of each watermelon rectangle, sprinkle with salt and pepper and grill on a sizzling hot grill for 1 minute each at the most, depending on the thickness.

* **Green tea**	** **Sencha Fukamushi**	*** **Gyokuro**
of your choice	green tea, Japan	green tea, Japan
The tea acquires more flavor, tones down the sweet notes of the dish.	The tea becomes sweeter, deeper and brighter, adds marine notes and enhances all flavors.	The tea deepens the food, makes it more complex, adds marine notes, all flavors are enhanced. The sweetness of the tea matches the remaining sugars of the melon.

Vegan tajine of aubergine, tomato and Assam tea

VG

Serves 6

20 g (0.70 oz) Assam, black tea from Northern India, or English Blend, or Shu Pu-Erh
600 ml (20 fl oz) filtered water
6 dried apricots, pitted
6 dried prunes, pitted
2 tbsp olive oil
2 red onions
3 cloves garlic
¼ or ½ red chili pepper
2 tsp coriander seeds
2 tsp cumin seeds
2½ cm (1 inch) ginger, peeled
zest of 1 orange
2 tsp granulated sugar
3 aubergines
2 cans peeled, cubed tomatoes 400 g (14 oz) each

Couscous
450 g (15,84 oz) couscous
400 ml (13 fl. oz) water
1 tsp ground cinnamon
olive oil
50 g (1.76 oz) unsalted, roasted and roughly chopped almonds
salt and pepper

Tea extract
Bring 600 ml (20 fl.oz) water to 95°C (203°F) and pour over the tea leaves. Cover and steep for 2 minutes.
In the meantime, cut the prunes and apricots into little pieces, transfer to a bowl. Pour the tea through a strainer over the fruit, cover and set aside. Discard the tea leaves, unless you use Shu Pu-Erh. In that case, keep the leaves for a second steep to drink with this food.

Vegetables
Wash and dry the aubergines, cut into chunks of about 2½ cm (1 inch) each. Peel the onions and cut in half and slice thinly.
Chop the peeled ginger finely, do the same with the peeled garlic.
Wash, dry and cut the chili pepper in half, remove seeds and membranes, slice thinly.
Heat a dry skillet, add the coriander and cumin seeds and roast until fragrant. Transfer the seeds into a mortar and pestle. Add sugar and grind into a powder.

In a large pot, heat 2 tbsp of olive oil, add the onions. When translucent, add garlic, ginger, chili and the freshly ground spices. Sauté over medium heat for a minute, then add the aubergines.
Stir well and fry over high heat for about 3 minutes. Add the tomatoes, stir well. Remove the prunes and apricots from the tea, cover the liquid and set aside. Add the fruit to the stew, cover, lower the heat and simmer, until the aubergines are soft and cooked.
Stir regularly and make sure the sauce doesn't boil too much.
While the vegetables are simmering, wash, dry and chop the coriander, parsley and mint. Add half of the mixed herbs to the vegetables after 25 minutes of simmering. Add the reserved tea to the vegetables, stir well, cover and simmer for another 10 minutes, or until the aubergines are soft. Season to taste.

>>

\>\>

Almonds

Preheat the oven to 175°C (350°F).
Line a baking sheet with parchment paper, spread out the almonds and roast until golden, about 10 minutes. Shake regularly for even roasting. Transfer them to a plate to cool off. Once cool, chop roughly.

Couscous

In the meantime, place the couscous into a large bowl. Rinse the couscous until the water becomes clear. Drain well. Bring 400 ml (13 fl. oz) water to a boil, add a large pinch of salt and splash of olive oil and pour over the couscous. Stir well and cover. Set aside for 5 minutes. Add 1 tbsp of oil and 1 tsp of cinnamon.

Finish

Just before serving, stir the couscous with a fork, mix in a handful of chopped mint. Transfer to a large serving bowl or dish, sprinkle with orange zest, the chopped almonds and half of the remaining chopped herbs. Sprinkle the other half over the vegetable stew. Serve couscous and stew in separate bowls.

Optional

Add lamb meatballs. Mix minced lamb meat with chopped onion, garlic and ras el hanout to taste. (Ras el hanout is a Moroccan blend of spices.) Fry in olive oil and add to the stew just before serving.

* English breakfast
black tea, blend
The tea becomes sweeter, softer, fresher, while the food is enhanced, becomes fuller, deeper.

** Shu Pu-Erh
(cooked), post-fermented tea, China
Second steep. The tea becomes softer, fruitier. The earthy notes contrast nicely with the acidity of the tomatoes and combine well with the aubergine and almonds. The stew becomes sweeter, fuller and deeper.

*** Da Hong Pao
dark rock oolong, China
The tea acquires more zest and depth, becomes more complex. The food acquires more umami, less sweetness, becomes deeper and fresher.

S PB

Vegan chocolate tea truffles

Makes about 25 truffles

225 g (7.93 oz) dark chocolate, at least 70%, chopped
12 g (0.42 oz) Earl Grey tea (or 6 tea bags)
120 ml (4.05 fl.oz) filtered water
100 g (3.3 oz) cocoa powder

Note: *Preparation time is at least 3 hours.*

Ganache
Melt the chocolate in a bain-marie. The bottom of the bowl should not touch the water. Stir until the chocolate is almost melted, then remove from heat.

Tea extract
Bring the filtered water to 95°C (203°F) and pour over the tea, steep for 2 minutes. Strain the tea over the bowl of melted chocolate and lightly press the tea leaves in the strainer to get all the moisture out. Stir until smooth. Line a bowl with cling film. Pour the ganache into the bowl, let it cool, cover and refrigerate for a few hours or overnight.

Finish
Place the cocoa powder in a large, wide dish or bowl. Take the ganache out of the fridge. With 2 dessert spoons or with clean, wet hands, make balls the size of an unpeeled walnut. Work quickly, as the chocolate will melt from the warmth of your hands. Or cut the ganache into similarly sized cubes. If the chocolate becomes too soft, place the bowl back in the fridge for about 10 minutes.
Roll the truffles through the powder carefully with a spoon, lift them gently out of the powder with a fork, carefully shake off the excess powder and place the truffle on a plate.
If you do not want to serve the truffles right away, store them in the fridge, covered.

Optional
You may also dip the truffles into melted chocolate first before dropping them in the bowl with cocoa powder. You will then get a crunchy chocolate layer in between the ganache and the cocoa powder. Let the melted chocolate cool down till about 33 - 35°C (91-95°F) before you dip the ganache balls into it, as the ganache will melt immediately if the chocolate is too hot.

* English breakfast
black tea, blend
The tea becomes fuller, creamier, acquires more flavor, makes the truffles taste deeper, more intense.

** Tieguanyin
oolong tea, China, Taiwan or Thailand
The tea becomes fuller, sweeter, creamier, while the truffles become lighter and brighter.

*** Darjeeling
first flush, black tea, India
The tea becomes fuller, creamier and sweeter, makes the truffles fruitier, brighter.

Grilled rhubarb with vegan Matcha cream and mango

Serves 4

1 can full-fat coconut milk of 400 ml (13.5 fl. oz)
½ tsp peeled and grated ginger
1 tsp Matcha
pinch salt
2 ripe mangoes
2 stalks rhubarb
4 tbsp granulated sugar
zest of 1 orange
vanilla sea salt (store bought or home made: add vanilla pith to coarse salt, shake and set aside for at least 2 days.)
optional: cacao nibs or toasted almonds

Note: Do not shake the can of coconut milk before opening it. The thick, creamy part usually floats on top, separated from the coconut water and it is the cream that you want for this recipe. Scoop it carefully out of the tin into a bowl and discard the coconut water. If the cream has not separated, then place the tin into the freezer for half an hour. This should do the trick.

Matcha cream
Mix 3 tbsp of the coconut cream with ginger and salt. Sift the Matcha over the cream and stir till bright green. Adjust to taste. Place in fridge, covered.

Rhubarb
Wash and dry the stalks of rhubarb, cut into 5 cm (2 inch) pieces. Place a dry, heavy skillet over high heat. Fold a sheet of aluminium foil twice lengthwise, place the rhubarb pieces on top, sprinkle with 2 tbsp of sugar and cover with a similar piece of aluminium foil folded twice. Squeeze the four sides together and place this parcel into the sizzling hot skillet. Cover, turn down the heat and bake until soft, but still holding its shape, 5 - 8 minutes. Take out with tongs, place onto a cutting board and remove the top foil. Ignite a blow torch, or, if you do not have one, preheat the grill. Sprinkle the rest of the sugar over the rhubarb and move the blowtorch over the rhubarb until the sugar turns brown, or place under the grill. This goes very quickly, so pay attention.

Mangoes
Peel the mangoes and cut lengthwise into slices of 3 mm (0.1 inch).

Orange
Wash and dry the orange. With a sharp peeler, cut off the skin without the white pith and slice in very thin strips, or use a zester.

Finish
Place a dollop of Matcha cream on each plate, followed by a slice of mango, the rhubarb and another dollop of cream. Garnish with vanilla salt, orange zest and orange ribbons. If you would like more crunch, add some cacao nibs or chopped almonds.

* **Earl grey,**
black tea, scented, blend
The tea acquires more depth, enhances the mango, makes the rhubarb fruitier, but also more astringent.

** **Bai Mudan**
white tea, China
The tea adds sweetness, softness and floral notes to the food, toning down the acidity of the rhubarb, connecting all flavors.

*** **Ruby #18**
black tea, Taiwan
The tea becomes brighter, fruitier, adds honey notes to the food, softens it, brings all flavors together and makes the food to taste less sharp and yet brighter.

Cheesecake with Matcha, yogurt and mango jelly

Serves 12

Pie crust
90 g (3.17 oz) unsalted butter
25 g (0.88 oz) granulated sugar
150 g (5.3 oz) cookies of your choice (graham crackers, digestives, ginger snaps, whole meal)

Filling
500 g (17.63 oz) cream cheese
400 g (14.10 oz) Turkish or Greek yoghurt 10% fat
150 g (5.3 oz) granulated sugar
1 leveled tbsp. Matcha
2 sheets gelatin, or 5 g (0.17 oz) powdered gelatin
pinch salt

Mango jelly
150 g (5.3 oz) mango, washed, peeled and cut into pieces
3 tbsp of water
75 g (2.65 oz) granulated sugar
1 tbsp lime juice
1 sheet gelatin, or 2,5 g (0.85 oz) powdered gelatin

1 to 2 tsp cocoa nibs

Note: This cheesecake needs a lot of waiting time, so make a day ahead.

Pie crust
Grease a springform pan with butter (8.66-9.44 inch). Place a piece of baking paper between the base and the ring and click the pan shut. Cut away the leftover baking paper.
Melt the butter over low heat.
Crumble the cookies in the food processor, blender, or with by rolling a rolling pin or bottle over a plastic ziplock bag filled with cookies. The crumbs must be fine like sand.
Mix in 50g (1.76 oz) sugar, add the hot melted butter. Stir until the sugar has dissolved.
Divide the mixture evenly over the bottom of the springform tin and press firmly until smooth and leveled.
Place in the fridge for at least an hour to set.

Filling
Soak the gelatin in a large bowl of cold water for 5 minutes.
Put the cream cheese in chunks into the food processor or blender, add the yoghurt, sugar and a pinch of salt.
Sift the Matcha over a bowl, add 2 tbsp hot, filtered water around 40 - 50°C (122 - 130°F). Stir until smooth and bright green and scoop this thick paste into the food processor. Pulse until well combined.
Place the gelatine sheets into a saucepan with 5 tbsp water over low heat. Stir constantly until the gelatin has melted completely. Do not let it boil, as it will become stringy.
Pour the gelatin into the yoghurt mixture in a thin stream with the food processor running.
Remove the springform pan from the refrigerator, pour the mixture into it and firmly tap the pan on the counter a few times to make any air bubbles disappear. Cover with cling film and chill for at least 3 hours.

>>

\>\>

Mango jelly

Let the gelatin soak for 5 minutes in plenty of cold water.
Purée the mango pieces with the lime juice in a blender or food processor. Add a pinch of salt and more juice to taste.
Place 75g (2.64 oz) sugar and 3 tbsp hot water in a small saucepan over low heat and stir until all the sugar has melted. Add this syrup to the mango pieces and pulse till blended.
Remove the gelatin sheet from the soaking water and place into a small saucepan with 5 tbsp hot water over low heat while stirring until all the gelatin has dissolved. Do not boil.

Let cool for 5 minutes and add in a trickle to the mixture in the running food processor.
Let cool for another 5 minutes.
Remove the springform pan from the refrigerator, pour the cooled mango purée onto the cheese cake, sprinkle with cocoa nibs.
Cover well with cling film and put in the fridge for at least 3 hours or overnight.

* English Breakfast
black tea, blend
The tea becomes full, creamy and also fruitier, makes the cake fruitier and deeper.

** Darjeeling
first flush, black tea, India
The tea becomes sweeter, fruitier. The cake becomes fruitier and fresher, acquires more flavor.

*** Feng Huang Mi Lan Dan Cong
dark oolong, China
The tea becomes fruitier, brighter, adds nutty notes, enhances and sweetens the mango, brings all flavors together.

S

Dairy-free chocolate cream with mango, lime and mint

Serves 6

Tea extract
8 g (0.28 oz) chai tea (4 bags)
brown sugar to taste

Chocolate cream
3 to 4 ripe avocados
200 ml (6.76 fl. oz) full-fat coconut milk
10 tbsp cocoa powder
3 tbsp honey
3 tbsp pomegranate molasses (available in Middle Eastern grocery stores)
pinch of salt

Fruit
2 mangoes
6-10 fresh mint leaves
juice and zest of 1 lime

1 tbsp cacao nibs
15 g (0.5 oz) unsalted peeled pistachios
optional: grated ginger or chili powder; toasted coconut flakes

Tea extract
Prepare the chai tea with 200 ml (6.76 fl. oz) filtered water at 95°C (203°F), steep for 2 minutes.
Strain the tea, discard the leaves or tea bags.
Add brown caster or cane sugar to taste.

Chocolate cream
Peel the avocados and remove the pit. Cut the avocado into chunks.
Place in a blender with the tea, coconut milk, cocoa powder, honey, pomegranate molasses, salt and the ginger or chili powder if you opt for those and pulse until smooth.
Season to taste. Cover, put into the refrigerator for at least an hour.

Fruit
Wash, dry and peel the mango. Cut into cubes or wedges or slices; whatever you prefer.
Roll up the mint leaves and cut into very thin strips.
Wash and dry the lime and grate the zest. (Only the green, not the white pith; that is bitter.)
Squeeze the lime.
Mix the mint, half of the grated lime and a splash of lime juice with the mango. Add more mint, zest and juice to taste.

Finish
Scoop a quenelle (an oblong shape) of avocado-chocolate cream on each plate. Divide the mango over the plates.
Garnish with cocoa nibs, pistachios, coconut flakes, mint leaves and zest.

Optional
Replace the coconut milk with crème fraîche.

* Earl Grey
black tea, scented, blend
The tea becomes fuller, softer, creamier, makes the dessert lighter, brighter, enhances the mint.

** Keemun
black tea, China
The tea becomes deeper, the dessert lighter, both brighter.

*** Shu Pu-Erh
(cooked), post-fermented tea, China
Both food and tea become fuller, creamier, sweeter, softer, mouth-filling.

Chocolate sorbet with red fruit and meringue

Serves 6

Sorbet
650 ml (21.97 fl.oz) water
200 g (7.05 oz) granulated sugar
125 g (4.40 oz) cocoa powder
ice cubes

Tea extract (optional)
10 g black tea (or 5 tea bags)
150 ml filtered water

Meringues
3 egg whites
pinch salt
150 g (5.3 oz) fine sugar
100 g (3.5 oz) icing sugar

Fruit
ripe red fruit to your liking: raspberries, blackberries, fresh, figs, strawberries
some mint leaves

Note: This recipe needs a lot of preparation time; start one day ahead.

Sorbet
Place water and sugar in a saucepan. Heat over low heat and stir until the sugar has dissolved. Add the cocoa powder and stir well. Let it steep for 15 minutes. Do not stir. Place a bowl in a larger bowl of ice cubes and pour the chocolate syrup into the inner bowl. Stir until the mass has cooled.
Put in the fridge for at least 6 hours or overnight, until the mixture is cold.

Tea extract
Place the tea leaves or bags in a glass jar, add the water, close firmly and place in the fridge for at least 6 hours. Strain over the chocolate syrup.
Note: in this case diminish the water you use to make the syrup by 100 ml, since you will add about 100 ml of tea extract to it.
Transfer the chocolate-tea syrup to an ice cream maker. When ready, transfer it to an airtight container and place in the freezer for at least 30 minutes.

Meringues
Preheat the oven to 110°C (230°F) and place a rack in the center of the oven. Beat the egg whites with the salt. Mix in the fine sugar very gradually with the mixer on half speed. When all sugar has dissolved, carefully fold in the sifted icing sugar. Beat until soft peaks form and hold their shape. The mixture has to be smooth and shiny.
Scoop or pipe eight round shapes of this mixture onto a parchment-lined baking sheet. About 1 heaped tbsp per shape. With the back of a spoon, make a dent into the mixture to form baskets.
Place the sheet in the oven and bake the meringues for 40 minutes or until dry to the touch.
Turn off the oven and leave the door slightly open by sticking a wooden spoon in between.
Allow to cool completely in the oven before removing them from the baking paper. The meringues will keep for weeks in an airtight container.

Finish
Scoop the sorbet into the meringues and decorate with red fruit and some mint.

Tea
Hot tea tends to clash with ice cream. Cold tea however often works fine. Try a sparkling cold brew made with white tea, oolong, or a gentle black tea, like Golden Yunnan or Ruby #18. For recipes, go to page 212.

Peach and oolong sorbet

Serves 4 - 6

15 g (0.52 oz) light oolong, e.g., Bao Zhong, Jin Xuan #12, Si Ji Chun, Tieguanyin
250 g (8.8 oz) granulated sugar
1 tsp vanilla essence
1 tbsp lemon juice
500 - 600 g (17.5 - 21.16 oz) peaches
½ egg white
1 tbsp granulated sugar

Note: This sorbet needs to be made at least one day in advance.

Sorbet
Wash and dry the peaches. Peeling is not necessary; they will be sieved later on. Remove the pits.
Purée the pulp in a high bowl. Add lemon juice, vanilla essence and sugar. Pour 100 ml (3.4 fl. oz) filtered water at 95°C (203°F) over the tea leaves and steep for 10 seconds. Strain, discard the liquid, add the wet leaves to the blended peaches. Cover and place into the refrigerator for at least 12 hours. Place your ice cream maker into the freezer if it is not there yet.

The next day
Push the purée with a spoon through a large, meshed sieve (or use a passe vite) over a large bowl and press firmly to get the most out of the pulp. There is still quite a bit of flavor left in the skins and tea leaves, so put your weight on it. Discard the pressed skins and tea leaves.
Transfer the purée to the ice cream maker and process into sorbet according to the manufacturer's instructions.
Beat ½ egg white. When it starts to get foamy and opaque, add 1 tbsp of sugar and continue beating until shiny and smooth and until stiff peaks form. Spoon into the sorbet mixture halfway through processing the ice cream, mix well and continue processing. When done, transfer to an airtight container and smooth it out with a spatula. Close the box tightly and place in the freezer to set for a few more hours.

Serve with Frisian cookies, for recipe go to page 124.

Tea
A cold sparkling tea of white or oolong tea goes well with this. For recipes see page 212.

Optional
Serve with a warm, grilled half peach filled with lemon mascarpone, see page 126.

Vanilla tea ice cream

Serves 4 - 6

8 g (0.28 oz) or 4 tea bags black tea, eg., Assam or English Breakfast
2 vanilla pods
100 g (3.5 oz) granulated sugar
400 g (14 oz) double cream
200 ml (6.76 fl. oz) full-fat milk
3 egg yolks
3 sprigs of mint

Note: *This ice cream needs to be made at least one day in advance.*

Vanilla tea ice cream
Scrape the pith out of the vanilla pods into the pan with the sugar and milk. Bring the milk with the sugar to a boil, stirring until all sugar has dissolved. Turn off the heat as soon as the milk boils, add the tea, stir, cover and set aside for 15 minutes.
Place the emptied vanilla pods inside the sugar jar, to scent your sugar.

Strain the milk. Since the tea has absorbed some of the milk, you have to weigh the remaining milk and add more milk until you reach 200g (7oz).
Beat the egg yolks and add the cream.
Add the tea milk to the mixture, stirring until well combined.
Cover and place into the refrigerator for at least 6 hours, or overnight.
Do you have an ice cream maker? Place it in the freezer at least 24 hours in advance.

After 6 hours or the next day
Turn on the ice cream maker and in a steady stream add the cream-milk-tea mixture. Transfer to an airtight plastic container and store in the freezer until ready to use. The fresher the ice cream, the better it tastes, so eat it within 3 days.

Do not have an ice cream maker?
After 6 hours (or more) of cooling in the fridge, place the container with the cream-milk-tea mixture in the freezer.
Take it out after 1 hour, stir well with a fork to break up the formed ice crystals and put back again.
Repeat this every hour until the mixture is firm and creamy.

Finish
Scoop the ice cream into homemade meringue nests or in frozen tall glasses, serve plain, or with hot chocolate sauce, or salty caramel sauce (recipe on the next page).

Tea
A cold sparkling tea of white or oolong tea goes well with this. For recipes see page 212.

Tip
Use Chai tea bags for an Indian touch.

S

Orange and black tea ice cream with salty caramel-ginger sauce

Serves 4 - 6

Ice cream
1 liter (34 fl. oz) good quality vanilla ice cream, store bought or home made
2 oranges
3 tbsp of orange-ginger marmalade
1 tbsp. soy sauce
tea extract, recipe on page 212

Caramel sauce
15 g (0.52 oz) fresh ginger, about 2½ cm (1 inch)
200 ml (6.76 fl.oz) double cream
1 vanilla pod
150 g (5.3 oz) granulated sugar
2 tbsp water
1 tsp honey
1 tbsp soy sauce
1 tbsp toasted white sesame seeds

Note: this recipe needs a lot of preparation time; start one day ahead, or 4 hours before serving.

Orange and black tea ice cream
Remove the ice cream from the freezer and set aside to soften a bit. Cut off the ends and skin of the orange, including the white pith, with a very sharp knife. Over a bowl, catch the juice and cut the wedges loose from the membranes, keep them in the juice.
Spoon the marmalade onto a large chopping board and remove the bits of rind and keep for garnishing. Place marmalade in a bowl, add the soy sauce, 4 tbsp of tea extract, and 1 tbsp of the collected orange juice. Stir until well combined and add to the softened ice cream. Cover and put back in the freezer for at least 3 hours.

Caramel sauce
Mix the double cream with a pinch of salt, the pith of the vanilla pod and the chopped ginger in a saucepan. Bring the cream to a boil, reduce the heat to its lowest point, cover and simmer for 10 minutes. Turn off the heat and let the mixture steep for another 10 minutes, covered. Strain, add the soy sauce and keep warm. Melt the sugar in a stainless steel, thick-bottomed pan over medium heat without stirring until it looks like honey. When the thermometer reads 165ºC (329ºF), turn off the heat, add the warm cream mixture a little at a time and stir until the caramel is smooth again. Be careful, this causes very hot bubbles, so add the cream slowly. This may take anywhere from 10 - 15 minutes, but keep a close eye on the temperature, as the right temperature is essential. Keep the sauce warm.
Note: the temperature will remain at a certain degree for a long time and suddenly rise.

Finish
Strain the orange wedges and divide them over ice cold plates. Scoop the slightly softened ice cream onto the plates, sprinkle with toasted sesame seeds and drizzle a bit of the warm caramel-ginger sauce over the ice cream.

Tea
Hot tea and ice cream tend to clash, something cold works better. You could try the Bombay Bubble cocktail, on page 217.

> **Tip**
> If there happens to be leftover sauce: serve the sauce the next day with marinated chicken thighs, baked crispy in the oven.
> Marinade for chicken: lime juice, honey, soy sauce, 2 cloves of garlic and some roughly chopped coriander stalks and leaves.

Matcha cream truffles

Yield: about 24 truffles

75 g (2.64 oz) granulated sugar
200 g (7 oz) double cream
1 vanilla pod
125 g (4.40 oz) unsalted butter at room temperature
3 g (0.10 oz) Matcha tea
250 g (8.8 oz) white chocolate
75 g (2.64 oz) cocoa powder

Note: *It is important that butter and cream are at the same temperature. If the mixture curdles (and starts to look like scrambled eggs) then one of the two is too cold. In that case, heat the mixture a bit in a bain-marie. If the mixture is runny, it is too warm. Cool the mixture down in a bowl with ice water and ice cubes. Whisk the mixture until smooth.*

Matcha cream
Cut open the vanilla pod, scrape out the pith and add it to the cream. Add a pinch of salt and the sugar, place the pan over medium heat and stir until all sugar has dissolved. Bring to a simmer and turn off the heat. Cover, set aside for 20 minutes. Sift the Matcha over the cream, stir till bright green, cover again and store in the fridge overnight.

Truffles
Cover a cutting board with parchment paper. Make sure it is not too big for the freezer.
Beat the butter gently with a mixer at half speed. Add the cream slowly, continue beating. Fill a piping bag with the mixture and pipe mounds the size of a walnut on the board. Place in the freezer for at least 45 minutes.

Chocolate
Chop the chocolate into uniform tiny pieces. Melt it using a bain-marie or double boiler while stirring regularly. The bottom of the bowl with the chocolate should not touch the boiling water, to prevent the chocolate from burning. It is the steam that does the trick.
Once the chocolate is almost melted, take it off the heat, allow it to cool off a bit. Wait till the chocolate reaches 30°C (86°F), else it will be too hot for the cream.

Finish
Take the tray with the dollops of cream out of the freezer. Slide a fork under a dollop and carefully dip the fork with the dollop into the melted chocolate. Shake off any excess chocolate from the fork, wipe the fork off along the edge of the bowl to remove excess chocolate. Carefully let the truffle slide off the fork into the bowl of cocoa powder. Do not touch it anymore, just scoop some cocoa powder over it with a spoon and let it dry. Wipe the fork clean and repeat until all dollops are covered with chocolate and cocoa powder.
Once they are dry, with a spoon scoop them carefully into a large sieve over a bowl and shake the sieve gently to remove any excess powder. Store the truffles in the refrigerator in a sealed box or freeze them.

* English breakfast, *black tea, blend*
The tea becomes fuller, creamier, deeper, makes the truffles lighter, brighter, intensifies the Matcha.

** Ceylon, *black tea, Sri Lanka*
The tea becomes fruitier, softer, makes the truffles lighter, brighter, intensifies the Matcha. Fresh aftertaste.

*** Darjeeling, *first flush, black tea, India*
The tea becomes creamier, sweeter, makes the truffles sweeter and fruity, the Matcha becomes less prominent.

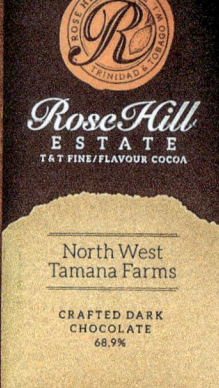

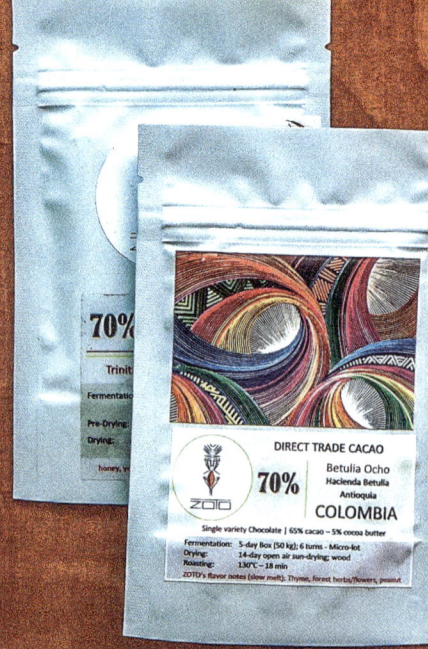

CHAPTER 8

Chocolate and tea

Chocolate is made from the almond-sized seeds of the fruit, or cocoa pods, that grow on the cacao tree, Theobroma Cacao. Each pod contains about 20 to 40 seeds, hidden in an aromatic, juicy white pulp that tastes like slightly like lychee. These cacao pods (some as large as a rugby ball) grow directly out of the tree trunk. They can have all sorts of colors, shapes and skins: bright orange, red, yellow, green and purple. Their shapes can be round, oval, ridged or almost smooth, a bit wrinkled or bumpy, slim or plump, and so on.

ORIGINS

The origin of cacao is in South America: more specifically, the Amazon River areas of Ecuador and Peru, around the Venezuelan Lake Maracaibo and in the foothills of the Venezuelan and Colombian Andes. The seeds were geographically spread out with the help of animals and birds, and slowly the trees came to be found further and further from their origins. Nowadays, cacao trees grow all around the world in an area roughly between 20 degrees north and 20 degrees south of the equator. The trees are harvested twice a year, and the fruit of one tree can be made into one kg of solid chocolate, on average.

HOW CHOCOLATE CAME ABOUT

As we now know for certain, humanity's love of chocolate started sometime around 3300 BC in the Ecuadorian Amazon region, very near the present-day border with Peru, where the Mayo-Chinchipe people then lived. The indigenous peoples used chocolate as a culinary ingredient, mixing the paste with chili, vanilla, herbs, flowers and many other aromatic substances. Archeologists have dug up remnants of ceramic vessels and kitchen tools, like mortar and pestles (metates), containing traces of Theobroma. This proves that the Mayo-Chinchipe people knew how to process the bitter and sour cacao beans into something edible and delicious.

Scientists traced the date back to 5,300 years ago with the use of Carbon-14 dating. It was already known that in Mesoamerica, between 1500 and 400 BC, the Olmec people, who lived in what is now Mexico, also used cacao as a food. They dried their staples, like corn, seeds and chili peppers in the sun, then roasted and ground them on stone slabs. At some point, they did the same with cacao beans, which taste very bitter when eaten raw but are edible when treated like corn kernels. The interior of the beans starts to ferment when dried in the sun, which changes the chemical composition of the bean and develops delicious flavors and aromas. After roasting, the Olmec people ground the oily beans, producing a kind of paste that could then be shaped into tasty, rich and nutritious balls that were dried for future use. And hence, chocolate was born. This did happen as early as 3300 BC!

Chocolate and spices mixtures like this still exist in Mesoamerican countries. I bought several delicious pastes, called moles, in Oaxaca, Mexico, and in surrounding countries. They still use this kind of chocolate in their dishes, porridges and drinks.

FOAMY CHOCOLATE DRINKS

The word 'cacao' is derived from the word 'kakawa,' which dates back to around 1000 BC when the Olmec culture was at its peak, and kakawa was the frothy chocolate drink that was used in sacrifices. In Olmec tradition, it could only be drunk by high priests and the nobility. It was literally a drink meant for the gods, and that is exactly what the Greek name for cacao, Theobroma, means; food of the gods. Linnaeus, who gave this name to the cacao tree, was probably aware of the fact that cacao had a divine significance for the original inhabitants of Central America. Or maybe Linnaeus considered it divine in taste as well, just like the Olmecs did.

The Olmecs, Toltecs, Aztecs and Mayas made cacao into a strong flavored drink, mixed with spices such as cinnamon, vanilla, peppers, etc. Sugar was unknown to them so if the drink was sweetened at all, then it was probably with honey and vanilla. Based on the reports of Spanish conquerors, it was mainly a very strong and bitter drink, which at first the Spanish did not like at all.

PRECIOUS CACAO BEANS

Cacao beans were also used as a form of currency, indicating the high value people of that time gave to it. According to records, a rabbit cost about 10 cacao beans, for example. A prostitute too. More about this and the history of cacao is to be found in the fascinating book *The True History of Chocolate*, by Sophie and Michael D. Coe. It is very detailed and compelling.

EDIBLE CHOCOLATE

Chocolate in solid form originated in the West in the late 19th century. Until then, chocolate had been only consumed as a hot beverage in Europe and North America. Cacao beans were ground and cooked with sugar and milk. Sometimes spices were also added, as the Spanish had seen the Aztecs do in Mexico.

Due to the high cacao butter content, this drink was very fattening and heavy. Approximately each cacao bean consists of half cacao solids and half cacao butter, which is pure fat. In 1828, Coenraad van Houten, a Dutchman, invented a hydraulic press for separating out the cocoa butter found in cocoa beans. After pressing, roughly 28% cocoa butter remained in the cacao mass. This created a fairly dry cake of cacao mass, which once ground, became a much less greasy base for chocolate milk, namely cocoa powder.

VARIETIES OF CACAO BEANS

In the past, it was assumed that there were only three main varieties of cacao pods: Criollo, Forastero and Trinitario. Genetic research shows that those varieties have sub-varieties with unique sets of genes, e.g., Nacional, Arriba, Calabacillo, Angoleta, Porcelana, Chuao, Choroní, Scavina, Amelonado, Amazon, Ocumare.

In the late 19th and early 20th centuries, the Nacional sub-variety was highly sought out in the West for making chocolate due to its complex floral notes. In 1916, a disastrous disease, known as Witches' Broom, almost eradicated the Nacional sub-variety. Farmers developed hybrid varieties to ensure variable harvests. The hybrids are more disease-resistant; unfortunately, they only contain about 30% of the original Nacional genes. However, around 2007, Jerry Toth, an American, started a rainforest conservation project in the rainforests of Ecuador, specifically Piedra de Plata, where the conservationists stumbled upon very old-growth cacao trees originating prior to 1916. When the trees were DNA tested, nine of them were 100% Nacional. A treasure had been found! They took cuttings from the trees and slowly but steadily brought the 100% Nacional back to life again. Great news for the cacao farmers! Their delicious chocolate is for sale under the name To'Ak.

CHOCOLATE MADE TRADITIONALLY

When the cacao pods are ready to be harvested, which happens twice a year, they are chopped off the tree with sharp blades on sticks, then cut open with chopping knives (machetes). The production process consists of several steps:

1. Fermentation

The pulp is spread out on banana leaves laid on the ground. The huge pile of pulp is covered with more banana leaves and left for five to eight days in the blazing heat of the tropical sun. Due to the high heat, the temperature inside the pile reaches about 45 to 50°C/113 to 122°F, causing the pulp to ferment. Eventually, it disintegrates and drains away, and a large pile of hot wet seeds is left. The fermentation process is very important for developing the final taste of the cacao.

2. Drying

The cacao beans are spread out onto huge tables, left to air dry in the sun for up to six days, and are turned regularly by hand to obtain an even drying.

3. Winnowing

They are then cleaned with hot air, the husks of the beans crack open and the inedible skins are removed. The remaining part is called the cacao nibs.

4. Roasting

The nibs are roasted in order to allow the acidic and bitter substances to evaporate and flavors develop.

5. Grinding

The nibs are then mixed with sugar (when milk chocolate is made, milk powder is also added) and ground until it turns into a homogenous, sticky paste: the cacao liquor or cacao mass. This has nothing to do with alcoholic liquor, it is just the technical term for this thick liquid mass.

6. Conching

The next step is conching: the liquor is rolled with heavy steel cylinders for about 24 - 72 hours. The conching ensures that the mass is completely smooth and velvety in structure, with all the particles melted together. This process was invented in 1879 by the Swiss chocolatier Rudolphe Lindt. Until then, chocolate had been fairly gritty and coarse. Lindt called it fondant chocolate, a term that is still in use. Fondant means melting.

7. Tempering

The mass is then tempered, in other words it is heated to a maximum of 50°C (122°F), after which it is poured over a cold, marble slab and is quickly scraped together. This process cools the chocolate back and ensures that the different crystals in the cacao butter dissolve, each at their own, different melting temperature. Once the mass is between 29 and 32°C (84 and 89°F), depending on whether what is being made is white, milk or dark chocolate, it is poured into moulds. During the hardening the mass has to shrink slightly, so that it can later be easily released from the moulds. If it is badly tempered, the chocolate will not come out of the mould.
For well tempered chocolate it is important that the percentage of cacao butter is high.

CACAO BUTTER

Each cacao bean consists of about half cacao mass and half cacao butter.
The precious cacao butter could be sold for the benefit of the cosmetics industry, because cacao butter is very good for the skin.
It can also be added to chocolate, which then becomes the so-called couverture chocolate. This is used for making chocolates. Because of the added cacao butter, the chocolate melts much better, there are more crystals in it, which makes it easier to temper and, as a result, easier to remove from the moulds.
Well-tempered chocolate also provides a beautiful shine and a snappiness that gives a pleasant texture.

INDUSTRIAL CHOCOLATE

In large chocolate factories there is no time for taking all these steps meticulously. Time is money, and the chocolate has to be sold cheaply and thus shortcuts are always necessary. Often the beans are very heavily roasted in order to burn away any injustices, with a bitter, flat and burnt taste as a result. All innate flavors and aromas go up in flames. In addition, a lot of sugar is added to compensate for the bitterness. Sometimes the percentage of cacao butter is lowered (because it yields a lot of money when sold) or completely replaced by the much cheaper (environmentally polluting) palm oil. Due to the blending of different beans (of different qualities), a generic flavor is obtained. The chocolate will always taste the same, and the consumers get exactly what they expect. This system also applies to most industrial coffee and tea.

SINGLE ORIGIN CHOCOLATE

In addition to supermarket chocolate, there is also chocolate made by micro-producers who carry out their craft with a lot of love, dedication and knowledge of their business. Their single origin chocolate is almost always of high-quality, and is complex in taste. Even a small piece of that kind of chocolate may cause a very intense, layered taste sensation. This chocolate is made artisanally and in small quantities, with high-quality cacao beans. This, by definition, makes it more expensive than the supermarket chocolate made in large factories from bulk, low-quality cacao beans. But more expensive is a relative term: as just a tiny piece of this chocolate goes a long way. Flavor-wise, it lasts much longer than cheap chocolate, which often loses its flavor right after swallowing, leaving an unpleasant and sticky aftertaste, which causes you to want to keep on eating it.

Single Origin means from one area. This may refer to a country, a region or even a village. The type and origin of the cacao bean used is usually stated on the packaging, as well as the percentage of cacao mass, milk, and sugar. Some chocolate makers make Bean to Bar chocolate. This means that they get involved with the production process from the moment of picking. The fermentation process is essential for the final taste and can make a huge difference. This kind of producer will decide for themselves how long and how they want the beans to ferment. This is actually a rare situation, because the decisions are usually made by the farmers themselves, without involvement from the producers. So if they do participate in the process in this way, it usually means they are very dedicated and care a lot about their product.

Test
Tasting tea and chocolate
Break off a small piece of the chocolate you would like to taste. Smell it first, then let it melt slowly in your mouth; do not chew it. Roll the piece around in your mouth and suck in some air. This way, you will taste more, as the oxygen promotes aromas to release themselves more readily. Pay attention to the texture, flavors and aromas. What do you notice? The aftertaste is important. The aromas of high-quality chocolate will linger a long time in the back of your throat, and you will be able to taste the chocolate for a long time, even if you have had just a tiny piece.

SUPERMARKET TEA WITH SINGLE ORIGIN CHOCOLATE

Due to its high sugar content, supermarket chocolate usually can be used with supermarket tea, as they are both blends with generic flavors, and are not very outspoken. Supermarket tea with single origin chocolate could, however, have an entirely different effect (see below). The tea may actually benefit, improve, from the complex flavors of the chocolate, but can also become extremely bitter and astringent. English Breakfast and some Ceylon tea, for example. I tasted each of these with a lot of single origin chocolate and it turned out that these astringent teas could only handle white and milk chocolate.

Every dark chocolate, even the very creamiest ones, strengthened the bitters in the tea and made the texture very astringent; my tongue felt like leather. Single origin dark chocolate seems to fare better with a sweeter black tea with honey and cacao notes and little to no astringency, like Taiwanese or some Chinese black teas.

If you want to stick to English Breakfast tea, then choose white or milk chocolate. The same goes for green supermarket tea, as their bitter notes and dry aftertaste pairs better with creamy milk and white chocolate than tart or powerful dry dark chocolate. Earl Grey is easier on dark single origin chocolate, because of its floral and citrus notes. It is softer, friendlier than English Breakfast or Ceylon tea.

SUPERMARKET CHOCOLATE WITH SINGLE ORIGIN TEA

Whether tea and chocolate are a good combination depends on the flavor profiles of the chocolate and tea that you use. If you have cheap chocolate with a lot of sugar, fat and milk powder, then it will be fine with any supermarket tea, be it black or green, as the taste of the chocolate is mainly sweet, with a sticky texture. Sugar suppresses flavors, therefore it is often not a good idea to use sweet, bland, supermarket chocolate with complex teas. There is a significant chance that this tea's delicate aromas will be pushed away by the sugars in the chocolate. However, sweet chocolate can be a solution to combine with bitter tea; even the more complex ones.

BULK AND BULK

Industrially made chocolate and industrially made tea often combine fairly well, as they are both rather flat in taste, straightforward, and without any complexity. The chocolate is mainly sweet, without a character of its own. The main goal in its production is quantity at low costs, rather than quality.

SINGLE ORIGIN CHOCOLATE WITH SINGLE ORIGIN TEA

There are also many high-quality teas and ditto chocolates, which are usually complex and intense in taste. They do not always match well. They can even severely clash. But there are also quite a lot of perfect matches to be expected. Discovering a harmonious and lasting combination of tea and chocolate feels like having your tastebuds dance like angels. On pages 192 - 197 are lists of tea and chocolate combinations that I like a lot.

On the next page you will find a handy tool: Taste With Colour®. This is a chocolate tasting flavor map designed by Hazel J. Lee, a British chocolate connoisseur and professional, who sees colors when she tastes chocolate.

If you are sensitive to colors, then this map could be very useful for you. Being an artist by trade, I like her idea of colored flavors very much. In a way, I think in colors too when I do my tastings.

The map works like this: if you taste something and your brain connects it to a certain color, then you can look in the area of that particular color to define what it is you actually taste. It is a tool to train your brain in developing your mental taste and flavor library, just like the flavor wheels on pages 56 and 248.
This map can also be used as a tool for tasting tea, or wine, coffee, or beer.

Image used with permission.

TASTE WITH COLOUR®
CHOCOLATE TASTING FLAVOUR MAP
BY HAZEL LEE

Pine, Rosemary, Basil, Jasmine, Lavender, Rose, Bubblegum, Raspberry, Cherry, Thyme, Herbal, Floral, Violet, Lychee, Rhubarb, Mint, Leafy, Coconut, Orange Blossom, Melon, Pink Peppercorn, Strawberry, Grassy, Cream, Peach, Grapefruit, Tomato, Green Tea, Vanilla, Orange, Chilli, Apple, Pistachio, Macadamia, Cashew, Fruity, Red Pepper, Gooseberry, Lime, Cheese, Tropical Fruit, Grapes, Green Banana, Honey, Pineapple, Apricot, Cranberries, Vegetal, Lemongrass, Butter, Lemon, Undergrowth, Olive, Hay, Banana, Passion Fruit, Blueberry, Mouldy, Alcoholic, Butterscotch, Ginger, Musty, Tobacco, Cinnamon, Almond, Blackberry, Mineral, Caramel, Bread, Metallic, Brownie, Nutmeg, Toffee, Peanut, Plum, Blackcurrant, Mushroom, Cocoa, Yeast, Malt, Smoky, Molasses, Marmite, Coffee, Maple, Cereal, Raisins, Prune, Fig, Leather, Brazil Nut, Nutty, Fudge, Rum, Clove, Hazelnut, Jammy, Liquorice, Earthy, Spicy, Dates, Walnut, Red Wine, Woody, Tonka, Tamarind, Overroasted, Toast, Truffle, Cardamom, Burnt, Balsamic, Muscovado, Dried Cherries, Tannic, Black Pepper, Game, Black Tea, Brown Fruit

#TASTEWITHCOLOUR   © 2021 HAZEL J LEE   @TASTEWITHCOLOUR

Tasting notes tea and chocolate

DARK CHOCOLATE	
CHOCOLATE	
Alkimia, *Cusco, Peru, 70%* **Flavor profile:** neutral, later on dry, rich, later on bright, grainy, sweet, slightly sour, fruity, nutty, spices; honey, citrus, peanut, cinnamon, clove, M-L	
TEA	
Sencha, *Kochi, Shikoku prefecture, Japan* **Flavor profile:** smooth to dry, rich and bright, sweet, bitter, umami, vegetal, herbaceous, maritime, fruity, M	**Ruby #18,** *black tea, Sun Moon Lake, Nantou County, Taiwan* **Flavor profile:** smooth, rich, sweet, earthy, herbaceous, fruity, sweets, spices, M
Effect: The tea becomes fruity, sweeter, acquires more umami. The chocolate becomes smooth, brighter, fruitier, effervescent.	**Effect:** The tea becomes sweeter, more floral, fuller, ends brighter. The chocolate becomes brighter, fruitier. Clean mouthfeel.
CHOCOLATE	
Cacao Hunters, *Arauca, Colombia, 70%* **Flavor profile:** smooth, silky, later on dry, bright, sweet, fruity, floral; passionfruit, pineapple, citrus, M-L	
TEA	
Mi Lan Xiang Feng Huang Dan Cong, *Chao-zhou, Guangdong province, China* **Flavor profile:** smooth, ends a bit dry, rich, sweet, umami, fruity, vegetal, floral, earthy, grains, sweets, M-L	**Bai Mudan,** *Fuding City, Fujian Province, China* **Flavor profile:** smooth, mellow, rich, later bright, subtle, sweet, floral, nuts, fruity, sweets, vegetal, grains, M
Effect: The tea and chocolate become very fruity, both acquire notes of gooseberry. The tea also acquires mineral notes.	**Effect:** The tea and chocolate become fruitier and blend together. Clean, bright, slightly dry finish.
CHOCOLATE	
Chocolate Tree, *Chililique, Peru, 70%* **Flavor profile:** dry, bright, later on rich, sweet, fruity, spices, herbal; passionfruit, pineapple, citrus, red fruit, cinnamon, mint, XL	
TEA	
Bai Hao Yin Zhen, *Shaowu City, Fujian province, China* **Flavor profile:** smooth, rich, creamy, sweet, vegetal, floral, sweets, fruity, grains, S.	**Wen Shan Baozhong** *Taipei County, Taiwan* **Flavor profile:** smooth and dry, rich and bright, sweet, slightly bitter, dairy, floral, fruity, vegetal, herbaceous, grains, nutty, spices, M
Effect: The tea acquires more depth, umami, spices. It tones down the acidic notes of the chocolate, brings more balance, emphasises notes of cinnamon.	**Effect:** The tea acquires cacao notes. It tones down the acidic notes of the chocolate, adds floral notes.

DARK CHOCOLATE	
CHOCOLATE	
Dick Taylor, *Sambirano Valley, Madagascar, 70%* **Flavor profile:** dry, bright and rich, earthy, fruity, nutty, spices, sweets; mango, raisins, clove, honey. In the finish stout beer, caramel, peanuts, L- XL	
TEA	
Tie Guan Yin heavy roast, *Longten, Taiwan* **Flavor profile:** smooth, rich, a bit bright, sweet, bitter, fruity, sweets, earthy, grains, floral, nutty, spices, L	**Shu (cooked) Pu Erh,** *Yunnan Province, China* **Flavor profile:** smooth, rich, sweet, umami, earthy, animal, sweets, herbaceous, vegetal, M-XL
Effect: The chocolate becomes very nutty, followed by bright fruitiness, a new flavor: licorice. The tea acquires notes of toast with honey. Both become more complex.	**Effect:** The tea makes the chocolate deeper and sweeter, enhances its earthy notes. The chocolate makes the tea fruitier, brighter, lighter.
CHOCOLATE	
Krak, *Madagascar, 70%* **Flavor profile:** dry, rich and bright, sweet, fruity, spices; citrus, red fruit, anise, L	
TEA	
Darjeeling, *second flush, Darjeeling, India* **Flavor profile:** neutral-dry, bright, crisp, floral, fruity, herbaceous, spices, M-L	**Mi Lan Xiang Feng Huang Dan Cong,** *Chao-zhou, Guangdong province, China* **Flavor profile:** smooth, ends a bit dry, rich, sweet, umami, fruity, vegetal, floral, earthy, grains, sweets, M-L
Effect: The tea and chocolate melt together, but remain their own characters. Mutual enhancement.	**Effect:** The tea makes the chocolate almost salty, umami, with notes of licorice. The chocolate makes the tea less fruity, more floral, especially notes of honeysuckle.
CHOCOLATE	
Marou, *Heart of Darkness, island of Tan Phu Dong, Mekong Delta, Vietnam, 85%* **Flavor profile:** smooth, later dry, rich and bright, sweet, umami, earthy, spices, floral, nutty; tobacco, ginger, hazelnut, XL	
TEA	
Tie Guan Yin *heavy roast, Longten, Taiwan* **Flavor profile:** smooth, rich, a bit bright, sweet, bitter, fruity, sweets, earthy, grains, floral, nutty, spices, L	**Dong Ding,** *Mei Shan, Nantou, Taiwan* **Flavor profile:** smooth and dry, rich and bright, sweet, slightly bitter, nutty, mineral, floral, sweets, vegetal, herbaceous, fruity, dairy, M-L
Effect: The tea and chocolate together cause new flavors: cinnamon and roasted coconut.	**Effect:** The tea brings out the floral notes of the chocolate, makes it lighter and brighter. The tea becomes creamy, with cacao meandering through.

DARK CHOCOLATE

CHOCOLATE

Pump Street Bakery, *Criollo, Madagascar, 70%*
Flavor profile: smooth, rich, meaty, sweet, earthy, fruity, spices, herbal; mushrooms, blackberries, pepper, eucalyptus, XL

TEA

Spicy White, *first flush, Kurseong valley, Darjeeling, India* **Flavor profile:** dry, slightly smooth, bright, crisp, sweet, bitter, floral, fruity, vegetal, herbaceous, M	**Dong Ding,** *Mei Shan, Nantou, Taiwan* **Flavor profile:** smooth and dry, rich and bright, sweet, slightly bitter, nutty, mineral, floral, sweets, vegetal, herbaceous, fruity, dairy, M-L
Effect: The tea becomes more floral, the chocolate less acidic, acquires floral notes, becomes balanced out. Rather dry aftertaste.	**Effect:** The chocolate acquires nutty and floral notes, becomes lighter and brighter. The tea becomes earthy, acquires umami and depth.

CHOCOLATE

Original Beans, *Beni wild harvest, Bolivia, 66%*
Flavor profile: smooth, rich and bright, sweet, fruity, spices; passionfruit, pineapple, cinnamon, M-L

TEA

Keemun, *Qimen County, China* **Flavor profile:** smooth, ends a bit dry, rich, sweet, umami, earthy, sweets, fruity, floral, grains, animal, L	**Bai Mudan,** *Fuding City, Fujian Province, China* **Flavor profile:** smooth, mellow, rich, later bright, subtle, sweet, floral, nuts, fruity, sweets, vegetal, grains, M
Effect: The chocolate becomes more intense, brighter, enhancement of the passion fruit notes. The tea becomes smokey, earthier, less sweet.	**Effect:** The chocolate becomes intensely floral, acquires notes of cookies, while the tea becomes fruitier and sweeter.

CHOCOLATE

François Pralus, *Tobago Estate W.I., 70%*
Flavor profile: smooth, ends a bit dry, silky, rich and bright, sweet, earthy, fruity, nutty; mushrooms, red fruit, peanut, L

TEA

Huo Shan Huang Ya, *Huo Shan County, Anhui Province, China* **Flavor profile:** smooth, bright, sweet, sour, umami, vegetal, fruity, earthy, grains, nutty, mineral, M	**Mi Lan Xiang Feng Huang Dan Cong,** *Chao-zhou, Guangdong province, China* **Flavor profile:** smooth, ends a bit dry, rich, sweet, umami, fruity, vegetal, floral, earthy, grains, sweets, M-L
Effect: The tea becomes earthier, nuttier, it brings all flavors together, makes the chocolate brighter, lighter, adds a hint of mint to the chocolate.	**Effect:** The tea acquires notes of aniseed, and more umami, the chocolate notes of bay leaf and licorice. Later on the entire sensation becomes very fruity, floral and umami, almost salty.

CHOCOLATE

Villa Kuyaya, *Arriba Nacional, Esmeraldas, Ecuador, 73%*
Flavor profile: dry, later on smooth, rich, sweet, animal, earthy, fruity, spices, floral; leather, cacao, red fruit, cinnamon, L-XL

TEA

Sencha, Kochi, *Shikoku prefecture, Japan* **Flavor profile:** smooth to dry, rich and bright, sweet, bitter, umami, vegetal, herbaceous, maritime, fruity, M	**Ruby #18,** *black tea, Sun Moon Lake, Nantou County, Taiwan* **Flavor profile:** smooth, rich, sweet, earthy, herbaceous, fruity, sweets, spices, M
Effect: The tea becomes deeper, acquires earthy notes, enhances the chocolate's earthiness. Clean palate afterwards.	**Effect:** The tea's aromas are enhanced, the chocolate becomes brighter and fruitier. Dry, clean, refreshing aftertaste.

DARK CHOCOLATE	
CHOCOLATE	
To'Ak, Nacional, *Rain Harvest 2017, Piedra de Plata, Ecuador, 76%* **Flavor profile:** smooth, rich, later on bright, sweet, fruity, floral, nutty, earthy; cherry, orange peel, pistachio, honeysuckle, mushrooms, L-XL	
TEA	
Nepalese black, *first flush, Hile, Dhankuta, Nepal* **Flavor profile:** smooth and dry, bright, crisp, sweet, slightly sour, fruity, sweets, earthy, nutty, floral, M	**Da Hong Pao,** *dark rock oolong, Wuyi Shan, Fujian, China* **Flavor profile:** smooth, ends a bit dry, rich, sweet, sour, umami, fruity, floral, sweets, earthy, herbaceous, grains, nutty, spices, mineral, L-XL
Effect: The floral notes of both tea and chocolate are enhanced. The tea becomes softer, rounder, sweeter, the chocolate more intense. Passionfruit and cacao in aftertaste.	**Effect:** The mineral and fruity notes of the tea are enhanced, the tea becomes very floral. The chocolate becomes very intense, with a very long aftertaste, floral, fruity, clean palate.
CHOCOLATE	
To'Ak, Nacional, *2015, aged in Tequila barrels, Piedra de Plata, Ecuador, 73%* **Flavor profile:** smooth, rich, sweet, earthy, floral, fruity; wood, tequila, honeysuckle, raisins, L-XL	
TEA	
Shu (cooked) Pu Erh, *Yunnan Province, China* **Flavor profile:** smooth, rich, sweet, umami, earthy, animal, sweets, herbaceous, vegetal, M-XL	**Dian Hong,** *Yunnan, China* **Flavor profile:** smooth, rich, sweet, umami, earthy, sweets, fruity, nutty, spices, L
Effect: The tea enhances the earthy and woody notes of the chocolate and deepens the tequila. The chocolate acquires the flavor of the tea and notes of raisin, adds umami and depth, warmth.	**Effect:** The tea acquires umami and depth, and a warming effect. The chocolate blends with the tea, both are enhanced, the tequila jumps out. Long, warm aftertaste of tea, chocolate and tequila.

MILK CHOCOLATE	
CHOCOLATE	
Chocolate Tree, *Marañon, Peru, dark milk, 60%* **Flavor profile:** mooth, rich, sweet, earthy, dairy, sweets; molasses, tobacco, condensed milk, caramel, coffee, M	
TEA	
Genmaicha-iri Matcha, *green tea mixed with Matcha and puffed rice; Ujitawara, Uji, Kyoto, Japan* **Flavor profile:** smooth, later on dry, rich, sweet, umami, nutty, grains, fruity, vegetal, herbaceous, maritime, earthy, M	**Jin Xuan #12,** *Alishan, Taiwan* **Flavor profile:** smooth, silky, rich, sweet, slightly bitter, dairy, floral, fruity, vegetal, herbaceous, M
Effect: Both tea and chocolate are enhanced and acquire more umami. The caramel matches the puffed rice. All flavors blend after a second sip.	**Effect:** The tea becomes brighter, lighter, fruity, the chocolate floral, creamier, sweeter. The aftertaste is bright, floral.

MILK CHOCOLATE	
CHOCOLATE	
Dick Taylor, *Sambirano Valley, Madagascar, 58%* **Flavor profile:** Flavor profile: dry, bright and rich, sweet, fruity; citrus, red fruit, caramel, M-L	
TEA	
Bi Luo Chun, *Dong Shan, Jiangsu Province, China* **Flavor profile:** smooth, rich, later dry and bright, sweet, slightly bitter, umami, vegetal, fruity, grains nutty, spices, mineral, M	**Earl Grey,** *black tea, scented with Bergamot citrus, blend* **Flavor profile:** dry, rich and bright, sweet, umami, floral, fruity, earthy, M-L
Effect: The tea becomes dryer, slightly salty, deeper. The chocolate becomes creamy, silky.	**Effect:** The tea becomes deeper, fuller, softer. The chocolate becomes very bright, its citrus notes enhanced. The aftertaste is floral, with both tea and chocolate in the background.
CHOCOLATE	
Fruition, *Marañon, Peru, dark milk, 68%* **Flavor profile:** dry, later on smooth, silky, bright, later on rich, sweet, earthy, fruity, floral, animal; hay, wet forest, mushroom, leather, stable, strawberry, raisins, L	
TEA	
Dong Fang Mei Ren, *oolong, Hsinchu County, Taiwan* **Flavor profile:** smooth, ends a bit dry, rich, sweet, floral, fruity, earthy, mineral, spices, M	**Da Hong Pao,** *dark rock oolong, Wuyi Shan, Fujian, China* **Flavor profile:** smooth, ends a bit dry, rich, sweet, sour, umami, fruity, floral, sweets, earthy, herbaceous, grains, nutty, spices, mineral, L-XL
Effect: The tea becomes fuller, sweeter, enhances the notes of red fruit in the chocolate. Together they taste like complex chocolate milk. Subtle notes of forest and cacao.	**Effect:** The tea becomes brighter, fruitier and enhances the notes of red fruit in the chocolate. Together they taste like flan with raspberries and cinnamon.
CHOCOLATE	
Labooko, *Nicaragua, 50%* **Flavor profile:** smooth, rich, dairy, nutty, sweets, fruity; butter, cream, chocolate toffee, biscuit, raisins, M	
TEA	
Huo Shan Huang Ya, *Huo Shan County, Anhui Province, China* **Flavor profile:** smooth, bright, sweet, sour, umami, vegetal, fruity, earthy, grains, nutty, mineral, M	**Nilgiri,** *Blue Mountains, India* **Flavor profile:** smooth, bright, sweet, fruity, floral, earthy, mineral, spices, M
Effect: The tea becomes sweeter, nuttier, fruity and makes the chocolate brighter, fruitier. Earthy notes in the finish.	**Effect:** The tea becomes sweeter, fuller, rounder, the chocolate lighter, with the flavor of tea added to it, fruitier as well.

MILK CHOCOLATE	
CHOCOLATE	
François Pralus, *Mélissa, criollo, 45%* **Flavor profile:** smooth, rich, bright, fruity, sweets; red fruit, honey, caramel, vanilla, M	
TEA	
Si Ji Chun, *Nantou, Taiwan* **Flavor profile:** smooth, rich and bright, sweet, bitter, a bit sour, floral, herbaceous, vegetal, sweets, fruity, nuts, dairy, M	**English Breakfast,** *blend* **Flavor profile:** dry to astringent, rich, ends bright, robust, bold, sweet, bitter, umami, fruity, sweets, earthy, spices, L-XL
Effect: The tea becomes more floral, creamier. The chocolate becomes both brighter and creamier, the notes of honey are enhanced.	**Effect:** The tea becomes more softer, sweeter, fruitier, rounder. The chocolate acquires more depth, becomes brighter, lighter, its fruity notes enhanced.

WHITE CHOCOLATE	
CHOCOLATE	
Coppeneur, *Bourbon Vanilla, Dominican Republic, 40%* **Flavor profile:** smooth, rich, silky, sweet, fruity, dairy, sweets; pineapple, butter, cream, caramel, M	
TEA	
Si Ji Chun, *Nantou, Taiwan* **Flavor profile:** smooth, rich and bright, sweet, bitter, a bit sour, floral, herbaceous, vegetal, sweets, fruity, nuts, dairy, M	**Dian Hong,** *Yunnan, China* **Flavor profile:** smooth, rich, sweet, umami, earthy, sweets, fruity, nutty, spices, L
Effect: The tea becomes creamier, sweeter and adds floral notes to the chocolate, making it brighter, less fatty, fruitier.	**Effect:** The tea becomes fuller, creamier, sweeter, cuts the fattiness of the chocolate, makes it brighter, lighter, fruitier.
CHOCOLATE	
Krak, *Hibiscus vanilla, criollo, 40%* **Flavor profile:** smooth, rich and bright, sour, sweet, fruity, floral, sweets, spices; raspberry, lemon, hibiscus, honey, vanilla, L-XL	
TEA	
Earl Grey, *black tea, scented with Bergamot citrus, blend* **Flavor profile:** dry, rich and bright, sweet, umami, floral, fruity, earthy, M-L	**Genmaicha-iri Matcha,** *green tea mixed with Matcha and puffed rice; Ujitawara, Uji, Kyoto, Japan* **Flavor profile:** smooth, later on dry, rich, sweet, umami, nutty, grains, fruity, vegetal, herbaceous, maritime, earthy, M
Effect: The chocola becomes very creamy, silky, and at the same time fruitier, zesty. The tea becomes smoother, softer, its citrus notes enhanced. When taken at the same time the sum total is bright, very fruity and silky.	**Effect:** The chocolate becomes fruitier, nutty, creamier and bright at the same time, like full fat yoghurt with granola. The tea becomes very fruity and bright, with notes of mint, then peppery, warming, sweeter. When taken at the same time the flavor becomes salty, umami and very fruity.

CHAPTER 9

Cheese and tea

Cheese has been made for centuries, and probably since humans started keeping and domesticating animals. Nomads kept fresh milk in the abomasum or the fourth stomach of cattle and camels. Over time, the milk eventually curdled due to rennin found in the abomasum. The milk did not spoil, but its structure, chemical composition and flavor changed. The resulting lumpy, curdled mixture was a very rudimentary form of cheese. Since then, cheese making has developed into what it is today. Before the invention of refrigeration, milk spoiled quickly, and cheese making was used to avoid wasting milk and to increase the milk's shelf life. In the Middle Ages, nobles travelled with cheese in their luggage, spreading the fame of certain cheeses, much like the Chinese monks in 800 AD who took powdered green tea on their travels through Asia and introduced tea to new people.

THE SEVEN CHEESE FAMILIES
- fresh cheese, e.g., mozzarella
- soft (young) cheese, e.g., Gouda
- semi hard (semi mature) cheese, e.g., Cheddar
- hard (mature to very mature) cheese, e.g., Parmesan
- white mould, e.g., Camembert
- red cheese, e.g., Époisse
- blue mould, e.g., Gorgonzola

CHEESY FACTS
- Compared with milk from cows and goats, sheep's milk contains the most fat, milk protein and salt.
- In semi-hard and hard cheeses, the lactose (milk sugar) is converted into lactic acid.
- Rennet is a complex of digestive enzymes in the abdominal stomach of an animal. But vegetarian rennet is also available, made from the thistle species of cardoon, or figs, mushrooms or citric acid.
- Raw milk cheese has gained a bad reputation because of the listeria bacteria that is. occasionally found in it. That is indeed possible, but the risk is just as big (or just as small) with pasteurized cheese, with only one annual death of listeria per three million inhabitants. The risk of catching listeria is almost zero in semi-hard and hard cheeses and slightly higher in soft cheeses.
- The characteristic brick color of red cheese, e.g., Munster, Époisse, Saint-Nectaire, reblochon and taleggio and its unmistakable scent reminiscent of old sneakers, are caused by bacteria such as Brevibacterium, Linens and Coryne. This type of cheese cannot be made without the presence of these bacteria. The Linens bacteria are related to the bacteria that love the microflora of our feet, hence the similar smell that red cheeses have.
- You should always keep cheese in parchment paper, never in plastic wrap, as the plastic suffocates cheese, and causes it to become damp, giving way to bacteria and fungi. Wrap your cheese in parchment paper and keep it in a cool place, preferably a cellar. If you do not have a cellar, then place it on the top shelf of the fridge, which tends to be the warmest spot. The ideal storage temperature differs per cheese, but is between 6 and 14°C (42 and 57°F). Soft, pasteurized cheeses are best at 6°C (42°F) and hard cheeses are best at 14°C (57°F).
- Preferably eat your cheese within a week of purchase. Once a wheel of cheese has been cut, its flavor and quality deteriorate considerably, even if you put the cheese in a cellar or on the top shelf of the fridge.
- Never store blue cheese in aluminium foil: the cheese dissolves the foil.

THE RIND: EDIBLE OR NOT?

White mould?	✔ Yes
Red cheese?	✔ Yes
Ash layer?	✔ Yes
Breadcrumbed cheese?	✔ Yes
Alcohol infused rind?	✔ Yes (only if younger than two months)
Herbs?	✔ Yes (only if younger than two months)
Natural rind?	✔ Yes (only if younger than two months)
Has the cheese ripened for two months or more?	✘ No
Blue cheese?	✘ No
Cheese linen?	✘ No
Paprika?	✘ No
Paraffin?	✘ No
Fat?	✘ No

EFFECT OF TEA ON CHEESE AND VICE VERSA

Tea and cheese can have a strong effect on each other. Both in a positive and negative sense. Many people would not dream of combining cheese with tea, yet when they finally do, they are very often pleasantly surprised by the result.
The heat of the tea melts the cheese in the mouth, causing it to release more aromas than when the cheese is just chewed and swallowed. Additionally, the compounds in the tea connect with the compounds in the cheese, sometimes resulting in a completely new or enhanced flavor or a different texture.

Tea is often served with cheese fondue. This works well because cold drinks such as wine, beer or water have a shock effect on melted cheese: the cheese shrinks due to the cold, causing it to become sticky and rubber-like and creating a big lump of solid cheese in the stomach. That is why it is not a good idea to eat ice cream as a dessert after a cheese fondue, as it may give the feeling that you have just swallowed a tennis ball.
By drinking hot tea with a fondue, the cheese stays soft, the aromas can be released more easily, you taste more, the texture is more pleasant, softer, velvety and it is not as heavy on the stomach.

Even with non-melted cheese, tea often works better than wine, for the very same reasons. Moreover, tea has a much more subtle flavor than wine, port or beer, which often makes the cheese stand out better.

CHEESE PLATTER WITH TEA

Build your platter from mild to medium to strong cheese. Always start the tasting with the mildest or freshest one and end with the strongest or intense cheese.
Use a maximum of 5 cheeses per platter and cut off small serving; otherwise, your palate and taste buds will get overwhelmed. The same applies to the teas: use small glasses and start with the lightest tea.
White tea is a good mouth cleanser, it neutralizes the flavors in your mouth, making it feel clean and fresh.
If serving several teas in one session is too much for you, just stick to one tea that is mild, mellow, not too outspoken, and smooth. For example, a soft, sweet green tea like Mao Feng, or a roasted green tea like Hōjicha. If black tea is more you thing, then choose a mellow, sweet and smooth black tea like Golden Yunnan or Honey Black.
If you prefer a white tea, then choose a stronger white, for example a Yue Guang Bai. I usually keep things simple and serve only one type of cheese after dinner, with just one matching tea.

An example cheese platter with matching teas

1. Bouygette, a slightly acidic, raw milk goat cheese from the South of France, preferably served with a cracker or some bread. Goes well with creamy, floral tea, like Jin Xuan #12 light oolong from Taiwan, but also with Jangwon, a complex green tea from Korea, with distinct marine and sweet vegetable notes.

2. Délice de Bourgogne, a triple-cream cheese, buttery, creamy, soft, with a peppery finish. The cheese pairs well with Yue Guang Bai from Yunnan, China. This tea is more outspoken than most white teas, bolder, quite earthy, with notes of hay, caramel, tobacco, vanilla, apricot and wood. The cheese makes the tea brighter, crisp, while the cheese itself becomes even creamier and fuller when combined with the tea. With the Jin Xuan #12 light oolong, both cheese and tea become fuller, sweeter, creamier and more intense in flavor.

3. Tête de Moine, a slightly sharp, raw cow's milk cheese from the Swiss Jura. This cheese should be cut into paper-thin curls with the girolle, a special device made for this cheese. Jangwon green tea and Jin Xuan #12 light oolong take off the cheese's sharpness, making the cheese rounder, fuller, and more voluptuous.

4. Époisse, a creamy red cheese from Burgundy, made with cow's milk that can be either raw or pasteurized, depending on the farmer who makes it. This full, velvety, runny, round, earthy cheese with its spicy finish should be eaten very ripe, with a spoon. Rock oolong goes well with it, e.g., Da Hong Pao, from the Wuyi Mountains in Fuijan, China. The mineral and complex character of this tea, with notes of dried stone fruit, honey and roasted grains, counterbalances this spicy and slightly mineral robust cheese.

5. Bleu des Basques, a sheep's milk blue cheese from the French Basque Country. It has sharp and spicy edges, and nutty notes. This cheese becomes gentler, more pleasant and sweeter when combined with rock oolong. My suggestion for a platter with this combination of cheeses: start with the Jin Xuan #12 light oolong for the first three cheeses and end with the Da Hong Pao rock oolong. This way, you will not make things too complicated. Serving different teas with five cheeses may be very interesting but quite demanding for your guests, who have already had dinner. Another, even easier option is to serve just one or two cheeses with only one type of tea.

HOW TO SERVE TEA WITH CHEESE

- Make sure everything for the tea is ready in advance, and that everything is weighed and covered. Tip: use my stress free method for easy steeping: cold brew tea extract topped with boiling water, see page 36 - 37.
- Remove the cheese from the fridge at least 30 minutes in advance for hard cheese, and around 20 minutes for soft cheese. This way, the cheese reaches the best temperature for consumption, leading to more flavor. The colder something is, the more difficult it is to taste it well. The ideal serving temperature for cheese is 15 - 17°C (59 - 62°F).
- Prepare and pour your tea 5 minutes before serving your cheese. Tea has more flavor when it has cooled down to about 55 - 60°C (131 -140°F).
- Do not serve grapes with cheese, as the grape skins ferment in the stomach. Raisins, however, are fine.
- If you insist on garnish with your cheese, then look at the classic combinations: Stilton with walnuts and celery, Manchego with quince jelly, Castelmagno with pear and black pepper, to name just a few.
- Do not forget the presentation: beautiful tea deserves to be served in beautiful recipients. Wine glasses are ideal.

THE BEST WAY TO CUT CHEESE

- Cut round-, conical-, pyramid-, or square-shaped cheese into wedges. This way, the rind is equally divided.
- Cut cylindrical cheese first into ½ inch slices, then cut each slice into wedges
- Cut cheese that has a wedge shape. of its own, like brie into little triangles and also into slices.
- Cut small goat cheese first in two, then slice it very thinly.
- Cut a slice of blue cheese lengthwise and diagonally.

EXAMPLES OF CHEESE AND TEA COMBINATIONS

On the following pages, you will find an overview of cheeses and teas which I think they go well together. This list is is simply a guide to help you with your tea and cheese pairings.Tastes differ and you may not agree at all with my recommended combinations. By all means, experiment and discover your own favorite pairings. That is the fun part!

Tasting notes tea and cheese

FRESH CHEESE
CHEESE
Mozzarella di bufala, *Italy, Italian buffalo's milk* **Flavor profile:** neutral, neutral, soft, slightly sweet, slightly salt, slightly earthy, dairy, animal, vegetal; cream, cow, grass, XS-S

TEA	
Yue Guang Bai, *Yunnan, China* **Flavor profile:** smooth, rich and bright, sweet, earthy, fruity, spices, floral, L	**Dong Fang Mei Ren,** *oolong, Hsinchu County, Taiwan* **Flavor profile:** smooth, ends a bit dry, rich, sweet, floral, fruity, earthy, mineral, spices, M
Effect: The cheese acquires more umami, more flavor, becomes floral. The tea becomes fuller, creamy, its earthy notes are stronger.	**Effect:** The cheese acquires nutty notes, more depth and flavor. The tea becomes sweeter, creamy, its spices notes enhanced.

WHITE SOFT CHEESE
CHEESE
Délice de Bourgogne, *France, cow's milk* **Flavor profile:** smooth, rich, bright finish, very creamy, sweet, fruity, dairy, animal, spices; citrus, cream, pepper, M

TEA	
Long Jing, West Lake, *Hangzhou City, Zhejiang province, China* **Flavor profile:** smooth, rich, later a bit bright, round, creamy, sweet, umami, vegetal, fruity, grains, nutty, maritime, M	**Huang Da Cha,** *Jinzhai County, Anhui Province, China* **Flavor profile:** smooth, ends dry, rich, sweet, umami, vegetal, earthy, fruity, grains, nutty, sweets, M
Effect: The cheese becomes softer, less acidic, acquires more depth and flavor, with vegetal notes. The tea becomes sweeter, softer, its vegetal notes enhanced.	**Effect:** The cheese becomes even creamier, very full and buttery, acquires more umami and depth. The tea becomes fuller, creamy, sweeter and acquires more umami as well.
Jin Xuan #12, *Alishan, Taiwan* **Flavor profile:** smooth, silky, rich, sweet, slightly bitter, dairy, floral, fruity, vegetal, herbaceous, M	**Keemun,** *black tea, Qimen County, China* **Flavor profile:** smooth, ends a bit dry, rich, sweet, umami, fruity, floral, grains, animal, sweets, earthy, L
Effect: The cheese and tea become both sweeter, creamier and all flavors are enhanced.	**Effect:** The cheese becomes sweeter, creamier, fuller and acquires smoky notes with a pleasant earthy bitter aftertaste. The tea becomes full, creamy and soft, like black tea with cream.

WHITE SOFT CHEESE

CHEESE

Camembert a.o.p., *France, raw cow's milk*
Flavor profile: smooth, rich, umami, salt, sweet, animal, dairy, earthy, spices; stable, cream, mushrooms, pepper, XL

TEA

Bi Luo Chun, *Dong Shan, Jiangsu Province, China* **Flavor profile:** smooth, rich, later dry and bright, sweet, slightly bitter, umami, vegetal, fruity, grains nutty, spices, mineral, M	**Bai Mudan,** *Fuding City, Fujian Province, China* **Flavor profile:** smooth, mellow, rich, later bright, subtle, sweet, floral, nuts, fruity, sweets, vegetal, grains, M
Effect: Both cheese and tea acquire more umami and depth, the cheese becomes smoother, while the tea becomes sweeter.	**Effect:** The cheese becomes nutty, creamier, sweeter, while the tea acquires more zest and umami.
Da Hong Pao, *dark rock oolong, Wuyi Shan, Fujian, China* **Flavor profile:** smooth, ends a bit dry, rich, sweet, sour, umami, fruity, floral, sweets, earthy, herbaceous, grains, nutty, spices, mineral, L-XL	**Goishicha,** *Otoyo, town, Kochi prefecture, Japan* **Flavor profile:** dry to neutral, rich and bright, sour, umami, sweet, dairy, animal, earthy, fruity, vegetal, herbaceous, M-L
Effect: The cheese becomes lighter, brighter, fruity, while the tea becomes full, creamy, sweet, with a clean palate afterwards.	**Effect:** The cheese becomes saltier, earthier, acquires more umami, while the tea becomes softer, less acidic, balanced. The aftertaste is bright, dry, fruity.

YELLOW SOFT CHEESE

CHEESE

Morbier, *France, cow's milk*
Flavor profile: smooth, rich, umami, salt, sweet, earthy, nutty, animal, dairy; mushrooms, hay, walnut, stable, cream, M

TEA

Huo Shan Huang Ya, *Huo Shan County, Anhui Province, China* **Flavor profile:** smooth, bright, sweet, sour, umami, vegetal, fruity, earthy, grains, nutty, mineral, M	**Dong Ding,** *Mei Shan, Nantou, Taiwan* **Flavor profile:** smooth and dry, rich and bright, sweet, slightly bitter, nutty, mineral, floral, sweets, vegetal, herbaceous, fruity, dairy, M-L
Effect: The cheese acquires more flavor, becomes earthier, animal notes are stronger, more aromatic. The tea becomes earthier, warmer, fuller, sweeter, acquires animal notes.	**Effect:** The cheese acquires more flavor, more umami, notes of beef stock. The aftertaste is floral. The tea becomes brighter, herbaceous and incorporates the flavor of the cheese. Clean palate.
Ruby #18, *black tea, Sun Moon Lake, Nantou County, Taiwan* **Flavor profile:** smooth, rich, sweet, earthy, herbaceous, fruity, sweets, spices, M	**Sheng (raw) Pu Erh,** *Lincang, Yunnan Province, China* **Flavor profile:** aged: neutral to smooth, rich and bright, sweet, sour, bitter, umami, earthy, vegetal, animal, herbaceous, spices, floral, fruity, M-L
Effect: The cheese becomes nuttier, stronger. The tea acquires more umami and becomes brighter. The aftertaste is earthy and sweet, with notes of ripe stone fruit.	**Effect:** The cheese becomes earthier, creamy and acidic, like sour cream. Its notes of hay are enhanced. The tea becomes softer, sweeter, brighter and nutty.

SEMI-HARD CHEESE	
CHEESE	
Emmenthaler, *France, raw cow's milk* **Flavor profile:** neutral, neutral, sweet, umami, salt, earthy, nutty, herbaceous; mushrooms, walnut, hay, M	
TEA	
Sheng (raw) Pu Erh, *Lincang, Yunnan Province, China* **Flavor profile:** aged: neutral to smooth, rich and bright, sweet, sour, bitter, umami, earthy, vegetal, animal, herbaceous, spices, floral, fruity, M-L	**Huo Shan Huang Ya,** *Huo Shan County, Anhui Province, China* **Flavor profile:** smooth, bright, sweet, sour, umami, vegetal, fruity, earthy, grains, nutty, mineral, M
Effect: The cheese becomes fruity, bright, earthier, while the tea becomes sweeter and fruitier.	**Effect:** The cheese acquires more umami and more flavor, and melts together with the tea, which becomes brighter and more vegetal. Bright aftertaste with both tea and cheese.
CHEESE	
Tête de Moine, *France, raw cow's milk* **Flavor profile:** dry, rich, umami, salt, sweet, animal, herbaceous, fruity, spices; rosemary, stable, fermented apple, pepper, M-L	
TEA	
Yue Guang Bai, *Yunnan, China* **Flavor profile:** smooth, rich and bright, sweet, earthy, fruity, spices, floral, L	**Hōjicha,** *roasted green tea, Tsukigase, Nara prefecture, Japan* **Flavor profile:** smooth, later on dry, rich, sweet, umami, nutty, grains, fruity, vegetal, herbaceous, maritime, earthy, M
Effect: The cheese becomes brighter, nuttier, sweeter, smooth, while the tea acquires more umami and becomes almost salty.	**Effect:** The cheese becomes smooth, sweeter, acquires nutty notes, while the tea becomes creamy, full, creamy, with more umami.

GOAT'S CHEESE	
CHEESE	
Bouygette, *France, soft, raw goat's milk* **Flavor profile:** dry and a bit smooth, bright and rich, umami, sour, salt, fruity, herbaceous, animal; lemon, rosemary, stable, M-L	
TEA	
Huo Shan Huang Ya, *Huo Shan County, Anhui Province, China* **Flavor profile:** smooth, bright, sweet, sour, umami, vegetal, fruity, earthy, grains, nutty, mineral, M	**Sencha,** *Kochi, Shikoku prefecture, Japan* **Flavor profile:** smooth to dry, rich and bright, sweet, bitter, umami, vegetal, herbaceous, maritime, fruity, M
Effect: The quite acidic cheese becomes creamy and brighter, like yoghurt. The goat aroma is enhanced. The tea becomes earthier, floral, more vegetal, with notes of courgette, sautéed in butter.	**Effect:** The quite acidic cheese becomes smooth and creamy, its goat aroma enhanced. The tea becomes brighter, floral, more vegetal, acquires more umami.

RED CHEESE
CHEESE
Époisse, *France, cow's milk* **Flavor profile:** smooth, rich, umami, salt, sweet, earthy, animal, vegetal, spices, nutty; mushrooms, stable, raw onion, pepper, walnut, XL

TEA	
Long Jing, *West Lake, Hangzhou City, Zhejiang province, China* **Flavor profile:** smooth, rich, later a bit bright, round, creamy, sweet, umami, vegetal, fruity, grains, nutty, maritime, M	**Dong Fang Mei Ren,** *oolong, Hsinchu County, Taiwan* **Flavor profile:** smooth, ends a bit dry, rich, sweet, floral, fruity, earthy, mineral, spices, M
Effect: The cheese acquires more umami and depth, becomes earthier, stronger, while the tea becomes sweeter and acquires more umami as well.	**Effect:** The cheese acquires more umami, becomes very intense in flavor, while the tea becomes sweeter, fuller, softer and creamy.

CHEESE
Li p'tit Rossê, *Belgium, raw cow's milk* **Flavor profile:** smooth, rich, umami, salt, earthy, vegetal, animal; mushrooms, raw onion, M-L

TEA	
Tie Guan Yin *heavy roast, Longten, Taiwan* **Flavor profile:** smooth, rich, a bit bright, sweet, bitter, fruity, sweets, earthy, grains, nutty, spices, L	**Bai Mudan,** *Fuding City, Fujian Province, China* **Flavor profile:** smooth, mellow, rich, later bright, subtle, sweet, floral, nuts, fruity, sweets, vegetal, grains, M
Effect: The cheese becomes sweeter, nutty and floral. The tea becomes bright at first, floral later on. All flavors blend in the aftertaste, the cheese creamy and nutty, the tea floral.	**Effect:** Both cheese and tea become creamy, sweet and nutty.

BLUE CHEESE
CHEESE
Gorgonzola dolce, *Italy, cow's milk* **Flavor profile:** smooth, rich and bright, sweet, salt, umami, earthy, dairy, spices; cave, mushrooms, cream, pepper, L

TEA	
Dian Hong, *Yunnan, China* **Flavor profile:** smooth, rich, sweet, umami, earthy, sweets, fruity, nutty, spices, L	**Shu Pu-Erh,** *post-fermented cooked tea, China* **Flavor profile:** smooth, round, rich, sweet, umami, earthy, animal, sweets, vegetal, L-XL
Effect: The cheese becomes lighter, brighter, fruity, the tea brighter, earthier, with more umami. Both fruity cheese and earthy tea in the aftertaste.	**Effect:** The cheese becomes sweeter and softer, the tea earthier, nutty and creamy, with more depth.

CHAPTER 10

Tea mixology

When tea is used as a basis for cocktails, the other ingredients will become more intense in taste and the cocktail as a whole will have a fuller texture. I tested this by preparing two almost identical cocktails, with just one difference: I added a bit of tea to one of them. The one made without tea turned out to be a lot thinner and lighter in taste, and more watery. The one made with tea was fuller, warmer and deeper and more intense in flavor. In order to get that effect, you do not have to actually taste the tea in the cocktail, the flavor enhancing effect is noticeable even without tasting the tea. This also works well with mocktails (alcohol-free cocktails).

THE QUALITY OF TEA FOR COCKTAILS

To make iced tea and cocktails, you do not necessarily need high-quality tea. It depends on how many ingredients you will use and whether the emphasis of the drink will be on the tea or on the overall taste. I only use quality teas for sparkling tea cocktails when I want to place an emphasis on the flavor of the tea and a minor but supporting role for any fruit I add. You would not want to blow away the delicate and complex flavors of the tea with too many other components, like sticky syrups and acidic fruit. So, if you like to use high-quality tea, then your base could be, for example, a light oolong like Ali Shan, or Si Ji Chun (Four Seasons), or a lightly roasted Tieguanyin. For an elegant mocktail, add a slice of ripe peach, the top of a lightly crushed tarragon twig and lightly sparkling water. If you want to turn it into a cocktail, add a measure of vodka and a drop of triple sec. If you'd rather make more exuberant cocktails with lots of fruit, syrups, juices, spices or fresh herbs, then simply use tea bags for those, as in that case you'll only need the tea's deepening and flavor enhancing qualities.

You could even use flavored tea as a base for that kind of cocktail.

LESS IS MORE

Search for the right balance. Strong seasonings such as rosemary, pepper, basil, lemon or star anise can be rather dominant, therefore be very cautious with such strong flavored components. You can always add some more of them, but once these have been added, there is no turning back. Excessive use of flavors and textures will flatten rather than enrich a drink, because they cause too much to happen in your mouth for your brain to cope with.
A minimum of three ingredients applies to a cocktail. There is no official maximum, but I recommend using no more than five to seven ingredients, including ice and tea.

BAR TOOLS

When you make a cocktail, you want to do it right. And it really is great fun to pretend you are a real bartender. Good tools are always half the battle, and this is also true when making cocktails. A shaker is indispensable, as is a muddler, a jigger, an ice bucket, ice tongs, a mixing spoon and strainer, a cutting board, a sharp knife, containers to hold pre-cut fruit and other ingredients, decoration material and stirrers and, as an optional extra: some fancy cutting tools for decorating.
On pages 214 - 217 you will find some recipes for cocktails and iced tea for inspiration.

ICED TEA SHOCK BREW STYLE

The fastest way to make a classic iced tea is to pour freshly steeped hot tea over ice cubes. The downside to this is that the tea will lose some of its flavor, but that is ok if you are going to mix in some other ingredients, for example, syrup, fruits and herbs. What is important to know is that you should split the amount of water you normally use for your tea in two: liquid and solid water, namely boiling water and ice cubes. For example: do you normally make 1 liter (34 fl. oz) hot tea with five tea bags? For iced tea use half a liter of hot water. Allow it to steep for the usual amount of time, then remove the five tea bags and pour the tea over 500 g (17 oz) ice cubes. This amounts to a liter (34 fl. oz) of water. So you have a total of one liter, of which half a liter is in liquid and half a liter is in solid form.

Classic iced tea recipe
for 1 liter (34 fl.oz) iced tea:
5 bags or 10 g (3.4 oz) Earl Grey tea
500 ml (17 fl.oz) filtered water at 90°C (194°F)
500 g (17 oz) ice cubes
2 sprigs lightly crushed mint
4 slices lemon
10 slices cucumber

Add the tea bags (or leaf tea) to a preheated pot and pour the hot water over the bags. Let it steep for 3 minutes. Remove the bags or strain the tea. Place $1/3$ of the ice cubes into a large glass jug. Place half of the lemon, cucumber and mint on top. Add another third of the ice cubes and place the other half of the lemon, cucumber and mint on top. Add the rest of the ice cubes and pour the hot tea over them. Wait until all the ice cubes have melted. Fill a tall glass with ice cubes and pour in the iced tea. Garnish with a sprig of mint. Do you want it sweetened? Try a dash of flavored syrup, for example cucumber, watermelon, or spicy mango flavor.

COLD BREW
A more recent version of iced tea is called cold brew, which is tea steeped in cold water. The colder the water, the more time the tea leaves need to release their aromas and flavors. This takes at least four to six hours. The advantage of making it like this is that the flavor becomes more complex than with hot brew and the tea does not become bitter. If you add some fruit, such as dried apricot, or fresh, ripe peach

or raspberries, then a very subtle, sweet and fruity layer is added to the tea during the cold steeping, without it becoming dominant. Another version is called sun brew, which has been around for ages in very hot places like Texas. The heat of the sun does the trick. This way of steeping needs less time, but also an outdoor temperature of at least 42°C (107°F).

THE COLD DRIP METHOD

A nice eye-catcher is a cold drip system. Originally designed for coffee, but also very useful for tea. This method produces very intense and smooth tea that is easy to make. Put 500 g (17.63 oz) ice cubes in the top container and 10 - 12 g (0.35 to 0.42 oz) tea leaves in the strainer. Set the speed to 45 drops per minute and wait about five or six hours. It is a very zen method, lovely to watch. Very slowly, literally drop by drop, the ice water drips through the tea, absorbs its flavors and drips down into the closed container at the bottom. You can then drink this tea pure, or on the rocks, with fruit, with herbs or mixed with sparkling water.

SPARKLING TEA

Mix a strong cold brew tea with sparkling water for a sparkling, refreshing drink. Start by making a cold brew tea extract according the fabulously fast and easy Mariëlla method (Page 34 for infographic). Simply place your tea leaves into the sterilized jar and then fill the jar with cold, filtered water up to the rim. Close the jar firmly and store it in the fridge for at least four hours. When the tea is ready, strain some of the extract over a high glass, and add cold sparkling water, about 1 part of tea extract to 3 - 4 parts of water. Hario ice tea bottles are very handy for this method.

Tea extract recipe
For 250 ml (8.5 fl. oz) tea extract:

10 g (0.35 oz) tea leaves
250 ml (8.5 fl. oz) cold, filtered water
optional:
1 ripe peach in pieces or other ripe fruit
of your choice
herbs, like mint, or basil, or tarragon.

Place all ingredients in a sterilized glass container, such as a jam jar. Close the jar firmly and store in the fridge for at least six hours or overnight. Strain into another sterilized jar, label it with the date and the type of tea. Add 3 or 4 parts of (sparkling) water to 1 part of extract and ice cubes to your liking.

Tip
- Green tea goes well with cucumber, lemon, (water) melon, mint
- Chinese black tea matches with strawberry, mango or peach
- White tea and green oolong can be used with almost all fruits, except banana. Never use bananas in iced tea
- Pu-Erh and dark oolong pair well with ripe stone fruits such as mango, peach or apricot

Recipes for long drinks, cocktails and mocktails

1 Inge's Infusion
Serves 6

Infusion
14 g (0.49 oz) dried Hibiscus leaves
1 liter (34 fl. oz) filtered water

10 strawberries, halved
6 small whole strawberries
6 sprigs of mint
ice cubes
optional: red currant berries
6 tall glasses

Make the infusion
Bring the water to a boil, then pour it over the Hibiscus leaves and 5 of the halved strawberries, cover and allow it to infuse for at least 5 minutes.
Strain, add the other 5 halved strawberries, then cover and let cool at room temperature.

Make the drink
Scoop some ice cubes into 6 glasses. Add one small strawberry and a slightly bruised sprig of mint to each glass. Fill the glasses up with the infusion and garnish with redcurrant berries.

2 Summer in the City
Serves 4

Tea extract
10 g (0.35 oz) Rock oolong, e.g., Da Hong Pao
500 ml (17 fl. oz) filtered water
Fresh fruit of your choice, e.g., peach, mango
1 cucumber, peeled
a sprig of verbena

a dash of ginger syrup
ice cubes
sparkling water
optional with alcohol: 15 ml (0.5 fl. oz) of Gin p.p
4 tall glasses

Make the tea extract
Wash and cut the pieces of fruit and transfer them to a sterilized jar or bottle with a wide neck. Cut the cucumber in half lengthwise. With a peeler, cut 4 very thin slices off the cucumber. Slightly bruise the sprig of verbena. Add the verbena and cucumber slices to the fruit, together with the tea leaves and the cold, filtered water. Close the bottle tightly and place in the fridge for at least 6 hours.
Strain and transfer into a sterilized bottle. Keep in the fridge until use.

Make the drink
Scoop ice cubes into a tall glass. Add a dash of ginger syrup. Add 100 ml (3.4 fl. oz) of the tea extract and stir. Fill the glass up with sparkling water. Repeat with the other glasses.
For a cocktail: add the Gin before you add the sparkling water and stir well.
Garnish to your liking with cucumber spirals, sprigs of mint, fresh verbena leaves or a slice of fruit.

3 Rock'n Roolong
Serves 2

Tea extract
10 g (0.35 oz) Rock oolong, e.g., Da Hong Pao
250 ml (8.5 fl. oz) filtered water

50 ml (1.7 fl. oz) white grape juice
dash apricot juice
dash ginger syrup
pinch clove
pinch salt
some drops Angostura bitters
4 ice cubes
optional with alcohol: 20 ml (0.65 fl. oz)
Vodka p.p and a dash of Triple Sec

2 chilled Gin glasses

Make the tea extract
Place oolong and water in a sterilized jar, close tightly and refrigerate for at least 6 hours. Strain over another sterilized jar or bottle, close tightly, keep refrigerated until use.

Make the cocktail
Fill a Boston shaker with ice cubes.
Add 50 ml (1.6 fl. oz) tea extract and 180 ml (6.5 fl. oz) of cold water.
Add grape juice, apricot juice, ginger syrup, clove, salt and Angostura bitters. Taste and adjust to liking.
For a cocktail: add the Vodka and Triple Sec. Shake.
Double-strain into the two chilled Gin glasses. Decorate with a slice of peach, some grapes or however you prefer.

4 Zesty Rosella
Serves 2

Infusion
3 g (0.1 oz) dried Hibiscus leaves
200 ml (7 fl. oz) filtered water of 100°C (212°F)
250 ml (8.8 fl. oz) cranberry juice
250 ml (8.8 fl. oz) Crodino sparkling herbal drink
10 ml (0.35 fl. oz) Macadamia syrup (Monin)
pinch chili pepper
pinch salt
strip orange peel
4 ice cubes
optional with alcohol: add 40 ml (1.4 fl.oz) Vodka and a dash of Triple Sec

2 tall glasses

Make the infusion
Bring the water to a boil, then pour it over the Hibiscus leaves, cover and allow it to infuse for at least 5 minutes. Strain and let cool.

Make the drinks
Scoop the ice cubes into the shaker.
Add the syrup, 10 ml (0.3 fl. oz) of the infusion, the cranberry juice, the pepper and salt.
For a cocktail: add the Vodka and Triple Sec. Shake.
Double-strain over two long drink glasses.
Add the Crodino sparkling drink and stir carefully with the cocktail spoon.
Twist and squeeze the orange peel over the drinks.
Garnish with a ribbon of orange peel, or half a slice of orange, in each glass.

5 Holy Smoky Mary

Serves 2

Tea extract
5 g (0.17 oz) Lapsang Souchong (smoked tea)
200 ml (6.7 fl. oz) filtered water

200 ml (6.7 fl. oz) tomato-vegetable juice
lime juice
lime wedge
a few drops of Tabasco
2 stalks of celery
ice cubes
optional with alcohol: add 20 ml (0.65 fl. oz) Vodka p.p

2 tall glasses

Make the tea extract
Heat the water to 90°C (194°F) and pour over the tea leaves. Cover and steep for 2 minutes. Strain and let cool completely.

Make the drink
Scoop 4 ice cubes into each long drink glass and pour 10 ml (0.3 fl. oz) of the tea extract into each glass.
Add 10 ml (0.3 fl. oz) of tomato-vegetable juice per glass, a squeeze of lime juice, some salt, some drops of Tabasco, to taste.
For a cocktail: also add the Vodka.
Add more salt, pepper or lime juice if needed.
Stir well with a stalk of celery in each glass.
Decorate with mini tomatoes, cucumber ribbons or slices and a wedge of lime.

6 Green Teatini

Serves 2

Tea extract
10 g (0.35 oz) green tea
250 ml (8.5 fl. oz) filtered water

40 ml (1.3 fl. oz) Gin
10 ml (0.3 fl. oz) lemon juice
2 olives
ice cubes
2 chilled Martini glasses

Make the tea extract
Place tea and water in a sterilized jar, close tightly and refrigerate for at least 6 hours. Strain over another sterilized jar or bottle, close tightly, keep refrigerated until use.

Make the cocktails
Pour 50 ml (1.7 fl. oz) of tea extract and 100 ml (3.4 fl. oz) of cold water and all other ingredients except the olive into a cocktail shaker filled with ice cubes.
Place one olive in each glass.
Shake the cocktail shaker well and divide over the two chilled Martini glasses.

7 Mojito Matcha Mocktail

Serves 2

1 lime, cut in wedges
12 mint leaves
2 tbs cane sugar
10 g (0.35 oz) Matcha
200 ml (6.7 fl. oz) filtered water
crushed ice
optional with alcohol: 30 ml of white Rum p.p

2 tumblers

Make the tea
Bring the water to 70°C (158°F).
Sieve the Matcha over a bowl.
Add a splash of the hot water and stir well until smooth. Add the remaining water while whisking thoroughly with a mini whisk or a traditional Matcha whisk (chasen). Add some crushed ice to cool down the tea.

Make the mocktails
In two tumblers, mix wedges of lime, sugar and mint. Crush with a muddler and stir.
Divide the cooled tea over the glasses, stir well, add more crushed ice and 100 ml (0.3 fl. oz) of cold soda water per glass.
Garnish with mint and a wedge of lime.
For a cocktail: add the Rum after muddling, but before adding the tea.

Bombay Bubble
Serves 2

Tea extract
2 tea bags of 2 g each with black tea
(or 4 g (0.14 oz) loose leaf tea
pinch cinnamon
pinch ground ginger
pinch nutmeg
pinch cardamom
pinch salt
250 ml (8.45 fl. oz) filtered water
at 100°C (212°F)

a dash of ginger syrup
Angostura Bitters
4 ice cubes
300 ml (10 fl. oz) cold sparkling water
2 orange peel ribbons
2 sprigs of mint
optional with alcohol: 40 ml (1.3 fl. oz)

2 chilled tumblers

Make the tea extract
Place the tea in a teapot or large mug.
Add the spices and the boiling water,
steep for 3 minutes.
Strain, cover and allow to cool completely.

Make the mocktails
Put ice cubes, ginger syrup, a few drops
Angostura Bitters and the tea extract into
a shaker.
For a cocktail: Add the Gin as well.
Shake and pour through a double strainer
into the chilled tumblers.
Fill up with ice cubes and sparkling water.
Garnish with citrus and mint.

CHAPTER 11

Tea in cafes and restaurants

How do you do your preparations for tea in your restaurant or cafe?
First of all, make sure your routing is in order: in one flowing movement go from picking up the tea ware, to adding tea and water, and then make your way to the customer with it.
The tea ware should be clean and easy to handle, the water should be soft, filtered, with a neutral pH value and preferably already at the correct temperature.
Tea must be stored in airtight tins, or caddies, that are easily accessible, labelled with the name and amount of tea per serving clearly marked on the caddy.

THE FOOLPROOF COLD BREW METHOD

This is the easiest and fastest preparation for tea and it is my favorite for cafes and restaurants. You simply use a cold brew tea extract, topped up with boiling water. It also works great at home for busy mornings during the week. I always have a few jars ready in my fridge, just in case.
I have tried this system many times, with only a few tables to a lot of tables to serving several kinds of tea all at once to a group of 100 guests and it worked perfectly. Planning one day ahead is needed for this version of mise en place. When reading how it works, it sounds way more complicated than it actually is. Just like learning how to ride a bicycle. It is actually a piece of cake. An infographic about this method is to be found on page 36 - 37.

THIS IS WHAT YOU DO:

Decide how many servings you might need the following day/evening. Have in mind the very maximum possibility, as the amount you will prepare will keep at least 10, but after opening 3 days.
Suppose you need 10 servings of tea A and 10 servings of tea B.
You want to serve the tea in wine glasses.
Say, you need 160 ml (5.4 fl. oz) tea per glass.
Therefore, the total amount of tea you will need is: 10 servings x 160 ml = 1600 ml (1.6 l, or 54 fl. oz) of tea for each kind of tea.
The ratio is 1 part tea extract to 3 parts of boiling water.
One glass of 160 ml (5.4 fl. oz) therefore needs 40 ml (1.35 fl. oz) tea extract and 120 ml (4 fl. oz) hot water.
This means you will need 400 ml (13.5 fl. oz) of tea extract for 10 servings.

If you want to make 1 liter (34 fl. oz) tea extract you will need 40 gram (1.35 oz) loose leaf tea leaf to 1 liter (34 fl. oz) soft, cold water. The tea leaf will absorb some of that water, so you will not end up with 1 liter exactly. It depends on the size of the leaf as to how much water will be absorbed by it. A bit of gentle squeezing of the tea leaves is allowed though.

For 1 glass with a content of 160 ml (5.4 fl. oz) you need 40 ml (1.35 fl. oz) extract.
This means, that with 1 liter of extract you will make approx. 22 - 23 glasses of tea, or about 3.5 to 3.7 liter of tea, while using 40 g (1.35 oz) of tea. This is about the same ratio of tea you would use when making hot tea the usual way.
A good thing about this extract is that the tea will not turn bitter due to the cold steep method, not even when cooling off. There is never a chance of over- or under-steeping or the need for a thermometer.
It works fast and foolproof.
Check if the ratio works well for your particular tea by simply preparing yourself a cup.
If you think the tea is too strong: adjust the ratio of water and write that down. Too weak? Add more tea extract and write it down.

If a guest thinks the tea is too strong or too weak, you just add extract or hot water.
All you need, is some prep time in the morning, or the night before. And make sure you add a sticker onto the jar or bottle, stating date and type of tea.

Let us say, for example, that you want to serve Sencha and Earl Grey black tea. Write this on two removable labels:

Info tea: Sencha, Japan
ratio per glass:
40 ml (1.35 fl. oz) tea extract
120 ml (4 fl. oz) hot water
Date:

Info tea: Earl Grey, blend, India, Sri Lanka
ratio per glass:
40 ml (1.35 fl. oz) tea extract
120 ml (4 fl. oz) hot water
Date:

ADVANTAGES:
- You will use the right amount of tea, which is good for both customer and profit.
- You can still adjust the flavor if the customer thinks the tea is too strong or too weak.
- Because you made it cold brew style, the tea will not become bitter when cooled off at the table. It actually still tastes good, even when cooled off completely.
- You may use the extract for both hot and cold tea. For iced tea you can use still or sparkling water.
- You can also use the extract in the bar, for cocktails.
- The extract can also be used for cooking in the kitchen (see chapter 6, page 130 for more info).

DISADVANTAGES:
It needs a change of mindset to get used to this system, as it is an entirely new approach to tea. However, once mastered, it is a piece of cake, foolproof and stress-free, with a very tasty and versatile tea as a result.

Note The foolproof method does not work wel with pressed teas, like Pu-Erh.

PREPARATION FOR SERVICE WITH TEA BAGS
If you work with tea bags, store each kind in a separate caddy. Label each one with the name of the tea, the length of steeping time and the correct water temperature. Do not intermix the caddies when they are empty. For example, the scent of Earl Grey tea will still linger in the empty caddy if you fill it up with a different tea. If you mix, them, then the new tea may absorb the scent of Earl Grey tea and as a result it will end up smelling and tasting like Earl Grey, instead of how it should smell and taste, and that is a thing you most certainly do not want.

If a tea is removed from the menu, make sure that the caddy used for that tea is washed until spotless and odorless. And pay special attention to drying it well, because they can rust quickly. Also, keep teapots as neutral in smell as possible and try using the same pot for scented teas. To make things easy, use stickers or labels with matching colors on both caddy and pot.

PREPARATION FOR LOOSE LEAF TEA

Loose leaf tea should be stored following the same guidelines as above. In addition, you should also ensure that you use the correct amount of loose leaf tea per serving. Most people tend to add too much tea, because when still dry, it can seem like there is not enough tea, and it is easy to forget that in water, tea increases three times in volume. Too large a scoop of tea makes the tea bitter and too bold, with the risk that your guest will not like the tea; this way you end up with an unhappy guest and it will cost you an unnecessary amount of tea, leading to less profit. However, using too little is not good either, as the tea will taste thin and weak. The key is to get the dosing just right. Read on for some suggestions.

THE MOST ACCURATE PREPARATION FOR LOOSE LEAF TEA

The best way to get the correct amount of tea per serving is by weighing it. You should weigh and prepare the portions in advance, as there will not be enough time to do it every time an order for tea comes in. Use a scale that weighs very accurately to 0.1 g (0.003 oz) and scoop each portion of weighed tea into paper filters, for example.
Fold the filters and slide them on a wooden skewer to keep them closed. Store them in a large, airtight tin until use.
Slide one filter off when an order comes in and shake the tea from the filter bag into the tea pot, tea glass or stainless steel filter. Another option is to use individual mini tins, one per portion. Make sure you label them, either with color codes or name stickers. Do not store skewers with different kinds of tea in the same container, as explained above.
Advantage: you always have the right amount of tea. Never too much, never too little, and you can grab one on the go.
Disadvantage: labour-intensive beforehand. Not suitable if you have a business with a high tea turnover.

A SLIGHTLY FASTER PREPARATION FOR TEA

If you get a lot of tea orders, you might have to compromise on the accuracy of the amount of tea used. In this case, just place a measurement spoon in each tea tin. With this spoon you can then easily measure the amount of tea you want per serving. That could be only one scoop, or it may be one and a half. That depends on the size of the tea leaves and the amount of tea per serving. A teapot will of course need more tea than a tea glass. Write on a label the name of the tea and the amount of scoops needed for one serving and stick the label onto the tin with the spoon inside it.
Advantage: less work involved than in the option above.
Disadvantage: it is slightly less accurate.

> **Tip**
> Save yourself a lot of trouble and use the fabulous foolproof cold brew method. Make sure to serve it fabulously too, from a lovely carafe into wine glasses. Your guests will be impressed!

THE RIGHT HARDWARE FOR SERVING TEA OUTSIDE THE HOME

How busy is your business? A well-functioning 250-seat or more type of restaurant may have less time to spend serving tea than a thirty-seat or less type of place. And in more exclusive restaurants, it may be of more importance to make time for guests, to elaborately advise them on wine, beer, coffee and tea than in a restaurant where turnover rate is more important. A good mise en place is essential for a fast and efficient working method, but knowledge of the product (and the serving material) is just as important.
In the catering industry it is important that work can be done quickly and efficiently with materials that look and feel attractive, but are also strong enough for frequent and intense use, and it is also vital that they are dishwasher safe.

TEXTURE

The texture of the material of the recipients used for drinks has a big effect on the guest's experience. A glass or cup with a thick rim is not pleasant to drink from. So, a general rule for recipients is the thinner, the better, but they should also be strong enough for intensive usage.

Double-walled glasses often have a thick edge, resulting in an unpleasant sensation, and they could also lead to burned lips, as it is hard to tell from the cool outside if the hot drink is already safe to drink. Apart from this, with this kind of glass, the tea stays too hot for a very long time to be safe to drink. This may lead to the undesired situation of one guest still waiting for their first cup of tea to be cool enough to drink, while another guest at the same table is already drinking a second cup of coffee.

With double-walled glass teapots, on the other hand, this effect is actually handy, because the tea stays hot for much longer than in an ordinary teapot. Unfortunately, double-walled glass is often very fragile. A good catering quality is therefore also of great importance in this case, but of course there is a price tag attached to that.

STACKING TO SAVE SPACE

Stackable tea glasses generally become ugly very quickly: full of scratches from stacking. Not to mention the brown rings in cups and glasses caused by limescale deposit in hot water in reaction to certain compounds in the tea. However, the latter can be easily solved by using filtered water with a neutral pH. This is important in any case when steeping tea, as it will taste much better. (See chapter 1).

Pottery or porcelain remains beautiful for longer even when stacked, but may have a rather rough and thick appearance. For tea ware, always make sure that the rim of the cup is thin. The design may be artisanal and sturdy, as long as the texture is pleasant.

STRAINERS

Large but narrow tea strainers are often difficult to clean: tea leaves remain behind, and they can only be removed by a powerful jet of water causing the dish washing staff extra work. Glass strainers are wider, but also have their disadvantages: there can only be a few slots at the bottom of the strainer. With more slots or holes, the glass would no longer be stable and would break very quickly. Because of the lack of enough holes in the strainer, the water passes through too slowly, resulting in a longer wait and a steep that is too strong. Another disadvantage of glass strainers is that tea leaves often get stuck in those slots, and it might take a lot of effort to remove them. The slots also turn brown after a while and will need extra cleaning with vinegar. In short: glass strainers look nice, but are not recommendable, especially not for businesses.

Crockery...
- ...must be shock-proof
- ...and dishwasher-proof
- ... must match the look and feel of the business and the guests
- ... should take up as little space as possible, and should preferably have little protrusions (spout, handle)
- ... has to provide a pleasant experience for the guests: texture is important. A thick rimmed glass or cup is unpleasant to drink from. The rim should be thin, without breaking too easily
- ... should not cause a hazard to guests, e.g., double walled glass, or glasses and cups without ears or handles. Wine glasses with stems are perfect for tea: they are thin rimmed and easy to hold, and are lovely for the guest's experience as well, much more so than cups and bowls

Water in the foodservice industry

As you know by now, it is essential to make tea with soft, clean fresh water with a neutral pH level. There are many kinds of filter systems, but the best system for tea is the reverse osmosis filter system. Not only at home, but also in the service industry. This system can be attached to the tap, to ensure a constant flow of filtered water and it can also be connected to a boiler, which maintains the water at the right temperature. There are all kinds of systems available, as different businesses need different solutions. Some businesses sell more tea than others, are bigger or need faster systems. To find the best solution for your business, it is best to talk to several companies that sell reverse osmosis systems. They will know what is available and which system is best for your situation.

Advantages

A reverse osmosis filter system gives you water that is not only perfect for tea, but also for the kitchen. Lots of restaurant kitchens already work with reverse osmosis, as it is much better for the machines and for the flavor of vegetables. What works well for tea, obviously also works well for vegetables, soups, stock, herbs and other food.

Purchasing tea

- Preferably, buy your tea from reliable tea companies with a good reputation.
- Start moderately: buy six different types of tea at the most, and do not buy more than 250 g (8.8 oz) each.
- Note down every day how much tea per type was sold. After a month, you will have a fairly good insight of how much is needed. Adapt your purchasing of tea accordingly.
- Buy an airtight caddy or canister for each different type of tea.
- Only extend your range of teas when you perceive a demand.

Storage of tea

- Preferably in an airtight tin with two lids: an outer and an inner lid.
- Glass jars are only useable when kept in the dark, as light affects the aroma and flavor of tea. Additionally, jars are heavy and breakable, so I would advise against glass jars altogether.
- Never store tea in plastic bags or boxes. Tea easily absorbs the smell of plastic and cardboard and this quickly becomes reflected in the taste.

Refills

- Only refill the tins when they are completely empty. Do not mix old and new tea.
- When filling the tin with a different tea, first wash and dry the tin thoroughly to make sure all aromas of the former tea have vanished.
- Keep a list of stock near the tea tins. Once a new package has been opened, make sure it is written down on the stock list. Check regularly if tea in stock is running out.

Packaging

- Beware of luxurious design packaging. Brands that spend a lot of money on their packaging, often love design and marketing more than they love tea. The more money is used for packaging, the less is spent on the product. A serious tea lover/tea merchant wants to spend most of the budget on his or her product, especially since the tea will have to be transferred to proper caddies and the packaging will then be discarded.
- Make sure the tea arrives properly packed, in sealed, lightproof and airtight packaging.

CHAPTER 12

Tea production

The youngest shoots of the tea plant are smooth, soft and delicate, and have a complex set of flavors, while the lower, larger leaves are thick, tough and will never be used, not even for the cheapest tea. The function of the lower, bigger leaves is to keep the plant healthy and strong. The young buds at the top are leaves that are not yet unrolled and are picked for the finest teas. The leaves are picked from the buds to about four or five leaves down maximum, depending on the type of tea and the cultivar used. Cultivar is short for the phrase cultivated variety. Through crossbreeding, tea farmers are able to develop new cultivars. These cultivars are created to achieve higher yields, more resistance to climate changes, diseases and pests, or to achieve desired flavor profiles. For some tea, only the bud is used, and for others only the leaves. For most tea, both the bud and the top two leaves are picked. The technical term for this is two leaves and a bud. However, there are also plenty of teas made with three leaves and a bud or only one leaf and a bud and even those made only from buds. Oolongs are made with the top four leaves, with or without the buds.

PICKING OF TEA LEAVES

Picking is often done by hand but can also be done by machine, which is not as selective, but much faster.
There are different types of machines to do the plucking, such as highly advanced machines, which are mainly used in countries like Japan, where the daily wages of pickers would be too high for a profitable yield from hand-picking. These machines are extremely expensive, even for Japanese standards, that is why the tea farmers often share them. They plant cultivars with different harvest times, so the machines are not needed at the same time. There are handheld machines with big bags attached to catch the cut leaves, and there are larger machines, with containers that suck in the cut leaves. The latter drive over the tea bushes and require accurate settings, so as not to cut too much or too little off the plants. But the use of driven machines is only possible in tea gardens situated on plateaus, of course. On steep mountainside plantations only hand-picking or handheld machines are used, as there is no way big driven machines can be used.
Because it is more and more difficult to find experienced tea pickers, the use of harvesting machines continues to increase, even in countries with low wage practices.

HOW IS TEA MADE?

When tea is picked, the leaves are still green. In order to keep them that way to make green and yellow tea, the enzymes responsible for the oxidation process must first be stopped. This is necessary because oxidation makes the leaves change both in color and flavor, just like with an apple when you take a bite out of it. By biting into an apple, the cells are broken and the cell juices are released and come into contact with oxygen. Two enzymes in those juices, oxidase and peroxidase, react immediately to the oxygen, starting the oxidation process. If you put the apple aside for a while, it will turn brown and taste different. That is called oxidation and this is exactly how it works for tea. Halting or preventing oxidation can be done through a heating process, whereby the cell juices are briefly but intensely exposed to a high temperature with steam or in a wok pan (known as pan firing), or both. The enzymes also will be stopped eventually when the tea leaves are left to wither for a long time. The leaves then lose so much moisture that the enzymes can no longer function properly and eventually give up. The leaves change color during this process, that is why long withering is not suitable for green or yellow tea. White tea is usually withered for a long time, both outdoors and indoors and is then just dried. The aromas will not be completely fixed, so white teas often loose their aromas faster than the other teas. The other types of tea are fixed during processing by means of heating, rolling and drying the leaves in ovens.

The final color (and flavor) of the tea therefore depends on the way of processing after picking. The top leaves of the plants are picked on the plantation, after which the leaves go to the factory as soon as possible, situated near the plantation. There, the tea will be processed into one of the six types of teas. They each have their own production process. You already read that white tea has the least production steps.

The tea with the most steps of production is oolong. The amount of steps needed to make a certain type of tea does not say anything about its final quality, as that depends on the total sum of the quality of the leaves, the experience and knowledge of the tea producer, the time of plucking, the amount of harvests per year, the height of the plantation, the amount of rainfall and sunshine and so on.

THE SIX TYPES OF TEA

GREEN TEA
YELLOW TEA
WHITE TEA
OOLONG TEA
BLACK TEA
PU-ERH TEA

PRODUCTION STEPS OF TEA

Picking of fresh tea leaf

WHITE TEA	GREEN TEA	YELLOW TEA	BLACK TEA	OOLONG TEA	PU-ERH TEA
Withering outdoors and indoors	Withering	Withering	Withering	Withering outdoors / Withering indoors	Withering
Drying by sun or oven	De-enzyming (Killing green) by wok, oven or steam	De-enzyming (Killing green) by wok	Rolling or cutting	Shaking	De-enzyming (Killing green) by wok < 50°C (122°F)
	Rolling	Smothering (yellowing)	Oxidation	Partial oxidation	Rolling
	Shaping	Rolling	Rolling	Short oxidation / Long oxidation	Drying (Mao Cha)
	Drying	Shaping	Shaping	De-enzyming (Killing green) by wok or oven	Steaming
		Drying	Drying	Shaping: twisting or ball-rolling	Fermentation
				Drying	
				Roasting, firing	At least 1 year / 45 days

GREEN TEA

Picking - withering - heating (stop oxidation) - rolling - shaping - drying

As explained above, green tea has to be heated first, to prevent oxidation of the leaves so that they remain green. The professional term for that is Killing The Green. A very strange name, as in fact the last thing you want to do is kill the green. I would rather call it Killing The Brown, but hey, I am not a tea farmer, so naming the process is not up to me. Another term used for this is de-enzyming which I think is more appropriate. The enzymes are not exactly killed but paralyzed. This de-enzyming can be done with steam or in woks, flat pans or ovens. Japanese tea makers do this by passing the leaves through a shower of steam, 30 to 40 seconds for light steaming, 50-70 seconds for middle steaming, and 120-200 seconds for long steaming, known as fukamushi or deep steaming. Some Japanese teas are both steamed and panfried, and very few are only panfried. The Chinese usually de-enzyme tea by pan firing, in a sizzling hot, huge wok, for a short period of time as the leaves should not be cooked or scorched. There are still other important processes to be done, like the development of flavors and aromas, which processes are carried out after Killing the Green, by means of bruising and/or rolling the leaves, causing the cells to tear and the cell juices to run free. The leaves are then rolled up again, or twisted, or folded, to lock in the flavors and aromas that are released when the cells break. The next step is to dry the leaves to prevent mould forming. Moisture is diminished down to 2 to 4 %. It is important to maintain a little bit of moisture, or else the tea would become brittle and crumble into dust, which is not desirable.

Tai Ping Hou Kui

Zhu Ye Qing

Mao Jian

Tamaryokucha

Bi Lo Chun

Long Jing

Mao Feng

YELLOW TEA

Picking - withering - heating (stop oxidation) - smothering - rolling - shaping - drying

The de-enzyming process is also carried out for yellow tea, since oxidation is not a feature of yellow tea. After de-enzyming, the hot leaves are wrapped in cloth or tarp to be smothered. The humid heat wants to escape, but there is no way out. Chlorophyll is broken down by the heat, the color changes from green to green-yellow, sometimes straw-colored, the aromas soften and become sweeter, and the leaf is then shaped and dried. Two yellow teas, the most expensive ones, Jun Shan Yin Zhen and Meng Ding Huang Ya, only contain buds. Two other less expensive yellow teas, Huo Shan and Huang Da Cha, also contain leaves.

Mogan Huang Ya

Huo Shan

WHITE TEA

Picking - withering for a long time - drying

For white tea, there is another form of de-enzyming: withering, over a period of days or weeks; first in the shade and later in the sun. As this takes up a lot of time, the leaves in the meantime slowly start to oxidize. Because the moisture in the leaf evaporates, the enzymes slowly but steadily run out of moisture and in the end can no longer do their job properly, and they dry out. White tea is therefore partly oxidized, but to what extent depends on the duration of withering and whether the leaves are big or small and whether it is made up of leaves and buds or only buds. The leaf is open and oxidizes more easily than the tightly rolled up buds. After withering, the only process white tea goes through is drying.

White tea originated in Fujian Province, China, specifically Fuding and Zhenghe, where the majority of white tea is still produced today. Nowadays, it is also produced in many other regions and also in other countries. The best-known white teas are made with the *Camellia sinensis sinensis* variety. Chinese white teas include Bai Hao Yin Zhen (Silver Needle), Bai Mudan (White Peony), Gong Mei (Tribute Eyebrow) and Shou Mei (Longevity Eyebrow). The first, made from a specific variety, Bai Hao Yin Zhen, contains only buds covered with silky white hairs (Bai Hao means white, fluffy hair). The second has both the bud and the two top leaves, is made from this same variety and also has those fluffy hairs, both on the leaf and on the buds. The third is of a lower quality, and often has broken leaves, fewer buds and larger differences in color. The fourth is of the lowest quality, has older, larger leaves, many broken pieces and even fewer buds. Shou Mei accounts for more than 50% of all white tea produced in China. Additionally, there is also Yue Guang Bai, in the West better known as White Moonlight. It is made from the top two leaves and the bud of a large-leaved *Camellia sinensis assamica* variety and comes from Yunnan, a tropical southern province in China. The tea leaf is left to wither much longer than usual and that process starts at night, hence the name. Due to the longer withering, the large buds are still silvery in color, but with a golden glow, and the leaves are almost black. This process makes the tea very aromatic and more complex in taste than the other white teas. White teas are also produced in countries other than than China, such as India, Nepal, Kenya, Taiwan, Sri Lanka and Malawi.

Spicy White, first flush, Darjeeling

Ali Shan White

Bai Mudan

Doke Silver Needle

Bai Hao Yin Zhen, aged, 2010

Bai Hao Yin Zhen

White Crescent

White Moonlight

OOLONG TEA

Picking - withering in the sun - further withering inside - shaking - partial oxidation - heating (stop oxidation) - rolling / ball rolling - drying - additional roasting

This tea requires more steps to produce than other teas, as you can see from the list above. Oolong is usually made with the top four leaves of the bush without buds, and it is a partially oxidized tea. After picking, the leaves are withered, usually in the sun or under a diffused sunroof, where aromas start to develop within the leaves. This makes the leaves more supple and pliable for the next steps. The freshly picked leaves are never rolled or shaken as this would risk breaking them.

After withering, the leaves are shaken, which bruises the outer edge of the leaves, initiating the oxidation process. Oxidation is more manageable thanks to this additional step, as it starts from the outside inwards, instead of all over the leaf at once. This shaking is traditionally done with large flat wicker baskets, or in large braided bamboo drums, and nowadays sometimes also by very careful rolling. The cell juices come into contact with oxygen and the oxidation process starts. This creates a thin brown edge around the outside of the leaf. The longer the enzymes remain active, the wider the edge becomes and thus the oxidation level of the leaf increases. The leaves are then spread out again, and they wither and oxidize even more, before being shaken again until the desired oxidation level is reached. The extent of this is determined by the tea master. He smells the leaves and knows: now we have to put the enzymes on hold. The oxidation levels of oolongs range from 10 to 80 percent. The leaves are placed briefly in hot, rotating drums, similar to a laundry dryer. The enzymes are stopped by the heat and the oxidation process stops. The leaves are spread out over a large cotton sheet, which is then rolled up for the rolling process to start. For the ball shape, the sheet is closed and rolled up tightly until a ball is formed. This is then pressed and kneaded inside an iron press. On a very small scale it is still traditionally kneaded by hand. This turns the leaves into balls inside the sheet. They are shaken loose from the sheet

Baozhong

Dong Fang Mei Ren

Da Hong Pao

Si Ji Chun

Feng Huang Milan Dancong

in the revolving drums, then scooped into the sheet again to return to the press for some further ball rolling. This is repeated very often. How often depends on the type of oolong that is made, the hand of the master and the price that the tea can yield. There are also half-ball shaped oolongs. Additionally, there is the elongated, twisted oolong. This one is carefully rolled by hand or machines without the use of sheets. This must be done carefully so as not to tear the leaves. Only the cells inside the leaf have to break to release the aromas and oxidation enzymes. The outside should remain as intact as possible, just like the ball-shaped oolong. Then the tea is dried in ovens and often roasted, also called fired. This makes the tea softer and more complex. Before the tea is packed, the stems are usually removed, but not always, as this is done by hand and as such very time consuming, making it expensive. Oolong is also known as Wulong, but as oolong is more often used in the west, I stick to calling it oolong.

BLACK TEA
Picking- withering - rolling - (or cutting in case of CTC) - complete oxidation - shaping - drying
The tea we call black, is named red tea by the Chinese. Calling it a red tea is much more apt, because when the tea is steeped it has shades of red, whilst in Western countries, it is the hard water that makes it almost black, not the tea itself. The Chinese consider post-fermented tea, or Hei Cha, to be black tea. Which makes sense, because it does become darker with each steep and sometimes it does indeed look as black as coffee. When black tea is mentioned in this book, it refers to Western black tea. When referencing Hei Cha, I use the phrase post-fermented. As soon as the picked leaf arrives at the factory, the tea is spread and left to wither. Thus, the leaves already lose 30 to 50% of their moisture, making them limp and able to be rolled more easily later on. The taste development also starts at this point, which is another reason that withering is an essential step. There are two methods of making black tea: the industrial method, known as CTC, which stands for Crush-Tear-Curl, and the traditional, or orthodox method.

CTC (CRUSH-TEAR-CURL) METHOD
This method was developed by the English in the 1930s in order to make large quantities of tea faster and more efficiently. Through a series of connecting machines, the leaves are first chopped, which accelerates the oxidation process. They are then transported by conveyor belts into large, shallow troughs. Warm, moist and oxygen-rich air is blown through the leaves, to accelerate oxidation even further. The duration of oxidation depends on several factors, such as the outside temperature, whether it is the rainy season, how long the leaf has been withered for, the size of the leaf, and the type of tea being made. When the desired level of oxidation has been reached, (usually 100 %) the leaves need to be dried. A full oxidation means a longer shelf life for the tea. The leaves are either placed on conveyor belts with holes blowing warm air through the bottom, or in ovens on perforated baking sheets or even, very occasionally, in the sun. After drying, the leaves are sieved by size and divided into four categories: dust, fanning, broken, and whole.
Dust: the smallest particles are called dust,

because they are as fine as dust. This grade is the cheapest category and used for tea bags given its fast release of flavor and color.
Fannings: consist of slightly larger pieces.
Brokens: this grade contains larger pieces than fannings.
Whole leaf: has the largest pieces of leaf, not necessarily whole leaves.

Sorting by size is especially important for flavor. If small particles are mixed with large ones, the release of flavors and color differ enormously, resulting in uneven flavors, causing the tea to be off balance.

ORTHODOX METHOD

In this case the leaves are first withered, then rolled softly, either by hand or machine. This careful rolling keeps the outside of the leaf intact, while the gentle movement tears the internal cells, releasing the cell juices and the oxidation process begins, albeit much slower than with CTC, as it is harder for the enzymes to make contact with the oxygen with the outer cells staying whole and the leaf practically intact. A very even, gentle and slow oxidation is the result.

FLAVORED TEAS

Flavored teas, such as Earl Grey, Lapsang Souchong, Jasmine etc. are not tea types in themselves, rather named that way due to the way they are processed, scented or flavored. The aromas of these varieties are added to the tea by literally covering the processed tea with fresh flowers or fresh Bergamot citrus peel (in the case of Earl Grey) or they are smoked above pine wood (in the case of Lapsang Souchong). These natural, labour-intensive methods are used for the more expensive teas, whereas the cheaper teas are aromatised with flavored additives.

English Blend

Honey Black

Ceylon

Lapsang Souchong unsmoked

Nepal Golden Needle

Assam

Nilgiri

Nepal Silver Tips

POST-FERMENTED TEA

Picking - withering - heating (stop oxidation) - rolling - sun baking - steaming/wetting - fermenting

This type of tea is the only one that goes through a process of deliberate fermentation. Black tea is often called fermented tea, but that is actually an incorrect denomination. Black tea, as explained previously, turns from green to brownish black because the leaves are oxidized, rather than fermented.

Fermentation is a natural process in which micro-organisms, either already present or intentionally added, such as bacteria, fungi or yeasts, start a chemical process in the absence of oxygen. The microorganisms develop due to heat and moisture, at the same time producing enzymes that change the acidity, taste, smell, appearance, digestibility and shelf life. This process makes the tea taste milder and sweeter, the scent becomes aromatic, ranging from bright and grassy to floral, nutty, woody or earthy and gives the tea a dark brown color. The longer the tea ferments, the softer and more complex the taste.

PRODUCTION

Picking is done manually, which is often quite a challenge, as most trees are several meters high, so climbing is mandatory. The pluck consists of one bud and three leaves. The fresh leaves are withered for a few hours, indoors or outdoors, depending on the weather. The leaves are heated in a wok to stop oxidation (kill-green), so that they no longer turn brown. They are then rolled by hand and placed in the sun to dry (sun-baked). This base tea is called "Mao Cha". Some literature speaks of a green tea, because this first phase is very similar to the production of baked green tea. An important difference however, is that Mao Cha has to be dried in the sun after heating and rolling. The Mao Cha is the base tea for Pu-Erh. After the sun drying it may be processed immediately for the fermentation process, or stored to be processed (years) later. Mao Cha has not yet been fermented; it is a semi-finished but indispensable product for the making of post-fermented tea.

Post-fermented teas contain many different aromas and flavors, but their basic aromas and taste are always earthy and woody.

Sheng Pu-Erh

Shu Pu-Erh

WHAT IS PU-ERH?

Pu-Erh is a special category within the post-fermented teas. Just like champagne, this tea may only be called as such if it has been made in the designated Pu-Erh area following strict guidelines about cultivar, location, processing method and so on. If one of those guidelines are not followed, the tea is Hei Cha, but not Pu-Erh. Compare it to champagne: if not made in the area of Champagne according strict guidelines and with a specific cultivar, it is not allowed to be called champagne, but should be called sparkling wine. All champagne is sparkling wine, but not all sparkling wines are champagne. The very same goes for Pu-Erh. The farmer may call it Pu-Erh when:

- The tea leaves from which the tea is made come from a tea tree from a designated area in Yunnan.
- The tea is made from the local variety Camellia sinensis assamica called Da Ye Zhong or 'Big Leaf'.
- The Mao Cha, or base tea for the production of Pu Erh, has been dried in the sun.

There are two types of Pu-Erh: Sheng and Shu (or Shou):

SHENG PU-ERH

Sheng is also called raw Pu-Erh. This refers to the natural fermentation that this type of Pu-Erh undergoes. For Sheng, the Mao Cha is first carefully weighed to the gram (the weight of Pu-Erh is also bound by rules). The most common Sheng Pu-Erh cake weighs 357 grams (13.22 oz), but they come in all kinds of shapes and sizes. The Mao Cha is then briefly heated over steam so that the leaves soften, which makes them easier to process. The moisture and heat also activate the micro-organisms (present in the tea, in the air and on the bag): they immediately start fermentation. The moist leaf is placed in a cloth bag and tightly but carefully tied by hand. The tea is then pressed into an even flat disc, called a cake or bing. Formerly this pressing was done by placing the bag under a heavy, flat stone, but nowadays this is done with a hydraulic press. The knot of the bag will dent the cake. The cake is removed from the bag and placed on a wooden rack to ferment. This happens in rooms where humidity and temperature are controlled. Heat is important to properly initiate and maintain fermentation. After a few hours to a few days (and sometimes even years) the cakes are individually wrapped in breathable paper and then wrapped with in total seven cakes, called bings, in dried bamboo leaf into a package, called a tong. This way the cakes continue to ferment slowly.

A young Sheng Pu-Erh often tastes bitter and a more mature Sheng Pu-Erh sweeter, with a softer texture. A young Sheng Pu-Erh has an astringent effect in your mouth, but when it gets older it becomes rounder and softer. The longer Sheng Pu-Erh ripens, the richer and more layered the flavors become.

SHU PU-ERH

Shu Pu-Erh, also called cooked or pile-fermented Pu-Erh, is a technique in which fermentation is activated in an artificial way to make fermentation go faster.

The "wòduí" or "wet piling" method is used for this. This was first used by the Menghei Tea Factory in 1972. For wet piling, the Mao Cha is placed on large piles, usually 70 cm (27.5 inches) high, but this can differ per factory. The tea is then moistened and covered with (linen) cloth. The temperature and humidity of the room are carefully monitored. The micro-organisms present in the room, on the cloth and in the tea, react to the moisture and heat and start the fermentation. The stacks of tea are regularly turned so that fermentation can take place gradually. This artificial method accelerates the fermentation enormously: in just 45 days (this can also vary slightly per factory) the fermentation is already finished. The Shu Pu-Erh is then pressed into bings, or small "Tuo Cha" or birds' nest for storage and aging, or dried and sold as loose Pu Erh.

Shu Pu-Erh has already undergone considerable

fermentation and has a soft and sweet taste, sometimes with an umami undertone. Shu Pu-Erh becomes richer in flavor as it gradually matures further.

CONTINUATION OF FERMENTATION

Like good wines, this tea gets better with age, provided it is stored under the right conditions: not too humid, not too hot or cold. The storage and further fermentation of Pu-Erh cakes, both Sheng and Shu, take place under controlled conditions of temperature and humidity. Basically, the cakes ferment best at a humidity of 70-80% at a temperature of 30°C (86°F). Despite the humidity and temperature being controlled, the production of Pu-Erh is a natural process and difficult to control. The development of the tea, the taste and the aromas therefore fluctuates in a natural way. A temperature above 45°C (113°F) is not desirable, as it will cause the tea to rot. A different storage method in which the humidity in the room is deliberately increased to 95% is "Shi Cang" or "wet storage". The higher the level of humidity, the faster the fermentation will proceed. This gives the tea an earthy, musty, mushroomy aroma. For some a delicacy, for others a no-go.
On average, Sheng Pu-Erh ripens for about 8 to 10 years before being sold for consumption, but can be kept much longer. Shu Pu-Erh is sold almost immediately for consumption.

ORIGIN OF POST-FERMENTED TEA

Nowadays, post-fermented teas are produced in a variety of countries from Malawi to Japan to Indonesia, but it originated in China, which is still the largest producer of post-fermented tea, although just a mere 3% of the total of Chinese tea production is post-fermented. In China, post-fermented tea is called "Hei Cha" or "Dark Tea". Hei Cha is produced in several Chinese provinces, including Hubei, Hunan and Sichuan. However, the most famous Hei Cha is Pu-Erh. This post-fermented tea comes from the southern province Yunnan, more specifically, from the area around the city of Pu-Erh. As that is the type of post-fermented tea most known in Western countries, I stick to the Pu-Erh version in this book when I talk about post-fermented tea.

JAPANESE POST-FERMENTED TEA

Goishicha is another type of post-fermented tea, only produced in Japan. Just a handful of farmers make this type of tea as it is very labour-intensive. Goishicha is acidic, fruitier and less earthy than Pu-erh. Typical aromas for Goishicha are sour cherry, buttermilk, citrus, malt, pickled ginger, chocolate and horse stable. The leaves are mainly handpicked once a year in June. Goishicha has been produced in the Kochi prefecture, located in the south of Japan, on Shikoku island for at least 400 years. Both the leaves of wild tea bushes, or Yamacha, and the leaves from tea gardens are used to made the tea.

The leaves are fermented twice. For the first fermentation session, the leaves are steamed, traditionally in wooden barrels over firewood. The leaves and stems are then separated by hand and fermented for one week by aerobic fermentation. This means there is still a bit of oxygen present in the process.

They are spread out indoors, under mats. For the second and anaerobic fermentation step, the leaves are stacked, 200 kg of leaves in total, and placed inside a wooden barrel and wrapped. Heavy stones are then placed on top of the leaves, up to 200 kg in total, to prevent oxygen from entering the stack.

The lactobacilli, naturally present inside the barrels, start to do their work. The weight presses the leaves tightly together into a thick cake. After a few weeks after the second fermentation process is complete, the leaves are cut up into squares of about 4 cm (1.20 inch) and spread out to dry for a few days in the sun. The dried pieces look a bit like the stones used in the board game Go, hence the name of the tea, Goishicha.

TAI PING HOU KUI (MONKEY KING) GREEN TEA

CHAPTER 13
Tea and health

Tea has several properties that are more beneficial to the body than wine:
- There are no calories in tea (provided of course you do not put sugar or milk in it)
- There is no alcohol in tea
- You stay clear and awake when you drink tea

Too much of anything is never good and this goes for tea as well. Many health claims are associated with tea, but the problem is that almost every study has different results, which can even differ per day.

TEA AND ANTIOXIDANTS
All teas contain antioxidants. But how much? Impossible to say, because here, the same applies as explained above. What we can be sure of is that because of its processing process, there are more antioxidants in green tea than in black tea. More about this can be found under the heading "Tannin or Catechin", on the next page. Antioxidants have a bitter taste, so green tea can taste more bitter than black, especially when steeped with very hot water. Bitter compounds get released more easily at high temperatures, so the hotter the water, the more readily the bitter compounds release themselves into your cup.

It is safe to say that one cultivar may contain much more or less antioxidants than another, but the variables are too large to draw solid, scientific conclusions. It is difficult to prove whether the antioxidants in tea actually do prevent diseases. Eastern cultures have been using tea as a medicine for thousands of years, and they wouldn't have been doing that if it had never ever helped. Experience is also worth something. It is definitely safe to say that tea is good for body and mind, but we cannot prove it. Nevertheless, there is...

> **... good news!**
> - It has been established that around 25 percent of dried tea is made up of antioxidants
> - Antioxidants are also found in wine and cocoa
> - Antioxidants are good for your skin because they prevent cell destruction. So, go ahead and have another cup of tea with a chunk of chocolate …

WHAT ARE POLYPHENOLS?
Polyphenols are chemical compounds found in all plant species. They have several functions, the main one being the plant's self-protection. Polyphenols also carry flavor, color and aroma. They are divided into different categories. Of these, flavonoids are the most important for tea, because they make up the largest component of the tea and are therefore the principal determinants of flavor.

Tea has about 30,000 different polyphenols, about the same amount as can be found in vegetables. Sunlight converts amino acids, which in themselves are sweet, into polyphenols, some of which are bitter and astringent. That is good news for the plant, because insects, just like humans, do not like bitter tastes. In fact, they are just as fond as us of sweet stuff, so polyphenols are a good means of defense against insects for the plant.

SUNLIGHT ADDS BITTERNESS TO TEA LEAVES, SHADE SWEETNESS
Tea grown in the shade gets less sunlight and therefore produces less polyphenols than tea grown in direct sunlight, and therefore the tea grown in the shade tastes sweeter. The same

goes for tea grown high in the mountains, where it is often foggy, because fog veils the sunlight. Most polyphenols are located in the delicate first bud and the first two leaves because their protection is more urgently needed. Each leaf further down receives less light and therefore less polyphenols. This does not matter so much because those leaves are already strong. What all this means is that the delicate buds and the upper two leaves contain most of the plant's protective substances, of which caffeine is a very important one. Although the top leaves contain more bitter components, they also have the highest complexity of other flavors and aromas, as not all polyphenols are bitter.

Some aromatic polyphenols are also intended as a defense mechanism for the plant. Linalool is one such flavor substance. Although linalool smells good to us humans, as it may smell like rose, wood, lavender or coriander, it deters insects. An exception to this rule is a Taiwanese oolong known as Dong Fang Mei Ren or Oriental Beauty. The Jacobiasca formosana is a tiny grasshopper-like insect that loves the leaves of the tea cultivar specifically used for its production. The plant does not know that the insect is immune to linalool, so in its defense against the insect's gnawing, the plant produces more and more linalool to scare off its attacker. However, the immune insect gnaws on, unperturbed. This gnawing incites a chemical reaction between the bug's saliva and the plant's linalool, which causes a change in color and aroma. The bug-bitten tea leaves acquire white stripes on their surface. During the production of the fresh, bug-bitten tea leaf a specific honey flavor arises that only occurs in this cultivar and is caused by that tiny little insect. Dong Fang Mei Ren is therefore by definition organic, because pesticides would destroy the animal and thus the intended aroma would not occur. Two other teas, Honey Black and Empress Gui Fei Oolong, are also made with bug-bitten leaves and have similar flavor profiles.

TANNIN OR CATECHIN?

Polyphenols are formed from amino acids under the influence of light and consist of various categories, of which the group of flavonoids is most abundant in tea. This group can be broken down into flavanols and they in turn into catechins. These flavanols change during the oxidation process. Green tea turns red-brown by oxidation and the tea tastes stronger. This is because the flavanols are converted from catechins to thearubigines by enzymes during oxidation. Their effect on our palate is very similar to those of tannins, as they are responsible for the astringent texture and somewhat bitter but pleasant taste of tea, which intensifies the flavor, making it richer and prolongs the aftertaste, and making the resulting tea easier to conserve. Tannins are present in wine, wood, rhubarb, cocoa and walnuts, but not in tea. In wine, when tannins are well balanced, the texture will be experienced as pleasant. The same goes for the thearubigines in tea. When there are too many, such as in cases when the tea is not balanced well during processing, then the tea might become unpleasantly astringent.

Thearubigines bind themselves to proteins. For example, those on the inside of your cheek, or on your tongue. This results in a specific effect: what was moist, suddenly feels dry, sometimes even astringent. Additionally, they bring body and volume to the tea, just like tannin does with wine. Thearubigines are present in black tea and in dark oolongs, but the amount and texture vary per tea.

In short: thearubigines are formed from catechins through oxidation, produced by specific enzymes, (oxidase and peroxidase). This process then leads to changes in color and taste.

EXAMPLES OF SMOOTH, SWEETER BLACK TEA (RELATIVELY FEW THEARUBIGINES):
- Yuchi Hong Yun, Taiwan
- Four Seasons Black, Taiwan
- Honey Black, Taiwan
- Lapsang Souchong, China
- Jin Jun Mei, China
- Keemun, China

EXAMPLES OF TARTER, MORE BITTER OR MORE ASTRINGENT TEA (MORE THEARUBIGINES):
- Assam, India
- English Breakfast, blend
- Irish Breakfast, blend
- Prince of Wales, blend
- Japanese black tea
- African black tea
- Ceylon, Sri Lanka
- Darjeeling, India
- Dian Hong (Golden Yunnan), China

The word tannin is derived from the Latin word "tannare", which means the tanning of skins. To tan skins, caustic acid is used to dry them. As described above, tannins in wine and thearubigins in tea have the very same effect on our cheeks and tongues. It is often thought that tannin or thearubigine are bad for us; however that is a myth. They might even have a calming effect on the stomach and intestines. Too much thearubigine can lead to constipation, because it can make the intestines too calm, stopping them from working. Also, too much thearubigine may prevent the absorption of iron and other minerals. This is because thearubigine and some other polyphenols can bind to minerals, including iron. If you do suffer from constipation or anaemia, drink black tea less often, or add a splash of milk to it. The calcium in milk binds to the thearubigine, which means that your body now can properly absorb minerals, such as iron.

CATECHINS

All antioxidants are polyphenols, but not all polyphenols are antioxidants. Antioxidants have gained a lot of attention over the past years because researchers claim that antioxidants do wonders for our skin and restore cells to prevent cell destruction. In this process, the catechins seem to play a major role. You read earlier that catechins originate from flavanols, a group that falls under flavonoids, which in turn are part of one of the many groups of polyphenols. So, to break down what we are talking about here: polyphenols> flavonoids> flavanols> catechins.

Catechins can also be divided into different subgroups, such as EGCG (epigallocatechin gallate), the most active in the field of warfare against free radicals. And tea contains a huge amount of EGCG. Researchers claim that free radicals cause illness, such as cancer, old age and the shrinking of skin cells. So it is not surprising that you see more and more tea-based skin creams popping up everywhere in stores and beauty parlors.

The flavonoids group also contains flavones, isoflavones and anthocyanins. Those are responsible for the smell, color and taste of tea. They are non-existent in old tea, because they are volatile. Antioxidants do, however, remain present, even in old tea, because they do not evaporate. Unfortunately, polyphenols, and thus antioxidants, are bitter and astringent. So old tea not only loses its smell, color and flavor complexity, but the bitter notes and astringency are also much more noticeable, because the volatile sweet, umami, floral and other aromatic compounds have disappeared. That is why most teas do not age well, lose flavor and become stale over time.

ANTIOXIDANTS IN GREEN TEA AND MATCHA

Green tea and Matcha are both green teas, but the methods of production, style of steeping and how they are consumed differ. When you drink Matcha, you actually consume the entire leaf, not just the infusion, as with all other teas. To make Matcha, the green tea leaf is ground into a fine powder that is mixed with water at 80 - 100°C (176 - 212°F), then whipped vigorously into a foamy, thick or thinner drinkable substance. Because you drink the entire leaf, you ingest more antioxidants and other compounds than when you steep tea leaves and only drink the infusion, discarding the leaves. Incidentally, cheaper Matcha has more antioxidants. That makes that they also taste more bitter, especially when they are older. For the more expensive varieties, tea is used from higher areas, where the plant needs less polyphenols for its protection and where the plant is shaded up to three weeks before it is plucked. This assures that the tea leaf is greener (more chlorophyll), contains more amino acids (less sunlight), and therefore tastes sweeter, contains more umami and is more refined and more complex.

WHAT DO AMINO ACIDS DO IN YOUR TEA?

Tea contains many amino acids, on average about 6% per cup of brewed tea. The most common of these is L-theanine, which only exists in tea leaves. This compound prevents the proper functioning of caffeine, and has a calming effect on our nervous system. Because the amino acid L-theanine counteracts the release of caffeine, while at the same time has a calming property, tea makes you alert, but not agitated.

We saw earlier that the amino acids in tea provide sweetness. Additionally, they are also responsible for umami and freshness and they counter the bitter taste of catechins. Serotonin is also found in small amounts in tea and, together with L-theanine, has a calming effect on the nervous system. Tea plants that have remained in the shade for the two to three weeks before picking, and have received less sunlight and therefore have developed a less bitter taste, remain sweeter and have more umami. This is basically because sunlight converts amino acids into bitter-tasting polyphenols, so with shade this happens much less, and the amino acids (sweet and umami) remain unaffected.

Amino acids summarized
L-theanine provides calmness and, together with the other amino acids, is also responsible for freshness, sweetness and umami. As a result, teas with an emphasis on sweet and umami flavors have a calming effect, such as the Japanese shade grown teas Gyokuro, Matcha and Kabusecha. These high-quality teas also contain less caffeine because they grow in higher, colder areas.

DOPAMINE

Small concentrations of dopamine can be found in tea, which improves the ability to concentrate, so you feel awake for much longer than when you drink coffee and not as agitated.

THEINE IS CAFFEINE

Caffeine is found in coffee, tea, yerba mate, cola and energy drinks such as Red Bull. It stimulates the heartbeat, the nervous system and the breathing of the person consuming it. It was previously thought that theine was different from caffeine, because the effect on the body is different. But we now know that this is due to the binding of L-theanine to the caffeine. Theine and caffeine are molecularly identical. So you can also use the word caffeine in relation to tea.

CAFFEINE IN SUMMARY

Every tea plant contains caffeine, and the processing of tea does not affect the amount of caffeine present. However, an exception to this rule is when the tea receives extra roasting. That diminishes the amount of caffeine, as the caffeine crystals stick to the sides of the roasting machine. When milk is added to tea, it breaks down the polyphenols in the tea, which negates the slowing effect that L-theanine has on caffeine. As a result, tea with milk has the same stimulating effect as coffee in terms of caffeine, albeit to a lesser extent, because a liter of coffee contains more caffeine than a liter of tea. Caffeine reduces fatigue, makes you alert and active. It also stimulates the metabolism. One drawback is that it can cause restlessness, palpitations, insomnia and addiction.

Tea...
- ...contains fluorine, which helps strengthening teeth
- ...contains caffeine, which stimulates digestion, is lipolytic and reduces fatigue
- ... contains L-theanine, which has a calming effect
- ... contains theobromine, which is a diuretic
- ... is a natural moisturizer, due to the minerals it contains

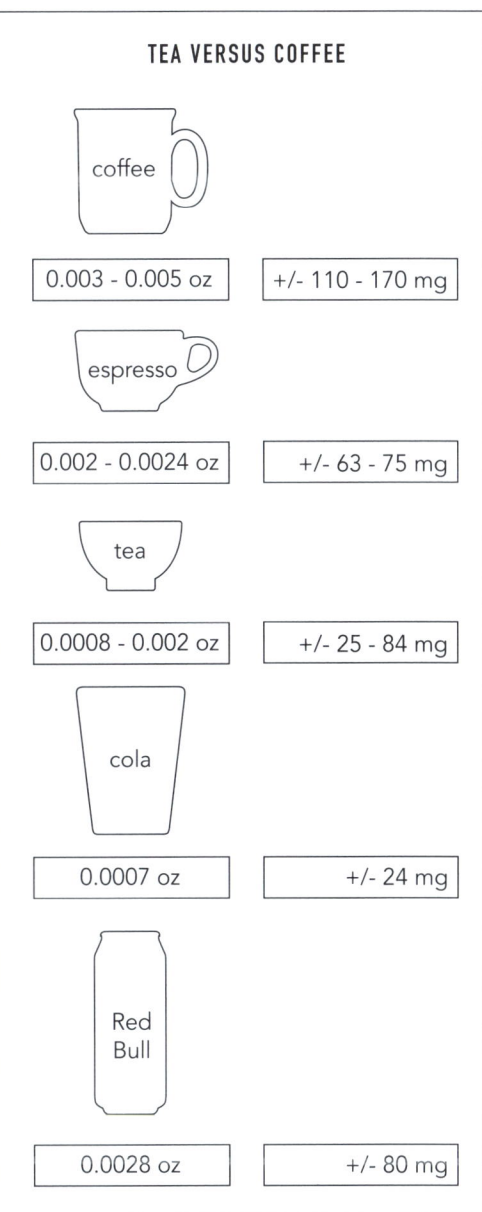

All tea types contain caffeine. It is sometimes claimed that white tea contains less or even no caffeine, but this only applies to the rather rare and expensive Yabao and Camellia ptilophylla varieties, see page 24. All other white teas contain caffeine. If you want to have tea without caffeine, it is best to drink herbal infusions, such as rooibos, nettle, verbena, ginger, mint, to name a few, which do not contain a trace of caffeine. Exceptions are the infusions yerba maté, guayusa and guaraná, all of which do contain a lot of caffeine.

Strongly roasted tea, such as Hōjicha, a Japanese green tea, has less caffeine. During the roasting process the caffeine crystals release themselves from the tea leaf and stick to the walls of the ovens. Likewise, roasted oolong also contains less caffeine than the unroasted version, but tea is never completely caffeine-free, unless the caffeine has been removed artificially or chemically. A white tea like Bai Hao Yin Zhen (Silver Needle) is made from only buds of the tea plant and is picked once a year, in the second half of March. These are the plant's very first buds after its four of five months of hibernation. Because the buds and leaves are still very tender and vulnerable, the plant produces extra caffeine for its protection, much more so than later in the year. However, this specific cultivar grows high up in the mountains, so it needs less caffeine to start with than tea from lower or tropical regions. Apart from this, there are other types of white tea, with leaves with other levels of caffeine content. In short, you cannot say that white tea contains more or less caffeine than other teas.

SUMMARY OF ACTIVE AND BENEFICIAL SUBSTANCES IN TEA

Amino acids
Amino acids are responsible for both umami and the sweet and bright taste of tea. Sunlight converts the amino acids into polyphenols by sunlight, and this changes the flavor, meaning that sweet becomes bitter. The amino acid L-theanine has a calming and soothing effect and inhibits the effect of caffeine.

Carbohydrates
Carbohydrates are fuel in the form of starch and sugars. They represent the energy source of the tea plant, and are necessary for the production of polyphenols, which protect the young leaves and initiate enzymatic processes.

Enzymes
Enzymes are proteins. Among the most important enzymes in tea are oxidase and peroxidase. These enzymes initiate the oxidation process of tea when the leaves are bruised, thus exposing the enzymes to oxygen, which activates them. Their work is intermitted by intensive, short-term heating and the oxidation process stops. By applying this heating before the stage when the leaves are bruised, the enzymes are annihilated before they can do their work and the leaf therefore remains green.

Methylxanthines
Methylxanthines include the polyphenols caffeine, theobromine and theophylline. The tea plant produces these three compounds in order to protect itself against insects, pests and diseases, they are diuretic and responsible for a bitter taste.

Pigments
The pigments carotene and xanthophyll give the oxidized leaves their orange or yellow color. Tea can also turn orange when the leaf is roasted. When the fluffy, white buds of tea are oxidized, they turn golden.

Polyphenols
Polyphenols contribute to a tea's astringency and bitterness. They include flavonoids. These are broken down into catechins, or antioxidants, of which EGCG is the most active and most abundant. Antioxidants in black tea are called thearubigines.

Vitamins and minerals
Tea contains 28 minerals, as well as vitamins B1 and C, but the latter is destroyed at temperatures above 30°C (86°F). The main minerals in tea are fluorine, potassium, zinc, nickel, copper, iron, magnesium, manganese, calcium and traces of sodium and aluminium.

Volatile compounds
Bearers of flavor, volatile compounds arise during the course of processing. Specifically, they appear during the processes of withering, bruising, oxidation and drying of the tea leaf. During these stages, the moisture inside fresh tea leaves largely evaporates, and the space between the compounds becomes much smaller, which can lead to chemical reactions at the point where they touch each other. In turn, this can lead to changes in aroma, color and flavor.

Some examples of these compounds are:
- Geraniol and Linalool, compounds that give off sweet-floral aromas such as linden flower, geranium, orchid, lily of the valley, rose, lavender, bergamot etc. Linalool also gives off herbal aromas such as coriander.
- Phenylacetaldehyde, a lactic acid compound, which also provides sweet-floral flavors. This compound is most significantly present in the Taiwanese variety Jin Xuan #12 light oolong, known in the west as milky oolong.
- Nerolidool, Benzaldehyde and Phenylethanol, compounds providing fruity aromas.
- B-ionone and n-hexanal, compounds giving off fresh aromas.

APPENDIX

Technical information about water

DRY RESIDUE

To measure the dry residue of water, it is heated to 180 degrees until all the water has evaporated and only the solids such as calcium, magnesium, sodium, potassium, chlorine, carbonates and sulphates remain. These are dried and weighed. The number of milligrams that these residues weigh together is called dry residue. For tea, the desired dry residue in water is 50 mg per liter or lower, with a neutral pH value of 6.5 - 7.

THE TDS METER

TDS stands for total dissolved solids: it measures the total dissolved solids in 1 liter of water, but what a TDS-meter actually measures is the conductivity, i.e. the conduction of the water. It does not literally measure the amount of solids in the water, but the degree of conductivity: the easier it goes, the harder the water is. The meter determines the degree of conduction with a conversion factor that differs per country because the composition and the amount of minerals varies per country. In the Netherlands this averages 0.6, but in Gothenburg, for example, it is 0.78. The result of that conversion is expressed in ppm: parts per million: the amount of solid particles per millionth of a liter = mg per liter. (1 liter of water weighs 1000 grams. 1 mg is a thousandth of 1 gram, so 1 liter of water weighs 1000 x 1000 mg = 1 million mg).

The TDS-meter indicates how many mg of negatively and positively charged ions are present in 1 liter of water, i.e. of the solids that are dissolved in it, but remain after evaporation. After all, solids do not evaporate. Examples of these ions are calcium, magnesium, sodium, potassium, chlorine, nitrate and others.

By the way, the measured value is mainly an indication, because the measurements often deviate due to the difference in the minerals present and the calibration of the meter itself. Therefore, it does not give an exact picture, but a push into the right direction: for tea you want a maximum TDS value of 50. Incidentally, the meter cannot see which solids are involved, because only a specialized laboratory can measure this with a gas chromatograph. On the labels of bottled water this is specified, but you can not measure it yourself from tap water.

HARDNESS OF WATER VARIES EVERYWHERE

The differences in water hardness per municipality are closely related to the type of soil in that area.

There is no calcium in sandy soil, so the groundwater of sandy soil is a lot softer than that of clay, for example, or calcareous soil. It is therefore advisable to inquire about your tap water. A lot of data can be retrieved via the websites of water companies, even by zip code. The most important things to pay attention to are in those lists:
- Total Hardness (Mg+Ca)
- Carbonate hardness (HCO_3)
- A good balance in Total Hardness and Carbonate Hardness
- pH value

The height of these values determines the taste of your tea after the water has been heated. The other values are much less important.

In a general sense* you would want water with the following values:
- Ca (calcium): 5 mg/l or less
- Mg (magnesium) 2 mg/l or less
- HCO_3^- (hydrogen carbonate): 20 mg/l or less

5 mg = 0.00017 oz.
2 mg = 0.00007 oz.
20 mg = 0.0007 oz.

*Some teas, such as certain oolongs, benefit from higher values, but it goes too far to name them here. Moreover, it is a matter of taste. Start with the suggestions above and find out for yourself the limits of what tea water is suitable for you.

MEASURING THE HARDNESS OF WATER

You can measure the total hardness (Mg + Ca) using drops. You dissolve them in 5 ml of water and it works like a litmus test: as you drip more, the water turns from red to green. The more drops you need, the harder the water is. You can buy those drops at an aquarium store, or online. There are also drops to measure the carbonate hardness. They work the same way, only the water turns from purple to yellow. The pH level is to be measured with a specific pH meter, also available at aquarium shops. They do not come cheap and need to be calibrated regularly. Some also have a TDS function on them. I bought mine at aquamastertools.com

Too much hassle for you, what with those drops and meters and all? Do not worry. Just stick to a proper water filter jug, and you will be fine. Provided you replace the filters on time and use the right filters, e.g., Maxtra Plus.

In short
H_2O is water
H^+ is hydrogen (acid gas)
CO_2 is carbon dioxide (acid gas)
$H_2O + CO_2$ can form HCO_3
HCO_3 is hydrogen carbonate
pH is the value assigned to the degree of acidity, neutrality or alkalinity of a substance
The lower the HCO_3 value, the lower the pH value.
Total hardness is Ca+Mg
Ca is Calcium (a solid, metal)
Mg is Magnesium (a solid, metal)

When water is heated, HCO_3 disintegrates into CO_3, CO_2 and H_2O
CO_2 (acid gas) evaporates when heated, because it is a gas. The acidity rises towards alkaline.
Tap water usually is too alkaline for tasty tea.

Flavor wheel

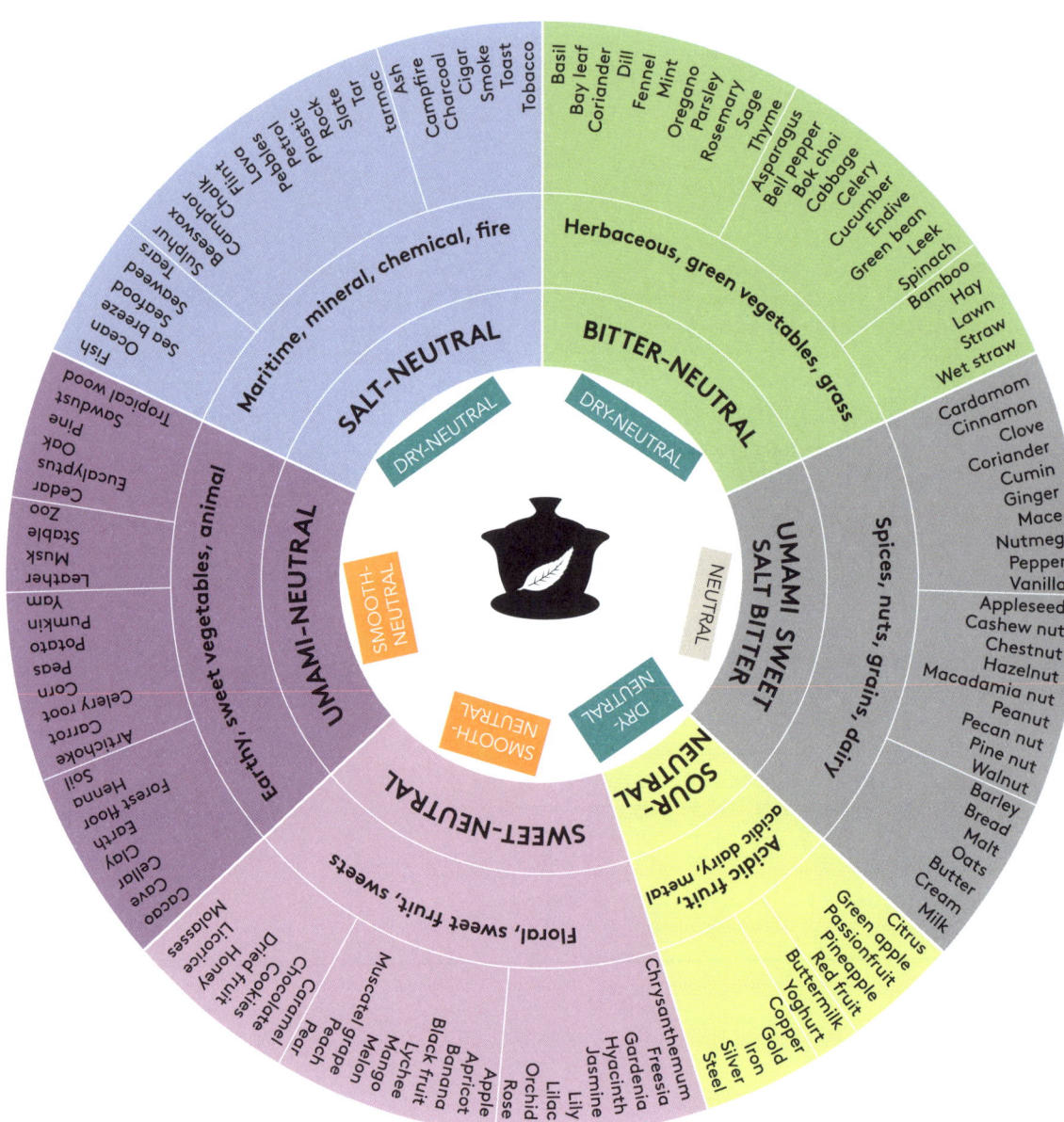

In this flavor wheel you will find a selection of the most common aromas one might taste in tea.

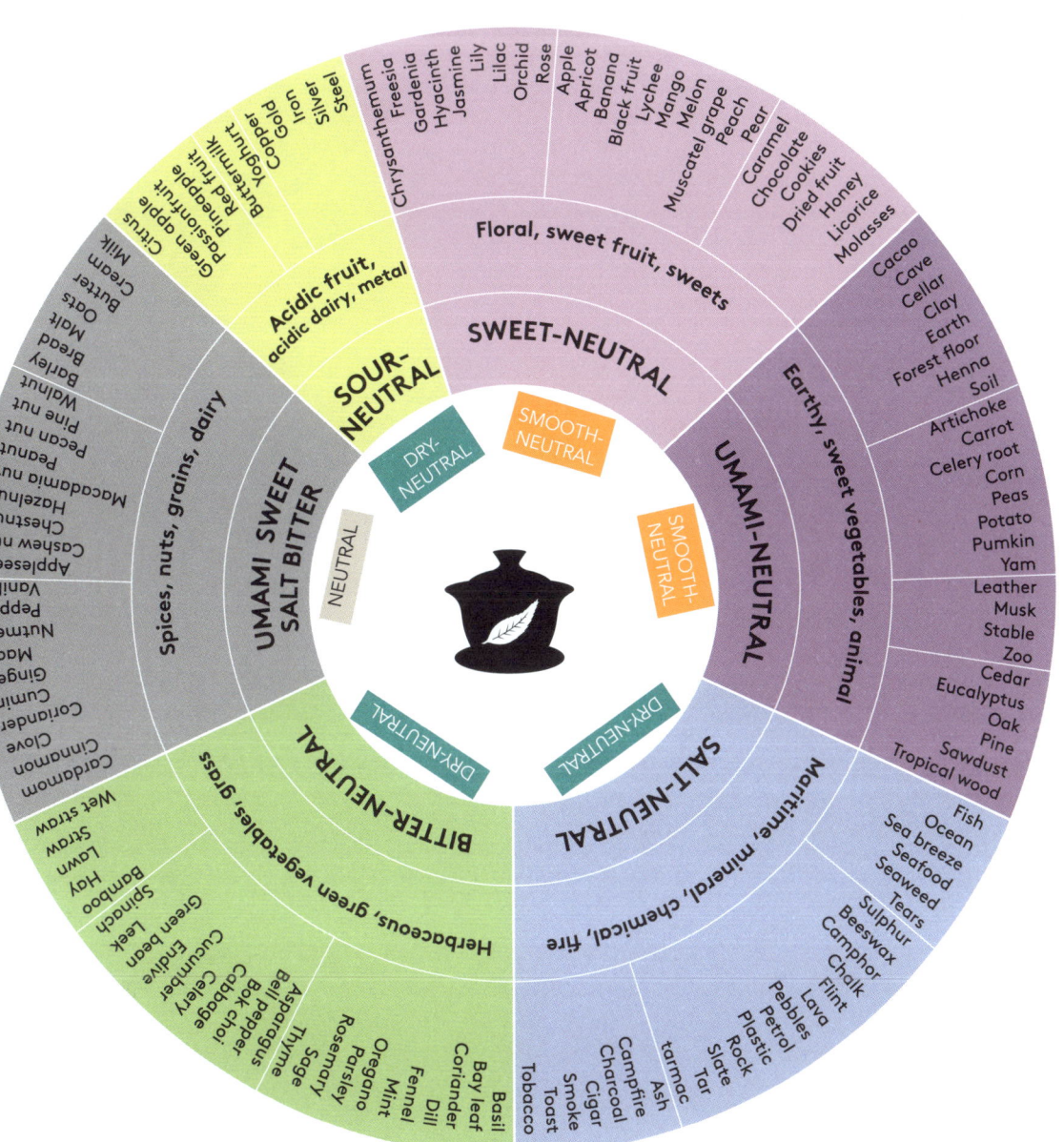

Example form for tasting notes

DESCRIPTION	TEA			
Name of tea				
Type of tea				
Flush, year				
Country of origin				
Other remarks				
Steeping method	WESTERN ○	EASTERN ○	FOOLPROOF METHOD ○	COLD BREW ○
	Weight of dry tea .... G (OZ.)	**Amount of water** ....DL (FL.OZ)	**Temperature** ....°C ....°F	**Steeping time** .... MIN/S

TEXTURE		TASTES		INTENSITY	
SMOOTH	○○○○○	SWEET	○○○○○	XS	○
DRY	○○○○○	UMAMI	○○○○○	S	○
NEUTRAL	○○○○○	SOUR	○○○○○	M	○
BOTH	○○○○○	BITTER	○○○○○	L	○
		SALT	○○○○○	XL	○

FLAVOR TYPE		EFFECT
BRIGHT	○○○○○	
RICH	○○○○○	
NEUTRAL	○○○○○	
BOTH	○○○○○	
MAIN NOTES		
FLAVOR PROFILE		

DESCRIPTION	TEA			
Name of tea				
Type of tea				
Flush, year				
Country of origin				
Other remarks				
Steeping method	WESTERN ○	EASTERN ○	FOOLPROOF METHOD ○	COLD BREW ○
	Weight of dry tea .... G (OZ.)	**Amount of water** ....DL (FL.OZ)	**Temperature** ....°C ....°F	**Steeping time** .... MIN/S

TEXTURE		TASTES		INTENSITY	
SMOOTH	○○○○○	SWEET	○○○○○	XS	○
DRY	○○○○○	UMAMI	○○○○○	S	○
NEUTRAL	○○○○○	SOUR	○○○○○	M	○
BOTH	○○○○○	BITTER	○○○○○	L	○
		SALT	○○○○○	XL	○

FLAVOR TYPE		EFFECT
BRIGHT	○○○○○	
RICH	○○○○○	
NEUTRAL	○○○○○	
BOTH	○○○○○	
MAIN NOTES		
FLAVOR PROFILE		

Example form for tasting notes tea, wine and food

DESCRIPTION	TEA	WINE	FOOD
Names tea, wine, food			
Type of tea, wine			
Flush, year			
Country of origin			
Other remarks			
Steeping method	WESTERN ○ EASTERN ○	FOOLPROOF METHOD ○	COLD BREW ○
	Weight of dry tea .... G (OZ.)	Amount of water ....DL (FL.OZ)	Temperature ....°C ....°F	Steeping time .... MIN/S

TEXTURE		TASTES		INTENSITY	
SMOOTH	○○○○○	SWEET	○○○○○	XS	○
DRY	○○○○○	UMAMI	○○○○○	S	○
NEUTRAL	○○○○○	SOUR	○○○○○	M	○
BOTH	○○○○○	BITTER	○○○○○	L	○
		SALT	○○○○○	XL	○

FLAVOR TYPE		EFFECT
BRIGHT	○○○○○	
RICH	○○○○○	
NEUTRAL	○○○○○	
BOTH	○○○○○	
MAIN NOTES		
FLAVOR PROFILE		

DESCRIPTION	TEA	WINE	FOOD
Names tea, wine, food			
Type of tea, wine			
Flush, year			
Country of origin			
Other remarks			
Steeping method	WESTERN ○ EASTERN ○	FOOLPROOF METHOD ○	COLD BREW ○
	Weight of dry tea .... G (OZ.)	Amount of water ....DL (FL.OZ)	Temperature ....°C ....°F	Steeping time .... MIN/S

TEXTURE		TASTES		INTENSITY	
SMOOTH	○○○○○	SWEET	○○○○○	XS	○
DRY	○○○○○	UMAMI	○○○○○	S	○
NEUTRAL	○○○○○	SOUR	○○○○○	M	○
BOTH	○○○○○	BITTER	○○○○○	L	○
		SALT	○○○○○	XL	○

FLAVOR TYPE		EFFECT
BRIGHT	○○○○○	
RICH	○○○○○	
NEUTRAL	○○○○○	
BOTH	○○○○○	
MAIN NOTES		
FLAVOR PROFILE		

Example form for tasting notes tea and food

DESCRIPTION	TEA			FOOD	
Name of tea - food					
Type of tea					
Flush, year					
Country of origin					
Other remarks					
Steeping method	WESTERN ○	EASTERN ○	FOOLPROOF METHOD ○	COLD BREW ○	
	Weight of dry tea .... G (OZ.)	Amount of water ....DL (FL.OZ)	Temperature ....°C ....°F	Steeping time .... MIN/S	
TEXTURE		**TASTES**		**INTENSITY**	
SMOOTH	○○○○○	SWEET	○○○○○	XS	○
DRY	○○○○○	UMAMI	○○○○○	S	○
NEUTRAL	○○○○○	SOUR	○○○○○	M	○
BOTH	○○○○○	BITTER	○○○○○	L	○
		SALT	○○○○○	XL	○
FLAVOR TYPE		**EFFECT**			
BRIGHT	○○○○○				
RICH	○○○○○				
NEUTRAL	○○○○○				
BOTH	○○○○○				
MAIN NOTES					
FLAVOR PROFILE					

DESCRIPTION	TEA			FOOD	
Name of tea - food					
Type of tea					
Flush, year					
Country of origin					
Other remarks					
Steeping method	WESTERN ○	EASTERN ○	FOOLPROOF METHOD ○	COLD BREW ○	
	Weight of dry tea .... G (OZ.)	Amount of water ....DL (FL.OZ)	Temperature ....°C ....°F	Steeping time .... MIN/S	
TEXTURE		**TASTES**		**INTENSITY**	
SMOOTH	○○○○○	SWEET	○○○○○	XS	○
DRY	○○○○○	UMAMI	○○○○○	S	○
NEUTRAL	○○○○○	SOUR	○○○○○	M	○
BOTH	○○○○○	BITTER	○○○○○	L	○
		SALT	○○○○○	XL	○
FLAVOR TYPE		**EFFECT**			
BRIGHT	○○○○○				
RICH	○○○○○				
NEUTRAL	○○○○○				
BOTH	○○○○○				
MAIN NOTES					
FLAVOR PROFILE					

Tasting notes tea and food pairing

FISH AND SEAFOOD	
FOOD	
Chinese mussels, with a ginger-lime sauce of mayonnaise and crème fraîche. **Flavor profile:** dry and smooth, rich and bright, umami, salt, a bit sweet, a bit sour, a bit bitter, maritime, dairy, fruity, M	
TEA	
Sencha, *Kochi, Shikoku prefecture, Japan* **Flavor profile:** smooth to dry, rich and bright, sweet, bitter, umami, vegetal, herbaceous, maritime, fruity, M	**Huang Da Cha,** *Jinzhai County, Anhui Province, China* **Flavor profile:** smooth, ends dry, rich, sweet, umami, vegetal, earthy, fruity, grains, nutty, sweets, M
Effect: The mussels acquire more umami, all flavors mingle. The tea becomes softer, sweeter and stands up to the food.	**Effect:** The mussels acquire more umami, become sweeter and fuller. All flavors come together. The tea becomes sweeter, softer, but stands up to the food.
FOOD	
Clams, with lemongrass and ginger. **Flavor profile:** smooth and neutral, rich and bright, salt, sour, slightly sweet, maritime, herbaceous, spices, M	
TEA	
Anji Bai Cha, *Huzhou City, Anji County, Zhejiang province, China* **Flavor profile:** smooth, rich, sweet, slightly sour, umami, dairy, floral, nutty, sweets, vegetal, fruity, S-M	**Wen Shan Baozhong,** *Taipei County, Taiwan* **Flavor profile:** smooth and dry, rich and bright, sweet, slightly bitter, dairy, floral, fruity, vegetal, herbaceous, grains, nutty, spices, M
Effect: The food acquires nutty notes, becomes fresh, with citrus notes. The tea acquires more umami, becomes brighter. The clams acquire vegetal notes, the aftertaste is bright, with a bit of mint. Tea and food come together, but both remain noticeable.	**Effect:** The tea adds vegetal and floral notes to the food, making it taste sweeter and stronger. The tea acquires more umami, more depth. The aftertaste is refreshing, floral.
FOOD	
Haddock, fried, with roasted almonds, juice and zest of Bergamot citrus fruit, steamed, but still crunchy Brussels sprouts and boiled potatoes. **Flavor profile:** neutral, rich and bright, umami, salt, bitter, sweet, maritime, earthy, fruity, floral, nutty, vegetal, M	
TEA	
Bi Luo Chun, *Dong Shan, Jiangsu Province, China* **Flavor profile:** smooth, rich, later dry and bright, sweet, slightly bitter, umami, vegetal, fruity, grains nutty, spices, mineral, M	**Huo Shan Huang Ya,** *Huo Shan County, Anhui Province, China* **Flavor profile:** smooth, bright, sweet, sour, umami, vegetal, fruity, earthy, grains, nutty, mineral, M
Effect: The fish remains succulent, acquires more umami and vegetal notes, The bergamot adds a slightly floral layer. The Brussels sprouts become nutty, floral, softer and bright. The tea becomes sweeter, brighter, more floral. Clean palate.	**Effect:** The fish remains succulent, becomes sweeter. The bergamot adds a slightly floral layer. The Brussels sprouts become nutty and sweeter. The tea becomes brighter, herbaceous.

FISH AND SEAFOOD

FOOD

Halibut in orange-tarragon-mustard-cream sauce, with Chinese cabbage, mushrooms, shallot, garlic, Italian parsley, zest of orange, mashed potatoes.
Flavor profile: smooth, rich, sour, umami, sweet, salt, maritime, earthy, vegetal, herbaceous, fruity, spices, dairy, M-L

TEA

Yue Guang Bai, *Yunnan, China* *Flavor profile:* smooth, rich and bright, sweet, earthy, fruity, spices, floral, L	**Sheng (raw) Pu Erh,** *Lincang, Yunnan Province, China* *Flavor profile:* aged: neutral to smooth, rich and bright, sweet, sour, bitter, umami, earthy, vegetal, animal, herbaceous, spices, floral, fruity, M-L
Effect: The tea stands up to the food, all flavors are deepened, sweeter, of both food and tea.	**Effect:** The tea enhances the cabbage, citrus and mushrooms, highlights umami, makes the sauce brighter, lighter, while the food makes the tea rounder, softer, sweeter, earthier.

FOOD

Langoustines, with harira (spicy Moroccan tomato-chickpea soup) and philo pastry.
Flavor profile: neutral and dry, rich, umami, salt, sweet, sour, maritime, vegetal, spices, grains, L-XL

TEA

Kabusecha, *Wazuka, Kyôto prefecture, Japan* *Flavor profile:* smooth, round, rich, mellow, umami, sweet, vegetal, herbaceous, fruity, dairy, maritime, L-XL	**Huang Da Cha,** *Jinzhai County, Anhui Province, China* *Flavor profile:* smooth, ends dry, rich, sweet, umami, vegetal, earthy, fruity, grains, nutty, sweets, M
Effect: The langoustines are enhanced, become sweeter, with more depth, with a touch of vegetal notes to them. The tea becomes rounder, sweeter, acquires more umami.	**Effect:** The langoustines are enhanced, become sweeter, with more depth, with a touch of nutty notes. The tea becomes rounder, sweeter, acquires more umami. Aftertaste is clean, fresh.

FOOD

Meagre (fish) with lobster, mushrooms, mayonnaise with seaweed and Jerusalem artichokes.
Flavor profile: smooth and neutral, rich, umami, sweet, salt, slightly bitter, maritime, earthy, vegetal, M-L

TEA

Yue Guang Bai, *Yunnan, China* *Flavor profile:* smooth, rich and bright, sweet, earthy, fruity, spices, floral, sweets, L	**Dong Ding,** *Mei Shan, Nantou, Taiwan* *Flavor profile:* smooth and dry, rich and bright, sweet, slightly bitter, nutty, mineral, floral, sweets, vegetal, herbaceous, fruity, dairy, M-L
Effect: The food is enhanced, acquired more umami, the fish becomes less fishy, but also a bit drier, so undercook the fish a bit in this case. The tea becomes sweeter and softer.	**Effect:** The seafood becomes lighter, brighter, sweeter, the Jerusalem artichokes acquire floral and nutty notes. The tea acquires more umami and becomes fuller, with a bright, vegetal edge.

FISH AND SEAFOOD

FOOD
Oysters, natural, raw. **Flavor profile:** *smooth, later dry, rich, later bright, sweet, salt, umami, maritime, mineral, L*

TEA	
Long Jing, *West Lake, Hangzhou City, Zhejiang province, China* **Flavor profile:** *smooth, rich, later a bit bright, round, creamy, sweet, umami, vegetal, fruity, grains, nutty, maritime, M*	**Wen Shan Baozhong** *Taipei County, Taiwan* **Flavor profile:** *smooth and dry, rich and bright, sweet, slightly bitter, dairy, floral, fruity, vegetal, herbaceous, grains, nutty, spices, M*
Effect: The oysters become sweeter, acquire more depth, the tea acquires more umami and becomes almost salty.	**Effect:** The oysters become more succulent, acquire more flavor, more depth. The tea becomes brighter, fruitier. Once the tea is cooled off, the oyster tastes more complex, acquires more umami, like beef stock, and a bit oily, almost like bacon. All flavors come together, with a clean and fresh finish.

FOOD
Pad Thai, with prawns, snow peas, mushrooms, bell pepper, fennel, mint, coriander, Thai basil, sesame seeds. **Flavor profile:** *neutral and smooth, rich and bright, bitter, sweet, salt, umami, maritime, earthy, grains, spices, herbaceous, nutty, vegetal, L*

TEA	
Jin Xuan #12, *Alishan, Taiwan* **Flavor profile:** *smooth, silky, rich, sweet, slightly bitter, dairy, floral, fruity, vegetal, herbaceous, M*	**Sheng (raw) Pu Erh,** *Lincang, Yunnan Province, China* **Flavor profile:** *aged: neutral to smooth, rich and bright, sweet, sour, bitter, umami, earthy, vegetal, animal, herbaceous, spices, floral, fruity, M-L*
Effect: The fish becomes softer, more succulent, the food in total enhanced. The tea becomes fruitier, brighter, while the lychee and coconut notes are stronger. The vegetables become brighter, more herbaceous, the noodles sweeter.	**Effect:** The tea makes the prawns sweeter and brighter, enhances the vegetables and the noodles, while becoming very bright and vivacious itself, with mint and basil in the background.

FOOD
Raw scallops, slightly blackened, with roasted cauliflower, avocado cream, sea lettuce, crunchy squid ink, harissa-oil (Harissa is Moroccan chili paste). **Flavor profile:** *neutral, rich, bright, umami, salt, sweet, maritime, earthy, vegetal, herbaceous, spices, L*

TEA	
Tie Guan Yin, *light roast, light oolong, Anxi, China* **Flavor profile:** *smooth and dry, bright, sweet, sour, bitter, floral, vegetal, herbaceous, fruity, mineral, metallic, M*	**Huang Da Cha,** *Jinzhai County, Anhui Province, China* **Flavor profile:** *smooth, ends dry, rich, sweet, umami, vegetal, earthy, fruity, grains, nutty, sweets, M*
Effect: The tea adds a floral layer, making the food lighter, brighter. The tea becomes fuller, creamier and acquires more umami. All flavors mingle but remain noticeable.	**Effect:** The scallops become fuller, sweeter, creamy. The tea becomes softer, brighter and sweeter, with a maritime note added.

FISH AND SEAFOOD
FOOD
Salmon-cucumber rolls, with chervil mayonnaise, green leaves, dill, coriander blossom, dill blossom. *Flavor profile:* neutral, neutral, umami, sweet, salt, animal, spices, grains, vegetal, herbaceous, M-L

TEA	
Sencha, *Kochi, Shikoku prefecture, Japan* **Flavor profile:** smooth to dry, rich and bright, sweet, bitter, umami, vegetal, herbaceous, maritime, fruity, M	**Ceylon Pusselawa,** *black tea, Pusselawa, Sri Lanka* **Flavor profile:** a bit smooth, dry, bright, sour, bitter, floral, fruity, earthy, M-L
Effect: The cucumber matches the notes of cucumber in the tea, the smoked sockeye salmon connects with the notes of seaweed in the tea. The tea is enhanced.	**Effect:** The tea becomes fuller, softer, sweeter, connects all flavors, enhances the food.

FOOD
Smoked mackerel, with roasted beetroot, boiled potatoes, lime mayonnaise, zest of lime, lollo rosso, lollo biondo, capers, toasted pine nuts, mint, ginger, Italian parsley. *Flavor profile:* smooth, oily, neutral and dry, rich and bright, umami, sour, bitter, salt, sweet, maritime, earthy, vegetal, nutty, fruity, herbaceous, spices, M-L

TEA	
Ceylon Nuwara Eliya, *Nuwara Eliya, Sri Lanka* **Flavor profile:** dry to astringent, brisk, bright, sour, fruity, earthy, herbaceous, spices, M-L	**Hōjicha,** *Bancha, roasted green tea, Tsukigase, Nara prefecture, Japan* **Flavor profile:** smooth, later on dry, rich, sweet, umami, nutty, grains, fruity, vegetal, herbaceous, maritime, earthy, M
Effect: The tea becomes mild, bright and soft. The beetroot becomes less sweet, acquires more umami and depth, capers, mint and pine nuts are enhanced. The mayonnaise becomes fresher, the fish less fishy, softer. Enhancement of smokiness.	**Effect:** The tea tones down the sharpness of the lime, makes the fish lighter, brighter, the beetroot less sweet, the potatoes and mint enhanced and brings all flavors together. The tea becomes creamy, sweeter, with stronger maritime notes.

FOOD
Sock eye salmon, with ricotta-lemon ravioli, broccoli in a white wine cream sauce with garlic, red onion, lemon juice and basil. *Flavor profile:* neutral and smooth, rich and bright, umami, sour, sweet, salt, animal, earthy, fruity, vegetal, smoky, L-XL

TEA	
Wen Shan Baozhong, *Taipei County, Taiwan* **Flavor profile:** smooth and dry, rich and bright, sweet, slightly bitter, dairy, floral, fruity, vegetal, herbaceous, grains, nutty, spices, M	**Earl Grey,** *black tea, scented with Bergamot citrus, blend* **Flavor profile:** dry, rich and bright, sweet, umami, floral, fruity, earthy, M-L
Effect: The tea enhanced mainly lemon and basil, softened the fish, made it less salty and creamy, connected all flavors and incorporated them, while still remaining noticeable, bright and floral.	**Effect:** The tea brings all flavors together, makes the pasta lighter, fruitier, softens the salmon. The tea acquires more depth and becomes fuller, softer.

VEGETARIAN FOOD	
FOOD	
Beet wellington, vegan, marinated and dried beet root in pastry, with mixed mushrooms-tomato-sauce, soy sauce, beet juice syrup and creamy cashew sauce. **Flavor profile:** smooth, rich, umami, sweet, sour, salty, earthy, nutty, grains, L	
TEA	
Da Hong Pao, dark rock oolong, Wuyi Shan, Fujian, China **Flavor profile:** smooth, ends a bit dry, rich, sweet, sour, umami, fruity, floral, sweets, earthy, herbaceous, grains, nutty, spices, mineral, L-XL	**Shu (cooked) Pu-Erh,** post-fermented tea, China **Flavor profile:** smooth, round, rich, sweet, umami, earthy, animal, sweets, vegetal, L-XL
Effect: The food acquires more depth, becomes lighter, fresher. The tea becomes sweeter, fuller. Tea and food do not mingle, but do match harmoniously.	**Effect:** Both tea and food acquire more depth, become earthier, sweeter, the mushrooms are enhanced. The aftertaste is clean.
FOOD	
Broccoli with pesto, served with tagliatelle. **Flavor profile:** smooth and neutral, rich, umami, bitter, salt, vegetal, grains, herbaceous, nutty, M-L	
TEA	
Hōjicha, roasted green tea, Tsukigase, Nara prefecture, Japan **Flavor profile:** smooth, later on dry, rich, sweet, umami, nutty, grains, fruity, vegetal, herbaceous, maritime, earthy, M	**Tie Guan Yin light roast,** light oolong, Anxi, China **Flavor profile:** smooth and dry, bright, sweet, bitter, sour, floral, vegetal, herbaceous, fruity, mineral, sometimes metallic, M
Effect: The tea becomes sweeter and softer, the food lighter, brighter, slightly nutty and it acquires more umami. The broccoli tastes softer, more subtle. All flavors come together.	**Effect:** The food becomes lighter, with a hint of floral, fruity and nutty notes, the basil and pasta are enhanced, the broccoli becomes sweeter. The tea becomes more vegetal, herbaceous, softer.
FOOD	
Brussels sprouts, roasted, with melted blue cheese, fried shallots and a dollop of crème fraîche, baked potatoes. **Flavor profile:** neutral, rich, umami, bitter, sweet, earthy, vegetal, dairy, M-L	
TEA	
Keemun, black tea, Qimen County, China **Flavor profile:** smooth, ends a bit dry, rich, sweet, umami, fruity, floral, grains, animal, sweets, earthy, L	**Gunpowder,** green tea, Zhejiang Province, China **Flavor profile:** neutral-bright, dry, sweet, bitter, sour, fruity, floral, earthy, vegetal, herbaceous, grains, nutty, fruity, mineral, metal, M-L
Effect: All flavors come together and are enhanced, acquire more umami. The tea becomes sweeter, brighter, rounder. Once the tea is cooled down, the cheese jumps out. In the aftertaste both tea and cheese are noticeable, rich and bright at the same time.	**Effect:** The food becomes lighter, brighter, the potatoes and the vegetal notes enhanced. The tea becomes sweeter, rounder, with more umami.

VEGETARIAN FOOD	
FOOD	
Cauliflower, with egg, yoghurt, tarragon and onion, recipe: Ottolenghi *Flavor profile:* neutral, rich and bright, sweet, umami, sour, earthy, dairy, herbaceous, M	
TEA	
Wen Shan Baozhong, *Taipei County, Taiwan* *Flavor profile:* smooth and dry, rich and bright, sweet, slightly bitter, dairy, floral, fruity, vegetal, herbaceous, grains, nutty, spices, M	**Ruby #18,** *Sun Moon Lake, Nantou County, Taiwan* *Flavor profile:* smooth, rich, sweet, earthy, herbaceous, fruity, sweets, spices, M
Effect: The tea adds floral notes to the food, herbs and pepper are enhanced, the dish becomes lighter, brighter, sharper. The tea acquires more umami, becomes sweeter, fuller. Clean and fresh palate.	**Effect:** The food becomes sweeter, softer, the spices are enhanced, acquires notes of cinnamon from the tea. The tea becomes less sweet, acquires more umami, more depth.
FOOD	
Cauliflower cream, with roasted, thinly sliced almonds, hazelnut-vanilla oil, pimentón and cacao nibs. *Flavor profile:* smooth, rich, creamy, sweet, umami, earthy, dairy, M	
TEA	
Da Hong Pao, *dark rock oolong, Wuyi Shan, Fujian, China* *Flavor profile:* smooth, ends a bit dry, rich, sweet, sour, umami, fruity, floral, sweets, earthy, herbaceous, grains, nutty, spices, mineral, L-XL	**Sheng (raw) Pu Erh,** *Lincang, Yunnan Province, China* *Flavor profile:* aged: neutral to smooth, rich and bright, sweet, sour, bitter, umami, earthy, vegetal, animal, herbaceous, spices, floral, fruity, M-L
Effect: The tea is dominant at first, then almonds and cauliflower return and stronger at that. The tea becomes sweeter, rounder, with notes of peach and licorice.	**Effect:** The tea enhances the almonds and mushrooms, highlights umami, makes the cauliflower brighter, lighter, while the food makes the tea rounder, softer, sweeter, earthier.
FOOD	
Cauliflower roasted, with toasted cumin seeds, olive oil, red onion ringlets, turmeric, cooked potatoes, grilled with cheese. *Flavor profile:* smooth and neutral, rich and neutral, umami, sweet, earthy, vegetal, dairy, spices, M	
TEA	
Long Jing, *West Lake, Hangzhou City, Zhejiang province, China* *Flavor profile:* smooth, rich, later a bit bright, round, creamy, sweet, umami, vegetal, fruity, grains, nutty, maritime, M	**Huang Da Cha,** *Jinzhai County, Anhui Province, China* *Flavor profile:* smooth, ends dry, rich, sweet, umami, vegetal, earthy, fruity, grains, nutty, sweets, M
Effect: The cumin, cheese, potato and onion are enhanced, the cauliflower remains the same. The tea becomes fuller, sweeter and acquires more umami.	**Effect:** The cumin, cheese, potato and onion are enhanced, the cauliflower becomes sweeter and earthier. The tea becomes fuller, sweeter and acquires more umami.

VEGETARIAN FOOD	
FOOD	
Cauliflower tandoori in yoghurt marinade with roasted tomatoes, cashew nuts and caramelized red onion. *Flavor profile:* neutral, rich and bright, sweet, umami, sour, earthy, dairy, nutty, vegetal, M	
TEA	
Jin Xuan #12, *Alishan, Taiwan* **Flavor profile:** smooth, silky, rich, sweet, slightly bitter, dairy, floral, fruity, vegetal, herbaceous, M	**Lapsang Souchong,** *unsmoked, Wuyishan, Fuijan, China* **Flavor profile:** smooth, rich, sweet, umami, vegetal, mineral, earthy, sweets, fruity, floral, M-L
Effect: Enhancement of onion and spices, while the dish all over becomes lighter, fresher. The tea becomes sweeter, softer, more floral.	**Effect:** The tea makes the food deeper, adding spices and cacao, enhancing nuts and onions. All flavors blend together. The tea acquires more umami and depth, becomes sweeter.
FOOD	
Courgette salad, with mint, coriander, sesame seeds and a miso -honey-lemon dressing, recipe: Yvette van Boven **Flavor profile:** neutral, rich, a bit bright, umami, bitter, sweet, sour, M	
TEA	
Dong Ding, *Mei Shan, Nantou, Taiwan* **Flavor profile:** smooth, and dry, rich and bright, sweet, slightly bitter, nutty, mineral, floral, sweets, vegetal, herbaceous, fruity, dairy, M-L	**Yue Guang Bai,** *Yunnan, China* **Flavor profile:** smooth, rich and bright, sweet, earthy, fruity, spices, floral, sweets, L
Effect: Courgette and dressing become deeper, warmer, more intense. The tea becomes fruitier, brighter.	**Effect:** The food becomes sweeter, softer, the spices are enhanced, acquires notes of cinnamon from the tea. The tea becomes less sweet, acquires more umami, more depth.
FOOD	
Fennel, beet root, red onion, sweet potato and garlic, roasted, served with a sauce of thick yoghurt, (10% fat) roasted garlic, mint, zest and juice of lemon, roasted, salted pecan nuts. *Flavor profile:* smooth rich, bright, sweet, umami, salt, sour, M-L	
TEA	
Earl Grey, *black tea, scented with Bergamot citrus, blend* **Flavor profile:** dry, rich and bright, sweet, umami, floral, fruity, earthy, M-L	**Yue Guang Bai,** *Yunnan, China* **Flavor profile:** smooth, rich and bright, sweet, earthy, fruity, spices, floral, sweets, L
Effect: The tea brings all flavors together, makes the food lighter, brighter, fruitier. The tea acquires more depth, more umami.	**Effect:** The entire dish becomes fuller, sweeter, acquires more umami. Later on it becomes fresher. The fennel becomes buttery, lemon and mint enhanced, clean and fresh palate. The tea acquires a bit of mint.

VEGETARIAN FOOD

FOOD
Parmigiana di Melanzane, fried aubergine, tomato sauce, mozzarella di buffala, Parmesan cheese, basil ***Flavor profile:*** *neutral, rich, sweet, umami, salt, sour, vegetal, fruity, dairy, earthy, herbaceous, M-L*

TEA	
Dong Ding, *Mei Shan, Nantou, Taiwan* ***Flavor profile:*** *smooth, and dry, rich and bright, sweet, slightly bitter, nutty, mineral, floral, sweets, vegetal, herbaceous, fruity, dairy, M-L*	**Earl Grey,** *black tea, scented with Bergamot citrus, blend* ***Flavor profile:*** *dry, rich and bright, sweet, umami, floral, fruity, earthy, M-L*
Effect: The food becomes lighter, brighter, nutty, the cheese is enhanced. The tea acquires more umami and becomes fuller, softer, creamy.	**Effect:** The food's acidic elements are enhanced, it becomes lighter, brighter, and the food acquires floral notes. The tea becomes more complex, acquires depth and umami.

FOOD
Portobello, stuffed, with broccoli, tomato, onion, garlic, egg, ricotta, crème fraîche, hazelnuts, hard cheese. ***Flavor profile:*** *neutral, rich, sweet, umami, salt, sour, earthy, vegetal, fruity, dairy, nutty, M-L*

TEA	
Shu Pu-Erh, *post-fermented cooked tea, China* ***Flavor profile:*** *smooth, round, rich, sweet, umami, earthy, animal, sweets, vegetal, L-XL*	**Lapsang Souchong,** *unsmoked, Wuyishan, Fuijan, China* ***Flavor profile:*** *smooth, rich, sweet, umami, vegetal, mineral, earthy, sweets, fruity, floral, M-L*
Effect: The mushroom is enhanced, the broccoli and tomato become softer, sweeter, the tomato acquires more umami, the cheese becomes sweeter, creamy. The tea becomes brighter, less sweet, more earthy.	**Effect:** The mushroom becomes sweeter, fresh, almost. The tea brings all flavors together, makes them deeper, taking off the edge of cheese and pepper. The crème fraîche becomes creamier. The notes of cinnamon in the tea are enhanced, the tea becomes brighter.

FOOD
Quiche, with Emmenthaler cheese and caramelized onions. ***Flavor profile:*** *dry, later smooth, rich, sweet, umami, salt, earthy, vegetal, fruity, M-L*

TEA	
Darjeeling, *first flush, Darjeeling, India* ***Flavor profile:*** *dry, bright, crisp, sweet, bitter, fruity, sweets, grains, vegetal, herbaceous, floral, M*	**Hōjicha,** *Bancha, roasted green tea, Tsukigase, Nara prefecture, Japan* ***Flavor profile:*** *smooth, later on dry, rich, sweet, umami, nutty, grains, fruity, vegetal, herbaceous, maritime, earthy, M*
Effect: The quiche as a whole is enhanced, the cheese becomes fuller, creamier, with more umami. The tea becomes sweeter, fuller and creamy.	**Effect:** The quiche acquires nutty notes, becomes lighter, brighter and acquires more umami. The tea becomes fuller, sweeter, with notes of toast and cookies.

VEGETARIAN FOOD

FOOD
Stir fried Brussels sprouts and noodles, with cucumber, mint, coriander, salted peanuts, spring onions, lime juice, soy sauce, sesame oil, garlic, recipe: Karin Luiten ***Flavor profile:*** *smooth rich, a bit bright, umami, bitter, sweet, salt, sour, vegetal, nutty, earthy, fruity, L*

TEA	
Kamairicha, *Ureshino, Kyushu, Japan* ***Flavor profile:*** *slightly dry, ends smooth and bright, sweet, slightly bitter, umami, floral, sweets, grains, vegetal, herbaceous, fruity, dairy, M-L*	**Yue Guang Bai,** *Yunnan, China* ***Flavor profile:*** *smooth, rich and bright, sweet, earthy, fruity, spices, floral, sweets, L*
Effect: The entire salad is enhanced, acquires more umami, while the tea becomes brighter and softer, mellower. All flavors blend and become an explosion of umami.	**Effect:** At first nothing much changes, but after a while the tea brings all flavors together and the finish is intense, with all flavors jumping up. The aftertaste is bright, refreshing, light. The tea becomes sweeter and brighter.

FOOD
Risotto with leek and mixed mushrooms, onion, garlic, hazelnuts, Parmesan cheese, butter. ***Flavor profile:*** *smooth rich, umami, bitter, sweet, salt, vegetal, grains, dairy, nutty, earthy, M*

TEA	
Huang Da Cha, *Jinzhai County, Anhui Province, China* ***Flavor profile:*** *smooth, ends dry, rich, sweet, umami, vegetal, earthy, fruity, grains, nutty, sweets, M*	**Wen Shan Baozhong,** *Taipei County, Taiwan* ***Flavor profile:*** *smooth and dry, rich and bright, sweet, slightly bitter, dairy, floral, fruity, vegetal, herbaceous, grains, nutty, spices, M*
Effect: The rice acquires more depth, more flavor and umami, becomes nutty. The leek becomes creamier, the mushrooms deeper and nutty. The tea becomes sweeter, fuller, acquires more umami.	**Effect:** The risotto acquires more umami, becomes lighter, brighter. The tea becomes fuller, sweeter, creamier and brings all flavors together. Fresh and clean palate.

FOOD
Sauerkraut, with mashed potatoes and mashed celeriac, sprinkled with chopped walnuts. ***Flavor profile:*** *smooth and dry, rich and bright, sour, bitter, umami, sweet, salt, vegetal, nutty, earthy, M*

TEA	
Huang Da Cha, *Jinzhai County, Anhui Province, China* ***Flavor profile:*** *smooth, bright, sweet, sour, umami, vegetal, fruity, earthy, grains, nutty, mineral, M*	**Hōjicha,** *Bancha, roasted green tea, Tsukigase, Nara prefecture, Japan* ***Flavor profile:*** *smooth, later on dry, rich, sweet, umami, nutty, grains, fruity, vegetal, herbaceous, maritime, earthy, M*
Effect: The tea makes the food less acidic, softer and enhances the celeriac root. The tea becomes fruitier, brighter, with a hint of fresh and fruity acidity.	**Effect:** The tea makes the food less acidic, softer and enhances the celeriac root. The nuts become sweeter. The tea becomes sweeter, rounder and softer, its flavor is added to the food.

VEGETARIAN FOOD	
FOOD	
Spinach, stir fried in garlic oil, with juice and zest of lemon, tarragon, hard cheese, boiled potatoes, a soft boiled egg and Maldon salt flakes. **Flavor profile:** neutral and dry, neutral and bright, umami, sour, bitter, salt, vegetal, fruity, dairy, herbaceous, M	
TEA	
Woojeoncha, *Jeju, Korea* **Flavor profile:** smooth, ends a bit dry, rich, creamy, sweet, umami, vegetal, earthy, fruity, nutty, dairy, mineral, maritime, M	**Jin Xuan #12,** *Alishan, Taiwan* **Flavor profile:** smooth, silky, rich, sweet, slightly bitter, dairy, floral, fruity, vegetal, herbaceous, M
Effect: The tea enhances garlic, egg and tarragon, makes the potato creamy and the spinach more vegetal. The tea becomes sweeter, brighter and acquires more umami.	**Effect:** The tea makes the spinach softer, rounder, adding floral notes, tones down the acidity of the lemon and enhances the cheese, salt and egg, while becoming more vegetal, more herbaceous and brighter itself.

MEAT AND POULTRY	
FOOD	
Carpaccio with water cress, Parmesan cheese and a dressing of Balsamic vinegar and maple syrup. **Flavor profile:** dry, rich and bright, umami, salt, a bit sweet, a bit sour, a bit bitter, animal, dairy, vegetal, fruity, sweets, L-XL	
TEA	
Shu Pu-Erh, *post-fermented cooked tea, China* **Flavor profile:** smooth, round, rich, sweet, umami, earthy, animal, sweets, vegetal, L-XL	**Assam,** *black tea, India* **Flavor profile:** dry, rich, robust, bold, sweet, bitter, umami, fruity, grains, sweets, earthy, animal, spices, herbaceous, XL
Effect: The food is enhanced, the meat acquires more umami, becomes sweeter, deeper, more intense. The tea becomes brighter, acquires more umami.	**Effect:** The meat and the lettuce become fuller, richer, deeper. The tea becomes softer, fuller, sweeter, less astringent. Bright aftertaste.
FOOD	
Fatteh by Nigella with minced meat, humus, baba ganoush, crispy flatbread, yoghurt-cucumber-mint-garlic sauce, charred bell pepper mixed with olive oil, lemon juice and coarse salt. **Flavor profile:** neutral, rich and bright, umami, sweet, sour, salt, animal, vegetal, grains, dairy, herbaceous, L	
TEA	
Ruby #18, black tea, *Sun Moon Lake, Nantou County, Taiwan* **Flavor profile:** smooth, rich, sweet, earthy, herbaceous, fruity, sweets, spices, M	**Dong Fang Mei Ren,** *dark oolong, Hsinchu County, Taiwan* **Flavor profile:** smooth, ends a bit dry, rich, sweet, floral, fruity, earthy, mineral, spices, M
Effect: The tea tones down the smokiness of the baba ganoush, makes it lighter, brighter, enhances the meat and the sauce, which also acquire more umami. The tea becomes deeper, sweeter, brighter with the yoghurt sauce.	**Effect:** The baba ganoush becomes brighter, lighter, melts together with the tea; clean palate. The meat becomes deeper, the spices enhanced, the bell pepper acquires more umami. The tea becomes sweeter and brighter.

MEAT AND POULTRY

FOOD

Fried bacon alongside Brussels sprouts, mashed with boiled potatoes, onion, garlic and mushrooms.
Flavor profile: *neutral, rich, umami, salt, bitter, sweet, animal, earthy, vegetal, L*

TEA

Tie Guan Yin *light roast, light oolong, Anxi, China* **Flavor profile:** *smooth and dry, bright, sweet, sour, bitter, floral, vegetal, herbaceous, fruity, mineral, metallic, M*	**Sheng (raw) Pu Erh,** *Lincang, Yunnan Province, China* **Flavor profile:** *aged: neutral to smooth, rich and bright, sweet, sour, bitter, umami, earthy, vegetal, animal, herbaceous, spices, floral, fruity, M-L*
Effect: The tea adds a floral layer to the mash, makes it brighter and enhances the bacon. The food makes the tea fuller, sweeter and adds some umami to it.	**Effect:** The tea enhances the bacon, garlic and mushrooms, brings on more umami, makes the mash of sprouts lighter, while the food makes the tea rounder, fuller, sweeter, earthier.

FOOD

Fried bacon alongside sauerkraut, mashed with boiled potatoes and celeriac root and a bit of Dijon mustard.
Flavor profile: *smooth and dry, rich and bright, slightly sharp, sour, umami, sweet, salt, earthy, vegetal, M*

TEA

Hōjicha, *roasted green tea, Tsukigase, Nara prefecture, Japan* **Flavor profile:** *smooth, later on dry, rich, sweet, umami, nutty, grains, fruity, vegetal, herbaceous, maritime, earthy, M*	**Lapsang Souchong,** *black tea, unsmoked, Wuyishan, Fujian, China* **Flavor profile:** *smooth, rich, sweet, umami, vegetal, mineral, earthy, sweets, fruity, floral, M-L*
Effect: The sauerkraut becomes softer, less acidic, the celeriac and bacon are enhanced. The roasting notes of the tea become warmer, stronger, the tea becomes sweeter, rounder and softer. The food acquires the flavor of the tea.	**Effect:** The sauerkraut becomes sweeter, softer, the bacon sweeter and deeper, with a hint of cacao and cinnamon. The tea becomes brighter, acquires more umami and more depth.

FOOD

Köfte in tomato sauce with Lebanese flatbread and yoghurt with mint, garlic, olive oil, lemon juice and cucumber.
Flavor profile: *smooth and dry, rich and bright, chewy and creamy, umami, sweet, sour, salt, animal, fruity, vegetal, grains, dairy, L-XL*

TEA

Da Hong Pao, *dark rock oolong, Wuyi Shan, Fujian, China* **Flavor profile:** *smooth, ends a bit dry, rich, sweet, sour, umami, fruity, floral, sweets, earthy, herbaceous, grains, nutty, spices, mineral, L-XL*	**Assam,** *black tea, second flush, Assam, India* **Flavor profile:** *dry, rich, robust, robust, bold, sweet, bitter, umami, fruity, grains, sweets, earthy, animal, spices, herbaceous, XL*
Effect: The notes of plum compliment the sauce and the meat. The food is enhanced, the tea becomes nutty and acquires more umami. The sum total becomes lighter, brighter.	**Effect:** The tea deepens the sauce, makes the köfte juicy, enhances the spices, the garlic and the bread. The yoghurt makes the tea bright and creamy, full, the other food deepens it.

MEAT AND POULTRY

FOOD

Lamb's neck stew, with Ras el Hanout, roasted root vegetables and couscous with mint and cinnamon.
Flavor profile: smooth and neutral, rich, umami, sweet, animal, earthy, spices, grains, vegetal, M-L

TEA

Mi Lan Xiang Feng Huang Dan Cong, *Chao-zhou, Guangdong province, China* **Flavor profile:** smooth, ends a bit dry, rich, sweet, umami, fruity, vegetal, floral, earthy, grains, sweets, M-L	**Dong Ding,** *Mei Shan, Nantou, Taiwan* **Flavor profile:** smooth and dry, rich and bright, sweet, slightly bitter, nutty, mineral, floral, sweets, vegetal, herbaceous, fruity, dairy, M-L
Effect: The food becomes deeper, more intense. The tea becomes deeper, acquires more umami, a hint of spices.	**Effect:** The spices are enhanced, the food becomes lighter, brighter, sweeter, acquires floral and fruity notes. The tea acquires more umami and becomes fuller, sweeter.

FOOD

Pancetta-chicory rolls, with potatoes, roux and cumin cheese.
Flavor profile: neutral and smooth, rich and bright, bitter, sweet, salt, umami, animal, earthy, dairy, spices, vegetal, L

TEA

Dian Hong, *Yunnan, China* **Flavor profile:** smooth, rich, sweet, umami, earthy, sweets, fruity, nutty, spices, L	**Yue Guang Bai,** *Yunnan, China* **Flavor profile:** smooth, rich and bright, sweet, earthy, fruity, spices, floral, sweets, L
Effect: The chicory becomes sweeter, velvety, the other ingredients acquire more umami, more depth. The tea connects all flavors, softens the texture, while itself becoming more woody, acquiring more umami. Enhancement of its spice notes.	**Effect:** The tea makes the food softer, sweeter and brighter, it cuts the fattiness of the pancetta, enhances cheese and cumin and cleanses the palate. The food makes the tea brighter, less sweet, more vegetal.

FOOD

Pasta Bolognese, with minced meat, chopped basil, green olives, pine nuts and Parmesan cheese.
Flavor profile: neutral, rich, a bit bright, umami, bitter, sweet, sour, animal, vegetal, fruity, herbaceous, dairy, nutty, M

TEA

Ruby #18, *black tea, Sun Moon Lake, Nantou County, Taiwan* **Flavor profile:** smooth, rich, sweet, earthy, herbaceous, fruity, sweets, spices, M	**Wen Shan Baozhong,** *Taipei County, Taiwan* **Flavor profile:** smooth and dry, rich and bright, sweet, slightly bitter, dairy, floral, fruity, vegetal, herbaceous, grains, nutty, spices, M
Effect: The tea and the sauce make each other lighter, brighter, with a clean palate. The tea's sweetness nicely counters the acidity of the tomatoes. Enhancement of all flavors.	**Effect:** The tea makes the saus lighter, more vegetal and herbaceous, enhances the pasta and the basil, connects all flavors and acquires more depth and umami itself.

MEAT AND POULTRY

FOOD

Ribeye, with a reduction of sage, oregano, smoked cinnamon, clove, powdered ginger, prunes, honey.
Flavor profile: neutral, rich, bright, umami, salt, sweet, slightly bitter, animal, fruity, vegetal, herbaceous, spices, L-XL

TEA

Earl Grey, black tea, scented with Bergamot citrus, blend **Flavor profile:** dry, rich and bright, sweet, umami, floral, fruity, earthy, M-L	**Yue Guang Bai,** Yunnan, China **Flavor profile:** smooth, rich and bright, sweet, earthy, fruity, spices, floral, sweets, L
Effect: The tea brings all flavors together, makes the food lighter, brighter, fruitier. The tea acquires more depth, more umami.	**Effect:** The entire dish becomes fuller, sweeter, acquires more umami. Later on it becomes fresher. The fennel becomes buttery, lemon and mint enhanced, clean and fresh palate. The tea acquires a bit of mint.

FOOD

Breast of chicken, roasted, with preserved lemons and green olives.
Flavor profile: neutral, rich and bright, umami, sour, slightly bitter, salt, animal, earthy, fruity, M

TEA

Dong Fang Mei Ren, oolong, Hsinchu County, Taiwan **Flavor profile:** smooth ends a bit dry, rich, sweet, floral, fruity, earthy, mineral, spices, M	**Hōjicha,** Bancha, roasted green tea, Tsukigase, Nara prefecture, Japan **Flavor profile:** smooth, later on dry, rich, sweet, umami, nutty, grains, fruity, vegetal, herbaceous, maritime, earthy, M
Effect: The tea becomes less sweet, acquires more depth and umami, enhances the food and makes it brighter, lighter.	**Effect:** The tea adds nutty and sweet notes to the food, tones down the sharpness of the lemon, makes the olives brighter, makes the chicken juicier, deeper, with more umami.

FOOD

Chicken pastries, Moroccan style, with Ras el Hanout, honey, roasted almonds and coriander.
Flavor profile: neutral, neutral, umami, sweet, salt, animal, spices, grains, vegetal, herbaceous, M-L

TEA

Da Hong Pao, dark rock oolong, Wuyi Shan, Fujian, China **Flavor profile:** smooth, ends a bit dry, rich, sweet, sour, umami, fruity, floral, sweets, earthy, herbaceous, grains, nutty, spices, mineral, L-XL	**Ceylon Pusselawa,** black tea, Pusselawa, Sri Lanka **Flavor profile:** a bit smooth, dry, bright, sour, bitter, floral, fruity, earthy, M-L
Effect: The tea becomes less sweet, acquires more depth and umami, enhances the food and makes it brighter, lighter.	**Effect:** The tea becomes fuller, softer, sweeter, connects all flavors, enhances the food.

MEAT AND POULTRY
FOOD
Chicken thighs, stewed in butter with shallot, garlic, bay leaf, leek, tarragon, Sherry; mashed potatoes. ***Flavor profile:*** *smooth, rich, sweet, umami, salt, animal, vegetal, herbaceous, M*

TEA	
Huo Shan Huang Ya, *Huo Shan County, Anhui Province, China* ***Flavor profile:*** *smooth, bright, sweet, sour, umami, vegetal, fruity, earthy, grains, nutty, mineral, M*	**Earl Grey,** *black tea, scented with Bergamot citrus, blend* ***Flavor profile:*** *dry, rich and bright, sweet, umami, floral, fruity, earthy, M-L*
Effect: The tea becomes fruitier, brighter, enhances the food, especially the tarragon, adds umami to the potatoes, makes the food lighter, brighter.	**Effect:** The tea deepens the food, adds floral and citrus notes, enhances chicken and mashed potatoes, while becoming itself softer, less bright, with more umami and depth.

FOOD
Chicken thighs, cooked in coconut cream, with garam massala and courgette, served with couscous and fresh herbs. ***Flavor profile:*** *smooth, rich, sweet, umami, salt, animal, spices, grains, vegetal, herbaceous, M-L*

TEA	
Spicy White, *first flush, Kurseong valley, Darjeeling, India* ***Flavor profile:*** *dry, bright, crisp, sweet, bitter, floral, fruity, vegetal, herbaceous, M*	**Assam,** *black tea, India* ***Flavor profile:*** *dry, rich, robust, robust, bold, sweet, bitter, umami, fruity, grains, sweets, earthy, animal, spices, herbaceous, XL*
Effect: The tea becomes brighter, fruitier, acquires more zest, adds its aromas to the chicken, enhances herbs and spices, adds depth and umami to the couscous.	**Effect:** The food becomes lighter and deeper at the same time, the spices and couscous are enhanced, the courgette becomes deeper but also slightly bitter, the chicken acquires more umami and so does the tea, which also becomes smoother, sweeter, rounder.

FOOD
Chicken thighs, stir fried, Indonesian style, with Balinese spices, sambal badjak (sweet chili paste), mixed vegetables, sweet soy sauce; rice. ***Flavor profile:*** *neutral, rich, umami, bitter, sweet, salt, animal, vegetal, grains spices, L*

TEA	
Dong Ding, *Mei Shan, Nantou, Taiwan* ***Flavor profile:*** *smooth and dry, rich and bright, sweet, slightly bitter, nutty, mineral, floral, sweets, vegetal, herbaceous, fruity, dairy, M-L*	**Shu Pu-Erh,** *post-fermented cooked tea, China* ***Flavor profile:*** *smooth, round, rich, sweet, umami, earthy, animal, sweets, vegetal, L-XL*
Effect: The tea becomes sweeter, fuller, rounder, less floral, but still bright, and it brings all flavors together, intensifies them, adds its roasting notes to the food, adds nuttiness.	**Effect:** The tea brings all flavors together, deepens the food, which also becomes sweeter, lighter. The tea becomes brighter, acquires more umami.

MEAT AND POULTRY

FOOD
Chicken thighs, stir fried, Thai style, with green curry paste, Nam Plâ (fish sauce), broccoli, bell pepper, carrot; rice. **Flavor profile:** *neutral, neutral, umami, sweet, salt, animal, vegetal, grains spices, L*

TEA	
Tie Guan Yin heavy roast, Longten, Taiwan **Flavor profile:** smooth, rich, a bit bright, sweet, bitter, fruity, sweets, earthy, grains, floral, nutty, spices, L	**Wen Shan Baozhong,** Taipei County, Taiwan **Flavor profile:** smooth and dry, rich and bright, sweet, slightly bitter, dairy, floral, fruity, vegetal, herbaceous, grains, nutty, spices, M
Effect: The tea adds nutty and floral notes to the food, enhances the spices, connects all flavors, clean palate afterwards. The tea itself becomes more vegetal, brighter, peppery.	**Effect:** The tea acquires more depth, more umami, makes the food brighter, lighter, adds umami to chicken, rice and vegetables.

FOOD
Duck breast and sauerkraut, with chanterelles, celeriac, BBQ gravy. **Flavor profile:** *neutral and smooth, rich and bright, umami, sour, sweet, salt, animal, earthy, fruity, vegetal, smoky, L-XL*

TEA	
Lapsang Souchong, smoked, Wuyishan, Fuijan province, China **Flavor profile:** smooth and dry, rich, umami, sweet, robust, mineral, earthy, sweets, fruity, XL	**Sheng (raw) Pu Erh,** Lincang, Yunnan Province, China (2010) **Flavor profile:** aged: neutral to smooth, rich and bright, sweet, sour, bitter, umami, earthy, vegetal, animal, herbaceous, spices, floral, fruity, M-L
Effect: The tea adds smoky notes, emphasizes the BBQ gravy, softens the sauerkraut, makes sauerkraut and celery root deeper, with more umami, becomes less smoky itself, fruitier.	**Effect:** The tea becomes fruitier, more acidic in a fruity way, acquires more umami, enhances the food, especially the chanterelles, makes the food sweeter and brighter, lighter.

FOOD
Duck in orange sauce, with sweet potatoes, puffed wild rice, Argan oil, deep fried fresh herbs. **Flavor profile:** *neutral, rich and bright, umami, bitter, sweet, salt, animal, earthy, fruity, herbaceous, grains, M*

TEA	
Da Hong Pao, dark rock oolong, Wuyi Shan, Fujian, China **Flavor profile:** smooth, ends a bit dry, rich, sweet, sour, umami, fruity, floral, sweets, earthy, herbaceous, grains, nutty, spices, mineral, L-XL	**Satemwa Black,** Shire Highlands Malawi **Flavor profile:** smooth and dry, robust, sour, bitter, umami, earthy, fruity, spices, XL
Effect: The tea becomes less sweet, deeper, stronger, fuller, with more umami, connects all flavors and enhances them.	**Effect:** The tea enhances the citrus of the food, deepens and enhances the duck, adds its own flavor to the potatoes, acquires nutty notes and more umami itself, becomes sweeter.

SWEETS	
FOOD	
Apricot-lemon-almond pie. *Flavor profile:* neutral, rich and bright, sweet, a bit sour, fruity, nutty, M	
TEA	
Mi Lan Xiang Feng Huang Dan Cong, Chao-Zhou, Guangdong province, China *Flavor profile:* smooth, ends a bit dry, rich, sweet, umami, fruity, vegetal, floral, earthy, grains, sweets, M-L	**Earl Grey,** black tea, scented with Bergamot citrus, blend *Flavor profile:* dry, rich and bright, sweet, umami, floral, fruity, earthy, M-L
Effect: Enhancement of apricots and almonds, the texture becomes smoother, juicier and lighter. The tea becomes fruitier and lighter, brighter.	**Effect:** The pie becomes fruitier and lighter, brighter. The tea becomes more complex, sweeter, fuller, rounder, creamy.
FOOD	
Cannoli limone *Flavor profile:* smooth, rich a bit bright, sweet, a bit sour, fruity, grains, M	
TEA	
White Whisper, Silver Needle, Nyeri region, Kenya *Flavor profile:* smooth, bold, rich, later bright, sweet, vegetal, floral, fruity, nutty, grains, M	**Lapsang Souchong,** unsmoked, Wuyishan, Fuijan, China *Flavor profile:* smooth, rich, sweet, umami, vegetal, mineral, earthy, sweets, fruity, floral, M-L
Effect: The cannoli becomes softer, less acidic, less sweet, brighter, with more balance. The tea becomes fruitier, brighter and connects all flavors.	**Effect:** The cannoli becomes sweeter, creamy, less acidic, with a hint of cacao and cinnamon. The tea becomes brighter, fruitier.
FOOD	
Chocolate-hazelnut cookies, recipe:Joy Wilson. *Flavor profile:* neutral, rich, sweet, grains, nutty, M	
TEA	
Dong Fang Mei Ren, oolong, Hsinchu County,Taiwan *Flavor profile:* smooth ends a bit dry, rich, sweet, floral, fruity, earthy, mineral, spices, M	**Hōjicha, Bancha,** roasted green tea, Tsukigase, Nara prefecture, Japan *Flavor profile:* smooth, later on dry, rich, sweet, umami, nutty, grains, fruity, vegetal, herbaceous, maritime, earthy, M
Effect: The cookies become lighter, brighter, hazelnuts enhanced. The tea becomes fuller, stronger.	**Effect:** The tea enhances the hazelnuts and the chocolate, while the tea itself becomes rounder, fuller, sweeter.

SWEETS
FOOD
Chocolate mousse, with mango coulis, mint. **Flavor profile:** smooth, rich a bit bright, sweet, a bit sour, earthy, fruity, herbaceous, M
TEA

Huang Da Cha, *Jinzhai County, Anhui Province, China* **Flavor profile:** smooth, ends dry, rich, sweet, umami, vegetal, earthy, fruity, grains, nutty, sweets, M	**Da Hong Pao,** *dark rock oolong, Wuyi Shan, Fujian, China* **Flavor profile:** smooth, ends a bit dry, rich, sweet, sour, umami, fruity, floral, sweets, earthy, herbaceous, grains, nutty, spices, mineral, L-XL
Effect: The mousse and mango coulis become fruitier, brighter, lighter, the mint blends with the tea. The tea becomes sweeter, fruitier and brighter.	**Effect:** The mousse becomes lighter, brighter, fruitier and acquires nutty notes. Enhancement of mint and mango. The mousse makes the tea creamy, while the mango and mint make it bright, light and fruity.

FOOD
Chocolate mud cake, flourless, with whipped cream and lemon zest. **Flavor profile:** smooth, rich, sweet, slightly sour, earthy, fruity, dairy, M
TEA

Keemun, *Qimen County, China* **Flavor profile:** smooth, ends a bit dry, rich, sweet, umami, fruity, floral, grains, animal, sweets, earthy, L	**Long Jing,** *West Lake, Hangzhou City, Zhejiang province, China* **Flavor profile:** smooth, rich, later a bit bright, round, creamy, sweet, umami, vegetal, fruity, grains, nutty, maritime, M
Effect: The chocolate is enhanced, becomes deeper. The cake makes the tea sweeter, fuller, deeper, with a hint of lemon in the aftertaste. Clean palate.	**Effect:** The pie becomes brighter, lighter, less sweet. The tea becomes fuller, sweeter, less vegetal.

FOOD
Milk chocolate mousse with espresso, raspberries, violets and almond crumble. **Flavor profile:** smooth and a bit dry, rich and bright, sweet, sour, earthy, fruity, nutty, slightly floral, M-L
TEA

Tie Guan Yin, *light roast, light oolong, Anxi, China* **Flavor profile:** smooth and dry, bright, sweet, sour, bitter, floral, vegetal, herbaceous, fruity, mineral, metallic, M	**Dian Hong,** *Yunnan, China* **Flavor profile:** smooth, rich, sweet, umami, earthy, sweets, fruity, nutty, spices, L
Effect: The tea adds floral notes, which combines nicely with the violets. The raspberries become brighter, a bit more tangy, the mousse brighter and lighter. Enhancement of chocolate, coffee and almonds. The tea becomes fuller, creamier, softer.	**Effect:** The mousse becomes lighter, brighter, the raspberries less acidic, deeper, the crumble enhanced. The violets disappear. The tea becomes sweeter, rounder, with nutty notes.

SWEETS	
FOOD	
Panna cotta of coconut, with salty caramel-ginger sauce. **Flavor profile:** *smooth, rich, sweet, slightly salt, umami, sweets, nutty, spices, L*	
TEA	
English Breakfast, *black tea, blend.* **Flavor profile:** *begins smooth, dry to astringent, rich, ends bright, robust, bold, sweet, bitter, umami, fruity, earthy, XL*	**Dong Ding,** *Mei Shan, Nantou, Taiwan* **Flavor profile:** *smooth and dry, rich and bright, sweet, slightly bitter, nutty, mineral, floral, sweets, vegetal, herbaceous, fruity, dairy, M-L*
Effect: The panna cotta becomes lighter, brighter, fruitier. The tea becomes fuller, creamier, softer and sweeter.	**Effect:** The tea makes the panna cotta brighter and sweeter, adds floral and nutty notes, enhances the coconut and the caramel. The tea becomes creamy and sweeter.
FOOD	
White chocolate mousse, with mandarin sauce. **Flavor profile:** *smooth, rich, sweet, slightly sour, earthy, sweets, fruity, M*	
TEA	
Genmaicha-iri Matcha, *green tea mixed with Matcha and puffed rice; Ujitawara, Uji, Kyoto, Japan* **Flavor profile:** *smooth, later on dry, rich, sweet, umami, nutty, grains, fruity, vegetal, herbaceous, maritime, earthy, M*	**Satemwa Black,** *Shire Highlands Malawi* **Flavor profile:** *smooth and dry, robust, sour, bitter, umami, earthy, fruity, spices, XL*
Effect: The mousse becomes lighter, brighter, fruitier, the sauce sweeter and brighter, the tea fuller and fruitier.	**Effect:** The mousse becomes lighter, brighter, acquires the flavor of black tea, the mandarin is enhanced. The tea becomes softer, fuller, rounder, sweeter, with citrus in the aftertaste; clean palate.

Tea characteristics

(The scores do not say anything about the quality of the tea!)

WHITE TEA

General characteristics: subtle; works very well as a neutralizer (or palate cleanser) between courses.
General profile: sweet, round, smooth, rich, neutral, floral, fruity, vegetal, sweets
Some more outspoken white teas combine well with fatty dishes, such as sausages. The tea breaks down fat and enhances the flavor of the food.

TEA	TEXTURE	FLAVOR TYPE	TASTE	MAIN NOTES	INTENSITY	CIRCLE SCORE
	○ = smooth ○ = dry ○ = neutral or both	○ = rich ○ = bright ○ = neutral or both	○ = sweet ○ = umami ○ = salt ○ = sour ○ = bitter	○ = cool ○ = warm ○ = neutral or both	XS S M L XL	○○○○○

Supermarket blend *Various countries, mainly China*
Flavor profile: neutral, neutral, subtle, sweet, bitter, floral, sweets vegetal; field flowers, honey, hay, XS-S

	○○○○○	○○○○○	○○○○○	○○○○○	XS	○○○○○

Bai Hao Yin Zhen *Shaowu City, Fujian province, China*
Flavor profile: smooth, rich, creamy, subtle, sweet, vegetal, floral, sweets, fruity, grains; grass, hay, wild flowers, rose, apricot, toasted brioche with apricot jam, cream pudding with dried fruit, S

	○○○○○	○○○○○	○○○○○	○○○○○	S	○○○○○

White Whisper *Silver Needle, Nyeri region, Kenya*
Flavor profile: smooth, rich, later bright, subtle, sweet, fruity, vegetal, floral, grains; peach, apricot, sweet corn, rose, barley, toasted brioche, M

	○○○○○	○○○○○	○○○○○	○○○○○	S	○○○○○

Bai Mudan *Fuding City, Fujian province, China*
Flavor profile: smooth, mellow, rich, later bright, subtle, sweet, floral, nuts, fruity, sweets, vegetal, grains; honeysuckle, chamomile, lilac, hazelnut, peach, apricot, melon, honey, hay, toasted bread, M

	○○○○○	○○○○○	○○○○○	○○○○○	M	○○○○○

Spicy White *first flush, Kurseong valley, Darjeeling, India*
Flavor profile: dry, a bit smooth, bright, crisp, sweet, bitter, floral, fruity, vegetal, herbaceous; field flowers, muscatel grape, melon, capsicum, hay, coriander, M

	○○○○○	○○○○○	○○○○○	○○○○○	M	○○○○○

Yue Guang Bai *Ming Le village, Jinggu county, Yunnan province, China*
Flavor profile: smooth, rich, later bright, sweet, creamy, umami, earthy, fruity, spices, floral, sweets, vegetal; henna, wood, sweet malt, autumn leaves, pipe tobacco, peach, apricot, cinnamon, honeysuckle, honey, soft caramel, vanilla, buttered fava beans, L

	○○○○○	○○○○○	○○○○○	○○○○○	M	○○○○○

GREEN TEA

General profile: mainly vegetal, slightly bitter-sweet, bright
General characteristics: Chinese green tea tastes mainly like sweet green vegetables and grains, Japanese green tea usually like umami-rich green vegetables and seaweed, depending on which green tea is used.

Supermarket blend *Various countries, mainly China*
Flavor profile: neutral, neutral, sweet, bitter, vegetal, herbaceous. XS-S

	○○○○○	○○○○○	○○○○○	○○○○○	M	○○○○○

Anji Bai Cha *Huzhou City, Anji County, Zhejiang province, China*
Flavor profile: smooth, rich, subtle, sweet, umami, slightly sour, dairy, floral, earthy, nutty, sweets, vegetal, fruity; cream, butter, magnolia, orchid, wood, macadamia nut, honey, white chocolate, lettuce hearts, snow peas, cucumber, citrus, strawberry jam, S-M

	○○○○○	○○○○○	○○○○○	○○○○○	M	○○○○○

GREEN TEA

Tai Ping Hou Kui *Tai Ping County, Anhui province, China*
Flavor profile: smooth, later dry, rich, later bright, mellow, sweet, bitter, umami, vegetal, fruity, earthy, nutty, grains, herbaceous, sweets; peas, cooked green beans, asparagus, green bell pepper, pear, guava, hay, cashew nut, almond, oats, a hint of eucalyptus, honey, M

○○○○●	○○○○○	○○○○●	○○○○○	M	○●○○○

Bi Luo Chun *Dong Shan, Jiangsu province, China*
Flavor profile: smooth, rich, later a bit dry and bright, round, creamy, sweet, bitter, sour, umami, vegetal, fruity, grains nutty, spices, mineral; baked chestnut, sautéed courgette, spinach, edamame, candied lemon, plum, toast, cookies, cashew nut, hazelnut, aniseed, nutmeg, flint, M

○○○○●	○○○○○	○○○○●	○○○○○	M	○●○○○

Long Jing, *West Lake, Hangzhou City, Zhejiang province, China*
Flavor profile: smooth, rich, later a bit bright, round, creamy, sweet, bitter, sour, umami, vegetal, fruity, grains, nutty, maritime, herbaceous; peas, corn, chestnut, raw courgette, spinach, edamame, lychee, toast, cookies, macadamia, oyster, aniseed, licorice, M

○○○○●	○○○○○	○○○○●	○○○○○	M	○●○○○

Gunpowder *Zhejiang Province, China*
Flavor profile: neutral to dry, a bit smooth, bright, sweet, bitter, sour, earthy, vegetal, herbaceous, grains, nutty, floral, fruity, mineral; wet pot soil, autumn leaves, wood, straw, broccoli, spinach, mint, cookies, almonds, lily, citrus, flint, smoke, M-L

○○○○○	○○○○○	○○○○●	○○○○○	M	○●○○○

Snow Shan Green *Ban Lien, Lao Cai, N-Vietnam*
Flavor profile: neutral to dry, bright, sweet, umami, bitter, floral, vegetal, herbaceous, fruity, sweets, earthy, mineral; wild flowers, kale, green bell pepper, sweet potato, sage, grapes, lychee, honey, cedar wood, hay, flint, M

○○○○○	○○○○○	○○○●○	○○○○○	M	○●○○○

Hōjicha (always roasted) *Tsukigase, Nara prefecture, Japan*
Flavor profile: smooth, later on dry, rich, sweet, umami, nutty, grains, sweets, fruity, spicy, vegetal, herbaceous, maritime, earthy; toasted hazelnuts, toast, caramel, honey pear, anise, black pepper, fried onion, roasted corn, seaweed, filter coffee, cedar wood, M

○○○○●	○○○○○	○○○●○	○○○○○	M	○●○○○

Sencha *Kochi, Shikoku prefecture, Japan*
Flavor profile: smooth to neutral-dry, rich-bright, sweet, bitter, umami, vegetal, herbaceous, maritime, fruity, sometimes dairy; grass, spinach, cucumber, parsley, basil, seaweed, seafood, citrus, peach, melon, soft boiled egg, butter, M

○○●○ ○	○○○○○	○○○○●	○●○○○	M	○●○○○

Kamairicha *Ureshino, Kyushu prefecture, Japan*
Flavor profile: starts off slightly dry, ends smooth, rich and bright, sweet, umami floral, sweets, grains, vegetal, herbaceous, fruity; freesia, oatmeal cookies, buttered toast, cucumber, white asparagus, lettuce heart, parsley, melon, M-L

○●○○○	○○○○○	○○○●○	○○○○○	M	○●○○○

Gyokuro *Fujieda, Shizuoka prefecture, Japan*
Flavor profile: smooth, ends dry, rich, bright finish, umami, sweet, vegetal, herbaceous, mineral, animal, fruity, dairy, maritime; spinach, courgette sautéed in butter, cucumber, parsley, sage, beef stock, crispy grilled chicken skin, honeydew melon, butter, shellfish, seaweed, mackerel, L-XL

○○○○●	○○○○○	●●●○○	○○○○○	M	○●○○●

Kabusecha *Wazuka, Kyôto prefecture, Japan*
Flavor profile: smooth, ends dry, rich, bright finish, mellow, umami, sweet, vegetal, herbaceous, fruity, dairy, maritime, earthy; fennel, spinach, braised courgette, dill, honeydew melon, peach, butter, cream, seaweed, oyster, pine wood, L-X

○○○●○	○○○○○	●●●○○	○○○○○	M	○●○○○

Woojeoncha *Jeju island, S-Korea*
Flavor profile: smooth, ends a bit dry, rich, ends a bit bright, creamy, sweet, umami, vegetal, herbaceous, earthy, fruity, nutty, dairy, mineral, maritime; vegetable broth, spinach, cucumber, citrus, melon, hazelnut, butter, rock, seaweed, wood, M

○○○○●	○○○○○	○○○●○	○○○○○	M	○●○○●

	YELLOW TEA					
General profile: General profile: sweet, smooth-neutral, neutral, nutty, vegetal, herbaceous, floral, earthy General characteristics: This tea is only manufactured in China, on Jun Shan Island in Hunan Province, in the Huo Shan area in Anhui Province, in the Meng Ding Shan area in Sichuan Province and in the Mo Gan Shan area in Zhejiang Province. Extra step in the process: smothering						
TEA	TEXTURE	FLAVOR TYPE	TASTE	MAIN NOTES	INTENSITY	CIRCLE SCORE
	O = smooth O = dry O = neutral or both	O = rich O = bright O = neutral or both	O = sweet O = umami O = salt O = sour O = bitter	O = cool O = warm O = neutral or both	XS S M L XL	OOOOO
Jun Shan Yin Zhen Jun Shan, Dong Ting Lake, Hunan province province, China **Flavor profile:** smooth, rich, sweet, floral, herbaceous, sweets; rose, chamomile, honeysuckle, chestnut, dried dill, eucalyptus, honey, S-M						
	OOOOO	OOOOO	OOOOO	OOOOO	M	OOOOO
Mo Gan Huang Ya Moganshan, Zhejiang Province, China **Flavor profile:** neutral, slightly smooth, neutral to bright, sweet, slightly bitter, vegetal, floral, mineral, sweets, earthy; sweet corn, wild flowers, beeswax, honey, hay, sandalwood, M						
	OOOOO	OOOOO	OOOOO	OOOOO	M	OOOOO
Huo Shan Huang Ya Huo Shan County, Anhui province, China **Flavor profile:** smooth, slightly dry, neutral to bright, sweet, sour, umami, vegetal, fruity, earthy, floral, mineral, grains, nutty; sweet corn, chestnut, steamed carrot, yam, red apple, pear, chocolate, honey, vegetable stock, hay, beeswax, toasted oats, freshly roasted hazelnut, cashew nut, sweet almond, M						
	OOOOO	OOOOO	OOOOO	OOOOO	M	OOOOO
Huang Da Cha Jinzhai County, Anhui province, China **Flavor profile:** smooth, ends dry, rich, ends bright, sweet, umami, vegetal, fruity, grains, mineral, earthy, nutty, sweets; spinach, hay, coffee, buttered toast with strawberry jam, charcoal, hay, hazelnut, caramel, chocolate, M						
	OOOOO	OOOOO	OOOOO	OOOOO	M	OOOOO
	OOLONG TEA, LIGHT					
General characteristics: oolongs are bruised for controlled oxidation by means of shaking or tumbling the fresh leaves. Level of oxidation could be anything between 10 and 80%, flavor anything between very green, crispy, grassy to deep, smooth, earthy and woody. General profile oolong, light: smooth and dry, bright, sweet, floral, vegetal, sometimes nutty, herbaceous General profile oolong, dark: smooth, rich, sweet, earthy, sometimes nutty, spices						
Wen Shan Baozhong Taipei County, Taiwan **Flavor profile:** smooth and dry, rich and bright, creamy, sweet, slightly bitter, a bit peppery, floral, dairy, fruity, vegetal, herbaceous, grains, nutty, spices; lily of the valley, rose, hyacinth, honeysuckle, butter, citrus, peach, grass, coriander, mint, cookies, raw white sweet almond, a hint of walnut, pepper, M						
	OOOOO	OOOOO	OOOOO	OOOOO	M	OOOOO
Si Ji Chun Nantou, Taiwan **Flavor profile:** smooth, slightly dry, rich and bright, sweet, bitter, a bit sour, floral, herbaceous, vegetal, sweets, spices, fruity, nuts, dairy; honeysuckle, gardenia, freesia, jasmine, coriander, oregano, cucumber, snow pea, vanilla, caramel, nutmeg, citrus, nectarine, coconut, almond, cream, butter, M						
	OOOOO	OOOOO	OOOOO	OOOOO	M	OOOOO
Qing Xin Li Shan, Taiwan **Flavor profile:** smooth and dry, rich and bright, sweet, bitter, floral, vegetal, dairy, herbaceous, fruity, sometimes nutty, hyacinth, rose, orchid, hay, peach, red apple, pear, honey, M						
	OOOOO	OOOOO	OOOOO	OOOOO	M	OOOOO
Jin Xuan #12 Ali Shan, Taiwan **Flavor profile:** smooth, ends slightly dry, silky, rich, ends slightly bright, sweet, slightly bitter, dairy, floral, fruity, herbaceous, vegetal; butter, cream, custard, lily, osmanthus, orchid, gardenia, peach, pear, apple, apricot, oregano, grass, broccoli, vanilla, M						
	OOOOO	OOOOO	OOOOO	OOOOO	M	OOOOO

OOLONG TEA, LIGHT						

Dong Ding *Mei Shan, Nantou, Taiwan*
Flavor profile: smooth and dry, rich and bright, sweet, slightly bitter, nutty, grains, sweets, floral, dairy, vegetal, herbaceous, fruity; freshly roasted hazelnuts, toast, honey, orchid, gardenia, butter, cream, vanilla roasted yam, pine, mint, peach, red and black fruit, M

	ooooo	ooooo	ooooo	ooooo	M	ooooo

Tie Guan Yin light roast *Anxi County, Fujian, China*
Flavor profile: smooth and dry, bright, sweet, bitter, sour, floral, vegetal, herbaceous, fruity, mineral, sometimes metallic; orchid, gardenia, rose, hyacinth, grass, wood, spinach, roasted broccoli, mint, green apple, red fruit, citrus, apricot, camphor, silver, M

	ooooo	ooooo	ooooo	ooooo	M	ooooo

OOLONG TEA, DARK

Dong Fang Mei Ren *Hsinchu County, Taiwan*
Flavor profile: smooth, ends a bit dry, rich, slightly bright, sweet, umami, floral, sweets, fruity, earthy, mineral, spice; elderflower, rose, geranium, honey, grapes, red currant, citrus, apricot, lychee, wood, rock, cinnamon, M

	ooooo	ooooo	ooooo	ooooo	M	ooooo

Tie Guan Yin heavy roast *Longten, Taiwan*
Flavor profile: smooth, slightly dry, rich, a bit bright, sweet, slightly bitter, fruity, sweets, earthy, grains, floral, nutty, spices; plum, stone fruit, red apple, dried fruit, pear, cherry, honey, caramel, dark wood, smoke, toast, orchid, pecan nut, cinnamon, L

	ooooo	ooooo	ooooo	ooooo	M	ooooo

Mi Lan Xiang Feng Huang Dan Cong *Chao-zhou, Guangdong province, China*
Flavor profile: smooth, ends a bit dry, rich, sweet, umami, fruity, sweets, vegetal, floral, earthy, grains, mineral; honey, sweet licorice, pear, dried apricot, raisins, cranberries, black plum, sweet potato, orchid, honeysuckle, cocoa, toast, rock, M-L

	ooooo	ooooo	ooooo	ooooo	M	ooooo

Da Hong Pao *Wuyi Shan, Fujian province, China*
Flavor profile: smooth, ends a bit dry, rich, sweet, sour, umami, fruity, floral, sweets, earthy, mineral, metal, herbaceous, grains, nutty, spices; peach, cherry, prune, orchid, butterscotch, caramel, brown sugar, cacao, tobacco, sandalwood, wet rock, charcoal, peat, pine, eucalyptus, freshly baked bread, hazelnut, cinnamon, clove, L-X

	ooooo	ooooo	ooooo	ooooo	M	ooooo

BLACK TEA

General characteristics: South East Asian black teas are usually sweeter, smooth, rounder and as such much less astringent than those from former English colonies. The Chinese call this tea red, because of the color of the steeped tea. Hong is Chinese for red.
General profile black tea: sweet, sometimes bitter, umami, dry, smooth, bright, neutral, rich, earthy, fruity, spices, mineral, floral

Honey Black #13 *Nantou County, Taiwan*
Flavor profile: smooth, rich, sweet, fruity; honey, chocolate, lychee, M

	ooooo	ooooo	ooooo	ooooo	M	ooooo

Ruby #18 *Sun Moon Lake, Nantou County, Taiwan*
Flavor profile: smooth, slightly dry, rich, slightly bright, sweet, spices, herbaceous, fruity, earthy; honey, cinnamon, mint, plum, exotic wood, M

	ooooo	ooooo	ooooo	ooooo	M	ooooo

Darjeeling, first flush *Darjeeling, India*
Flavor profile: dry, slightly smooth, bright, slightly rich, crisp, sweet, bitter, floral, fruity, grains, vegetal, herbaceous; pink rose, muscatel grape, pear, brioche, asparagus, freshly cut grass, mint, coriander, M

	ooooo	ooooo	ooooo	ooooo	M	ooooo

Nepalese black, first flush *Hile, Dhankuta, Nepal*
Flavor profile: smooth and dry, bright, crisp, sweet, slightly sour, floral, fruity, sweets, vegetal, herbaceous, nutty; orange blossom, field flowers, muscatel grape, citrus, honey, wood, hay, hazelnut, M

	ooooo	ooooo	ooooo	ooooo	M	ooooo

BLACK TEA						
TEA	TEXTURE	FLAVOR TYPE	TASTE	MAIN NOTES	INTENSITY	CIRCLE SCORE
	O = smooth O = dry O = neutral or both	O = rich O = bright O = neutral or both	O = sweet O = umami O = salt O = sour O = bitter	O = cool O = warm O = neutral or both	XS S M L XL	OOOOO
Darjeeling, second flush *Darjeeling, India* **Flavor profile:** neutral to dry, bright, crisp, umami, sweet, slightly sour, floral, fruity, earthy; orange blossom, muscatel grapes, yellow plum, citrus, exotic wood, M-L						
	OOOOO	OOOOO	OOOOO	OOOOO	M-L	OOOOO
Nepalese Imperial Black *Hile, Dhankuta, Nepal* **Flavor profile:** smooth and dry, rich and bright, umami, sweet, slightly bitter, fruity, grains, spices, earthy, vegetal, sweets, nutty; citrus, strawberry, grapes, toast, roasted oats, mulling spices, wood, bell pepper, pumpkin, yam, honey, brown sugar, milk chocolate, walnut, M-L						
	OOOOO	OOOOO	OOOOO	OOOOO	M-L	OOOOO
Kericho *Western Highlands, Kenia* **Flavor profile:** slightly smooth, dry, ends slightly astringent, bright, sour, sweet, bitter, earthy, vegetal, sweets, fruity; malt, exotic wood, chocolate, citrus, M-L						
	OOOOO	OOOOO	OOOOO	OOOOO	M-L	OOOOO
Lapsang Souchong, unsmoked *Wuyishan, Fuijan province, China* **Flavor profile:** smooth, rich, sweet, umami, vegetal, sweets, mineral, earthy, fruity, floral, grains, nutty; yam, milk chocolate, honey, molasses, pebbles, pine wood, mushroom, straw, orange, peach, lychee, orchid, rose, violet, brioche, almond, peanut, M-L						
	OOOOO	OOOOO	OOOOO	OOOOO	M-L	OOOOO
Dian Hong *Feng Qing County, Yunnan, China* **Flavor profile:** smooth, ends a bit dry, rich, ends a bit bright, sweet, umami, slightly bitter, earthy, vegetal, sweets, fruity, spices, nutty; malt, wood, honey, molasses, raisins, black currant, apricot, pear, a hint of citrus, walnut, L						
	OOOOO	OOOOO	OOOOO	OOOOO	L	OOOOO
Keemun *Qimen County, China* **Flavor profile:** smooth, ends a bit dry, rich, sweet, umami, earthy, sweets, fruity, floral, grains; smoke, malt, cacao, stone fruit, orchid, rose, toast, L						
	OOOOO	OOOOO	OOOOO	OOOOO	L	OOOOO
Lapsang Souchong, smoked *Wuyishan, Fuijan province, China* **Flavor profile:** smooth and dry, rich, robust, umami, sweet, mineral, sweets, earthy, fruity; smoked pine, charcoal, resin, incense, tar, dark chocolate, silvery ripe stone fruit, brandy, XL						
	OOOOO	OOOOO	OOOOO	OOOOO	XL	OOOOO
Nilgiri *Blue Mountains, India* **Flavor profile:** smooth, ends dry, bright, sweet, slightly bitter, umami, fruity, floral, nutty, vegetal, earthy, mineral, spices; raisins, red fruit, blackberry, fig, plum, orchid, walnut, wood, rock, cinnamon, M						
	OOOOO	OOOOO	OOOOO	OOOOO	M	OOOOO
Ceylon Nuwara Eliya *Nuwara Eliya, Sri Lanka* **Flavor profile:** dry to astringent, brisk, bright, sour, bitter, sweet, slightly umami, fruity, herbaceous; citrus, plum, raisins, mint, eucalyptus, M-L						
	OOOOO	OOOOO	OOO	OOOOO	M-L	OOOOO
Ceylon Pusselawa *Pusselawa, Sri Lanka* **Flavor profile:** dry to astringent, bright, sour, bitter, sweet, slightly umami, floral, fruity, vegetal spices; rose, citrus, wood, cinnamon, L						
	OOOOO	OOOOO	OOOO	OOOOO	L	OOOOO

BLACK TEA

Ceylon Uva *Uva, Sri Lanka*
Flavor profile: dry, mellow, bright, sweet, umami, sour, herbaceous, fruity, earthy, sweets; eucalyptus, mint, citrus, pine wood, malt, honey, L-XL

ooooo	ooooo	ooooo	ooooo	L-XL	ooooo

Assam *Assam, India*
Flavor profile: begins smooth, dry to astringent, rich, ends bright, robust, bold, sweet, bitter, umami, fruity, grains, vegetal, sweets, earthy, spices; raisins, citrus, toast, biscuity, wood, honey, malt, soil, clove, XL

ooooo	ooooo	ooooo	ooooo	M	ooooo

Benifûki Wakoucha *Takachiho, Nishiusuki District, Miyazaki prefecture, Japan*
Flavor profile: smooth, later dry, rich, ends a bit bright, sweet, umami, floral, fruity, vegetal, earthy, mineral; orchid, orange blossom, peach, grapes, wood, oak, resin, L-XL

ooooo	ooooo	ooooo	ooooo	M	ooooo

Satemwa Black *Shire Highlands Malawi*
Flavor profile: smooth and dry, rich, ends a bit bright, robust, sweet, sour, bitter, umami, earthy, fruity, spices; malt, wet leaves, cacao, citrus, dried fruit, cinnamon, XL

ooooo	ooooo	ooooo	ooooo	M	ooooo

POST-FERMENTED TEA RAW
POST-FERMENTED TEA COOKED

General characteristics: strong, earthy and animal aroma. The Chinese call this tea black, due to the very dark, often blackish color of the steep. The higher qualities become better the longer they are allowed to ripen. This process may take up to many, many years. During aging a constant temperature is adamant.

Sheng (raw) Pu Erh *Lincang County, Yunnan province, China*
Flavor profile: dry to astringent when young, neutral to smooth when aged, bright and light when young, rich and complex when aged, sweet, sour, bitter, umami, earthy, vegetal, sweets, animal, herbaceous, spices, fruity; forest leaves, hay, wood, smoke, pipe tobacco, silage, camphor, yeast, henna, kale, mushrooms, licorice, burnt caramel, honey, stable, zoo, sage, mint, eucalyptus, pepper, citrus, stewed apple, M-L-XL

ooooo	ooooo	ooooo	ooooo	M-L-XL	ooooo

Shu (cooked) Pu Erh *Lincang County, Yunnan province, China*
Flavor profile: smooth, rich, sweet, umami, earthy, animal, sweets, herbaceous, vegetal; wet leaves, autumnal forest, clay, cave, henna, cellar, mushrooms, soil, dark tobacco, leather, stable, sometimes fishy, honey, caramel, molasses, maple syrup, eucalyptus, cough syrup, potato skin, roasted pumpkin, roasted yam, M-L-XL

ooooo	ooooo	ooooo	ooooo	M-L-XL	ooooo

Goishicha *Otoyo town, Kochi prefecture, Japan*
Flavor profile: dry to neutral, rich and bright, sour, umami, sweet, dairy, animal, earthy, fruity, vegetal, herbaceous; buttermilk, yoghurt, goat stable, straw, silage, autumnal forest, soil, balsamic vinegar, dried hibiscus, sour cherry, citrus, dried fruit, sour plum, purslane, lemongrass, verbena, M-L

ooooo	ooooo	ooooo	ooooo	M-L	ooooo

Index recipes

Plant based
Jackfruit stew with celery root and bell pepper 118
Mashed potatoes, purslane, basil, almonds 70
Pulled jackfruit, BBQ sauce, coleslaw 74
Pumpkin curry, tomato, dirty Chai 150
Roasted sweet potatoes, broccoli, tahini 72
Satay of vegetables, noodles 110
Tofu, cauliflower, tomato, Angostura sauce 102

Vegetarian
Beetroot, lemon, Parmesan cheese 108
Courgettes, mushrooms, Camembert 82
Crustless pie, broccoli, tomato, Parmesan cheese 78
Fennel, samphire, walnuts, feta 104
Lentils, aubergine, bell pepper, celeriac 84
Pasta, broccoli, tomato, Camembert 90
Pea mousse, lemon, mint, cheese wafers 80
Portobellos, spinach, pecans, cheese 94
Pumpkin, mushrooms, Gorgonzola, pecans 92
Roasted cauliflower, Camembert, almonds 88
Roasted vegetables, lemon-yoghurt-mayo 87
Silken tofu stuffed cabbage 100

Fish-seafood
Fish, cauliflower, tomato, Angostura sauce 102
Haddock, leek, beetroot, pomegranate 96
Haddock, Pimentón, lentils, aubergine, bell pepper, celeriac 86
Hake stuffed cabbage 98
Monkfish, fennel, samphire, feta 104
Prawn risotto, spinach, lemon, basil 106

Meat-poultry
Bresaola, Parmesan cheese, lemon 108
Chicken, broccoli, roasted sweet potatoes, tahini 72
Chicken fatteh, chickpeas, tomato, bell pepper, almonds 114
Chicken, leek, Noilly Prat cream sauce 117
Chicken, roasted vegetables, lemon-yoghurt-mayo 87
Chicken satay, vegetables, noodles 110
Chorizo, roasted cauliflower 86
Courgettes, mushrooms, bacon, 82
Crustless pie, broccoli, bacon, tomato, Parmesan cheese 78
Lamb stew, celeriac, bell pepper 118
Mashed potatoes, purslane, bacon, basil 70
Merguez lamb sausages, lentils, aubergine, bell pepper, celeriac 86
Merguez lamb sausages, roasted sweet potatoes, broccoli, tahini 72
Pea mousse, lemon, mint, crispy bacon 80
Pig's neck, BBQ sauce, coleslaw 76
Pumpkin, minced meat, mushrooms, pecans 92

Sweets
Frisian thumbprint cookies 124
Lime meringue pie 128
Mariëlla's brownies 120
Orange almond cake with cacao nibs 122
Roasted summer fruit with mascarpone 126

COOKING WITH TEA

Plant based
Caramelized chicory, Pu-Erh, mushroom gravy, hazelnuts, mashed potatoes 140
Fennel, orange, hazelnuts, tea dressing 158
Tajine, aubergine, tomato, tea 164
Vegan oysters 144
Vegan sashimi 160

Vegetarian
Asparagus with tea butter 138
Caramelized chicory, Pu-Erh, cheese wafers, mashed potatoes and mushroom gravy 140
Pumpkin curry, tomato, dirty Chai 150
Strawberries, asparagus, Matcha butter 154

Fish-seafood
Cod, beetroot, tarragon, Matcha 148
Fish burger, Matcha-tarragon mayonnaise 156
Pumpkin curry, prawns, tomato, dirty Chai 150
Razor clams, snow peas, tea, tarragon butter 152

Meat-poultry
Asparagus, ham, tea butter, 138
Beetroot, avocado, Parma ham, tea liqueur 136
Chicory, Pu-Erh, bacon, mushroom gravy 142
Pumpkin curry, chicken, tomato, dirty Chai 150
Tajine, minced lamb, aubergine, tomato, tea 166
Turkey burger, Matcha-tarragon mayonnaise 156

Sweets
Plant based
Chocolate cream, mango, lime, mint 172
Grilled rhubarb, coconut-Matcha, mango 168
Vegan chocolate tea truffles 167

Dairy or egg based
Cheesecake, Matcha, mango jelly 170
Chocolate cream, mango, lime, mint 172
Chocolate sorbet, tea, meringue, fruit 174
Matcha cream truffles 180
Orange and black tea ice cream, salty caramel-ginger sauce 179
Peach and oolong sorbet 176
Vanilla tea ice cream 178

Cocktails
Bombay Bubble 217
Green Teatini 216
Holy Smoky Mary 216
Inge's Hibiscus and strawberry Infusion 214
Mojito Matcha Mocktail 216
Rock'n Roolong 215
Summer in the City 214
Zesty Rosella 215

Ice tea recipes
Classic iced tea recipe 211
Cold brew 35, 36, 37, 40, 130, 132, 211, 212, 219, 220

Cold brew in alcohol 132
Cold drip 212
Iced tea shock brew style 210
Sun brew ice tea 212

Various recipes
Ambient brew 35
Foolproof cold brew method 35, 36, 37, 219
Smoking with tea 132
Steeping tea Western style 38, 40
Steeping tea Eastern style 39, 40

TASTING NOTES TEA AND FOOD WITHOUT RECIPES

Plant based
Beet Wellington 260
Cauliflower cream, almonds, hazelnut-vanilla oil, pimentón and cacao nibs 261
Courgette salad, miso-honey-lemon dressing, herbs, sesame seeds 262
Sauerkraut, mashed potatoes, mashed celeriac, walnuts 264

Vegetarian
Broccoli, pesto, tagliatelle 260
Brussels sprouts, roasted, fried shallots, blue cheese, baked potatoes 260
Cauliflower, egg, yoghurt, onion, tarragon 261
Cauliflower, roasted, cumin, fried red onion, turmeric, cheese, potatoes 261
Cauliflower tandoori, yoghurt, tomato, cashew nuts, caramelized onions 262
Fennel, beet root, red onion, yam, garlic, all roasted, yoghurt, mint, lemon, pecan nuts 262
Parmigiana di Melanzane, aubergine, tomato, mozzarella di buffala, Parmesan cheese, basil 263
Portobello, broccoli, tomato, garlic, egg, ricotta, hazelnuts, Parmesan cheese 263
Quiche, Emmenthaler cheese, caramelized onions 263
Stir fried Brussels sprouts, noodles, cucumber, herbs, spring onion, peanuts, lime, soy 264
Risotto, leek, mushrooms, hazelnuts, Parmesan cheese, butter 264
Spinach, garlic, lemon, tarragon, Parmesan cheese, egg, boiled potatoes 265

Fish and seafood
Chinese mussels, ginger- lime mayonnaise, crème fraîche 256
Clams, lemongrass, ginger 256
Haddock, roasted almonds, Bergamot citrus, Brussels sprouts, boiled potatoes 256
Halibut, orange-tarragon-mustard sauce, Chinese cabbage, mushrooms, shallot, mashed potatoes 257
Langoustines, spicy tomato-chickpeasoup, Phyllo pastry 257
Meagre, lobster, mushrooms, seaweed mayonnaise, Jerusalem artichokes 257
Oysters 258
Pad Thai, prawns, snow peas, mushrooms, bell pepper, fennel, herbs, sesame seeds 258
Raw scallops, slightly blackened, cauliflower, avocado, sea lettuce, harissa oil 258
Salmon-cucumber rolls, chervil-mayonnaise, herbs, mezclun 259
Smoked mackerel, roasted beet root, boiled potatoes, lime-mayonnaise, capers, lettuce, ginger, pine nuts 259
Sock eye salmon, smoked, ricotta-lemon ravioli, broccoli, wine-cream sauce, basil 259

Meat and poultry
Carpaccio , water cress, Parmesan cheese, Balsamic vinegar, maple syrup 265
Fatteh, minced meat, humus, baba ganoush, flatbread, yoghurt, cucumber bell pepper 265
Fried bacon, Brussels sprouts, mashed with boiled potatoes, onion, garlic, mushrooms 266
Fried bacon, sauerkraut, mashed with boiled potatoes and celeriac, mustard 266
Köfte, tomato sauce, flatbread, yoghurt, mint, cucumber, lemon, garlic 266
Lamb's neck stew, Ras el Hanout, roasted vegetables, couscous, mint, cinnamon 267
Pancetta-chicory rolls, boiled potatoes, roux, cumin cheese 267
Pasta Bolognese, minced meat, basil, olives, pine nuts, Parmesan cheese 267
Ribeye, sage, oregano, smoked cinnamon, clove, ginger, prunes, honey 268
Breast of chicken, roasted, preserved lemons, green olives 268
Chicken pastries, Moroccan style, Ras el Hanout, roasted almonds, honey, coriander 268
Chicken thighs, butter, shallot, bay leaf, leek, tarragon, Sherry, mashed potatoes 269
Chicken thighs, cooked in coconut cream, garam massala, courgette, couscous, herbs 269
Chicken thighs, stir fried, Indonesian style, vegetables, sweet soy sauce, rice 269
Chicken thighs, stir fried, Thai style, green curry, broccoli, bell pepper, carrot, rice 270
Duck breast, sauerkraut, celeriac, chanterelles, BBQ gravy 270
Duck in orange sauce, yam, puffed wild rice, Argan oil, deep fried herbs 270

Sweets
Apricot-lemon-almond pie 271
Cannoli limone 271
Chocolate-hazelnut cookies 271
Chocolate mousse, mango coulis, mint 272
Chocolate mud cake 272
Milk chocolate mousse, espresso, raspberries, violets, almond crumble 272
Panna cotta of coconut, salty caramel-ginger sauce 273
White chocolate mousse, mandarin sauce 273

Index

Acidic: 25, 28, 30, 31, 49, 50, 54, 61, 67, 186, 202, 210, 237
Acknowledgments 296
Alkaline 30, 31, 33, 34, 247
Amino acids 52, 130, 239, 240, 242, 245
Analyzing flavor 54
Antioxidants 239, 241, 242, 245
Aromas 16, 26, 49, 52 - 55, 223, 237, 239, 240, 245
Aromas flavor wheel 57, 248, 249
Aromas overview 55
Astringency 15, 49, 50, 64, 189, 241, 245
Bibliography 292
Black tea (Chinese, Hei Cha) 233, 236, 237
Black tea (Western) 16, 22, 23, 24, 28, 33, 38, 50, 51, 61, 188, 201, 212, 228, 233 - 235, 239, 241, 245, 279 - 281
Books about tea: 292Cacao 22, 55,188
Cacao beans 184 -187
Cacao butter 186
Cacao nibs 122, 168, 172, 186, 261
Caffeine 15, 51, 240 - 45
Calcium 10, 29 - 32, 45, 241, 245 - 247
Camellia cambodia 26
Camellia crassicolumna 26
Camellia ptilophylla 26
Camellia sinensis 12, 16, 26, 28, 287
Camellia sinensis assamica 16, 26, 28, 231, 236
Camellia sinensis sinensis 16, 26, 28, 231
Camellia taliensis 26
Carbohydrates 245
Catechins 240, 241, 242, 245
Cháhuá 26
Cheese 48, 50, 51, 54, 55, 200 - 207
Chocolate 186, 187, 188, 189, 191 - 197
Chocolate tasting flavor map 191
Cocktails 9, 11, 29, 76, 210, 214 - 216, 220, 285
Cold brew 35, 36, 40, 69, 130, 132, 135, 211, 212, 219, 220
Cold drip 212Complexity 29, 42, 52, 62, 189, 240, 241
Cooking techniques 52, 62, 67
Cooking with tea 130 - 132, 284
CTC (Crush, Tear, Curl; Cut, Twist, Curl) 233, 234
Cultivar 12, 16, 227, 236, 239, 240, 244
De-enzyme 229
Dry residue 32, 34, 42, 246
Enzymes 200, 227, 229, 230, 232, 233, 234, 240, 245
Geraniol 245
Hardness of water 29, 34, 246
Hei Cha 233, 236, 237
Finish 52
Flavor profile 53, 54, 61 - 63, 66, 202 - 207, 192 - 197, 256 - 273
Flavor type 46, 48, 50, 52 - 54, 58, 59, 61 - 63, 66, 276 - 281
Flavor wheel 49, 53, 54, 57, 245, 246,
Green tea 10, 16, 18, 19, 20, 28, 33, 35, 38, 39, 40, 50 - 52, 60, 131, 132, 200 - 202, 212, 228, 229, 238, 239, 242, 244, 276, 277
Herbal tea 26
Herbal infusion 26
Ice tea 29, 37, 211, 21
Intensity 13, 46, 48, 52 - 54, 58, 59, 61 - 63, 66, 251, 276 - 281
Ion exchanger 31
Iron 241, 245
Jacobiasca formosana 240
Killing the green 229
Length 52
Linalool 240, 245
Main notes (main aromas) 48, 53, 54, 58, 59, 66, 67, 276 - 281
Magnesium 10, 29 - 32, 45, 245 - 247
Memory 47, 48
Methylxanthines 245
Minerals in tea 241, 243, 245
Oolong 12, 16, 21, 22, 28, 38, 39, 51, 61, 202, 210, 212, 228, 232, 233, 240, 244, 245, 278, 279
Orthonasal 49
Oxidase 227, 240, 245
Oxidation 227 - 235, 240, 245, 278
Peroxidase 227, 240, 245
pH value 28, 30, 33, 38, 40, 43, 130
Pigments 245
Plant based 9, 69, 74, 116, 130, 131, 135, 142,144, 146, 160, 164, 167,168, 260, 284
Polyphenols 50, 239, 240 - 245
Post-fermented tea 24, 25, 28, 48, 61, 66, 233, 235 - 237, 281
Production process 16, 42,185, 187, 228
Pu-Erh 28, 35, 38 - 40, 51, 61, 66, 212, 220, 228, 235 - 237, 281
Recipes: 284, 285
Retronasal 49
Reversed osmosis 30, 31
Senses 17, 47, 48, 60
Steeping tea 10, 33 - 40, 45, 219 - 223
Steeping time 12, 33, 35, 38 - 40, 47, 130, 220
Storage of tea 66, 223, 237
Tannins 50, 240, 241
Tap water 30
Tastes (the 5 tastes) 47, 48, 49, 51, 52, 53, 54, 57, 59, 64, 67, 276 - 281
Tasting notes cheese 202 - 207
Tasting notes chocolate 192 - 197
Tasting notes example forms 251 - 253
Tasting notes food 256 - 273
TDS meter 246
Tea bags 10, 38, 42, 43, 130, 210, 211, 220, 234
Tea characteristics 276 - 281
Tea extract 35 - 37, 40, 130, 131, 132, 202, 212, 219, 220
Tea plantations 286
Tea shops, addresses 219, 222, 286 - 291
Tea storage 66, 223, 237
Tea type 38, 39, 67
Tea varieties 16, 18 - 25
Tea ware 286, 291,
Temperature 12, 16, 29, 33 - 35, 38, 39, 40, 45, 47, 131, 186, 200, 212, 219, 223, 227, 233, 236
Terroir 12, 16
Texture 13, 15, 35, 48 - 54, 58, 59, 61 - 63, 66, 132, 186 - 189, 201, 210, 222, 236, 240, 276 - 281
Thearubigines 240, 241, 245
Theine 26, 242
Theobroma 184, 185
Tisane 26
Types of tea, the six- 11, 16, 28, 66, 228
Umami 48
Vegan 9, 74, 116, 130, 131, 144, 146, 160, 164, 167,168, 260, 284
Vegetarian 69, 135, 200, 260 - 265, 284
Vitamins 245
Volatile compounds in tea 130, 241, 245
Water 29 - 34, 40, 45, 246, 247
Water filter 30 - 32, 247
White tea 16, 18, 25, 28, 38, 39, 51, 66, 201, 202, 212, 228, 230, 231, 244, 245, 276

Wine and tea 12,16
Yabao 26, 27, 244
Yellow tea 20, 28, 38, 39, 51, 227, 228, 230, 278

Examples of green tea:
Anji Bai Cha, China 18, 70, 256, 276
Bi Lo Chun (Green Snail Spring), China 229
Dragon Well (Long Jing), China 12, 18, 204, 207, 229, 258, 262, 272, 277 Green Bamboo (Zhu Ye Qing), China 80, 117, 229
Green Snail Spring (Bi Lo Chun), China 229
Gunpowder, China 19, 40, 80, 87, 90, 94, 112, 146, 261, 277
Gyokuro, Japan 19, 146, 152, 162, 242, 277
Hōjicha, Japan 12, 16, 19, 61, 72, 80, 87, 96, 112, 117, 138, 148, 201, 206, 244, 259, 260, 264, 265, 266, 268, 277
Jangwon, Korea 104, 202
Kabusecha, Japan 20, 242, 257, 277
Long Jing (Dragon Well), China 12, 18, 204, 207, 229, 258, 262, 272, 277
Mao Feng (Yellow Mountain Fur), China 90, 100, 201, 229
Mao Jian (Misty New Top), China 229
Matcha 12, 138, 148, 152, 154, 156, 168, 170, 180, 181, 242, 273
Misty New Top (Mao Jian), China 229
Monkey King (Tai Ping Hou Kui), China 19, 152, 229, 238, 277
Sencha, Japan 16, 19, 60, 96, 102, 104, 106, 131, 148, 157, 192, 194, 206, 220, 256, 259, 277
Sencha Fukamushi, Japan 60, 162, 229
Tai Ping Hou Kui (Monkey King), China 19, 152, 229, 238, 277
Tamaryokucha, Japan 82, 106, 229, 291
Yellow Mountain Fur (Mao Feng), China 90, 100, 201, 229
Zhu Ye Qing (Green Bamboo), China 80, 117, 229

Examples of yellow tea:
Huang Da Cha, China 20, 106, 204, 230, 256, 257, 258, 262, 264, 265, 272, 278
Huo Shan Huang Ya, China 20, 194, 196, 205, 206, 230, 256, 269, 278
Meng Ding Huang Ya, China 230
Mo Gan Huang Ya, China 20, 30, 230, 278
Jun Shan Yin Zhen, China 20, 30, 230, 278

Examples of white tea:
Ali Shan White, Taiwan 231
Bai Hao Yin Zhen (Siver Needle), China 12, 18, 192, 231, 244, 276Bai Mudan (White Peony), China 18, 126, 168, 192, 194, 205, 207, 231, 276
Doke Silver Needle, Darjeeling 231
Siver Needle (Bai Hao Yin Zhen) 12, 18, 192, 231, 244, 276
Spicy White, first flush, India 18, 194, 231, 269, 276
White Crescent, Nepal 231
White Moonlight (Yue Guang Bai) China 18, 88, 94, 96, 102, 108, 142, 150, 201, 202, 204, 206, 231, 257, 262, 263, 264, 267, 268, 276
White Peony (Bai Mudan), China 18, 126, 168, 192, 194, 205, 207, 231, 276
White Whisper, Kenia 18, 271, 276
Yabao, China 26, 27, 244
Yue Guang Bai (White Moonlight), China 18, 88, 94, 96, 102, 108, 142, 150, 201, 202, 204, 206, 231, 257, 262, 263, 264, 267, 268, 276

Examples of light oolong tea:
Baozhong, Taiwan 12, 21,72, 192, 232, 256, 258, 260, 261, 264, 268, 270, 278
Dong Ding Mei Shan, Taiwan 21, 66, 82, 87, 94, 100, 112, 193, 194, 205, 257, 262, 263, 267, 270, 273, 279
Iron Goddess of Mercy (Tieguanyin), China, Taiwan, Thailand 12, 21, 22, 40, 66, 102, 122, 157, 167, 176, 210, 279
Si Ji Chun (Four Seasons), Taiwan 21, 120, 176, 197, 210, 232, 278

Qing Xin, Li Shan, Taiwan 21, 278
Jin Xuan #12 (Milky oolong), Taiwan 12, 21, 146, 148, 154,176, 195, 202, 204, 245, 258, 265, 278
Four Seasons (Si Ji Chun), Taiwan 21, 120, 176, 197, 210, 232, 278
Milky oolong (Jin Xuan #12), Taiwan 12, 21, 146, 148, 154,176, 195, 202, 204, 245, 258, 265, 278
Tieguanyin, (Iron Goddess of Mercy), China, Taiwan, Thailand 12, 21, 22, 40, 66, 102, 122, 157, 167, 176, 210, 279
Wenshan Baozhong, Taiwan 12, 21,72, 192, 232, 256, 258, 260, 261, 264, 268, 270, 278

Examples of dark oolong tea:
Big Red Robe (Da Hong Pao), China 22, 92, 126, 136, 166, 195, 196, 202, 205, 214, 215, 232, 260, 261, 267, 269, 271, 272, 279
Da Hong Pao (Big Red Robe), China 22, 92, 126, 136, 166, 195, 196, 202, 205, 214, 215, 232, 260, 261, 267, 269, 271, 272, 279
Dong Fang Mei Ren (Oriental Beauty), Taiwan 21,196, 204, 207, 232, 240, 266, 268, 272, 279
Mi Lan Xiang Feng Huang Dan Cong (Phoenix Dancong), China 22, 192, 193, 194, 267, 271, 279
Oriental Beauty (Dong Fang Mei Ren), Taiwan 21,196, 204, 207, 232, 240, 266, 268, 272, 279
Phoenix Dancong (Mi Lan Xiang Feng Huang Dan Cong), China 22, 192, 193, 194, 267, 271, 279

Examples of black tea:
Assam, India 12, 23, 76, 164, 178, 234, 265, 267, 269, 281
Benifûki Wakoucha, Japan 24, 281
Ceylon, Nuwara Eliya, Sri Lanka 23, 51, 61, 188, 189, 234, 241, 259, 280
Ceylon, Pusselawa, Sri Lanka 23, 51, 61, 188, 189, 234, 241, 259, 269, 280
Ceylon Uva, Sri Lanka 24, 51, 61, 78, 188, 189, 234, 241, 281
Darjeeling first flush, India 22, 50, 53, 61, 104, 116, 122, 128, 138, 167, 171, 180, 264, 279
Dian Hong (Golden Yunnan), China 23, 195, 197, 207, 241, 267, 273, 280
Golden Yunnan (Dian Hong), China 23, 195, 197, 207, 241, 267, 273, 280
Earl Grey, blend 10, 13, 61, 76, 108, 116, 120, 122, 124, 126, 128, 142, 151, 154, 158, 167, 168, 172, 189, 196, 197, 211, 220, 234, 260, 263, 268, 269, 271
English Breakfast, blend 10, 13, 82, 86, 88, 92, 94, 118, 130,142, 150, 166, 167, 171, 178, 180, 197, 188, 189, 241, 273
Honey Black, Taiwan 24, 116, 201, 234, 240, 241, 279
Jin Jun Mei, (Golden Eyebrow), China 241
Keemun, China 23, 86, 172, 194, 204, 241, 261, 272, 280
Kericho, Kenia 24, 280
Lapsang Souchong (smoked), China 23, 216, 234, 241, 270, 280
Lapsang Souchong (unsmoked), China 23, 234, 241, 262, 263, 266, 271, 280
Nepalese Black, first flush, Nepal 22, 279
Nepalese Imperial Black, Nepal 23, 280
Nilgiri Black, India 22,196, 234
Ruby #18, Taiwan 24, 118, 120, 158, 168, 174, 192, 194, 205, 261, 266, 268, 279
Satemwa Black, Malawi 24, 271, 273, 281

Examples of post-fermented tea:
Goishicha, Japan 25, 61, 205, 237, 281
Sheng (raw) Pu Erh China 24, 206, 235 - 237, 257, 258, 261, 266, 270, 281
Shu (cooked) Pu ErhChina 25, 61, 82, 86, 92, 108, 118, 140, 142, 151, 154, 160, 164, 166, 172, 193, 195, 207, 235 - 237, 260, 263, 265, 270, 28

Addresses of teashops and tea institutes

On these pages you will find an overview of teashops, tea webshops, tea schools, tea gardens and tea magazines worldwide. This list is by no means complete; far from it. It is a small selection of addresses I collected with the help of many tea friends all over the world, but there are many more shops to be found. Most teashops also sell tea ware and often have a webshop as well. So do most tea plantations. The best advice I can give you is: wherever you buy your tea, make sure it is from someone who loves tea, knows lots about it and treats the product and its makers with respect.

TEA BLOGS

The Tea Crane, www.the-tea-crane.com/blog/
Tea Epicure, teaepicure.com/blog/
Tea for me, please, www.teaformeplease.com
The Tea Squirrel, teasquirrel.com
Tea Geek, www.teageek.net/blog/

TEA BOOK CLUB

www.teabookclub.org

TEA COMMUNITY, ONLINE

gjtea.org
specialityteaeurope.com
steepster.com

TEA MAGAZINES

Eighty Degrees, www.readeighty.com
Tea Journey Magazine, teajourney.pub
Tea Biz, tea-biz.com

TEA PLANTATIONS (often webshop as well)

Australia

Brynhill, Atherton Table Lands, Near Atherton, Queensland, www.brynhill.com.au
The Daintree Tea Company, Mossman, Queensland, daintreetea.com.au
Nucifora Tea Estate, 2535 Palmerston Highway East Palmerston, Queensland, www.nucifora.com.au
Tassie-T, Tasmanian grown tea, 3 Kadina Close, Allens Rivulet, Tasmania, www.tassie-t.com.au

China

Wuyi Rock Tea Factory, Man tuo Yan Road 14-1, San gu district, Wuyishan City, Fujian Province, www.wuyiorigin.com
And many more

France

Filleule des Fées, Trébihan, 56440 Languidic, Brittany, filleule-des-fees.fr
Les jardins de la Plantisserie, 1 rue du Pont, 56150 Guénin, Brittany, email: la_plantisserie@icloud.com
Sainte-Marie, 44170, Treffieux, email: thomas@pioka.pink

Germany

Tschanara Teagarden, Wirtsspezard 14, 51519, Odenthal-Scheuren, tschanara-teagarden.de
Wudang Daoist Tea Garden, Immserstr. 22, 31061, Alfeld, www.liu-tea-art.com

India

Glenburn Tea Estate, Darjeeling, glenburnteaestate.com
Gopaldhara Teas, gopaldharaindia.com
Makaibari, www.makaibari.com
Teabox, www.teabox.com
Tea Gardenia, www.teagardenia.com
Tea 'n' Teas, teanteas.com

Italy

Piantagione Livio Zacchera, Premosello Chiovenda, via Milano, www.compagniadellago.com
Il Giardino del tè, Via Intra Premeno 148 - I28921, Antoliva Verbania, Lake Maggiore, www.lacameliadoro.com

Nepal

Jun Chiyabari, junchiyabari.com

New Zealand

Zealong, 495 Gordonton Road, Hamilton, zealong.com

Sri Lanka

Amba Estate, Ambadandegama, Bandarawela, BD 90108, www.ambaestate.com
Pedro Tea Estate, Nuwara Eliya, Central Province, Sri Lanka

Switzerland

Casa del Tè Monte Veritá, Via Collina 84, CH-6612 Ascona, www.casa-del-te.ch

The Netherlands
Het Zuyderblad, De Branten 12, 6027 NL, Soerendonk, www.hetzuyderblad.nl
UK
Jersey
Jersey Fine Tea, Jersey, Channel Islands, www.jerseyfinetea.com
Scotland
Windy Hollow Farm, Trinity Gask, By Auchterarder, Perthshire PH3 1LL, www.windyholloworganics.co.uk
USA
Hawaii
Maui Tea Farm, 18303 Haleakala Hwy, Kula, HI 96790, mauiteafarm.com
Maunakea Tea, maunakeatea.com
Big Island Tea, www.bigislandtea.com
Alabama
Fair Hope Tea Plantation, 12424 Lyter Ln., Fairhope, AL, fairhopeteaplantation.com

TEA SCHOOLS
Australia
Australia Tea Masters, 107 Ryrie Street, Geelong 3220, VIC , australianteamasters.com.au
Canada
International Tea Education Institute, CP5 Succursale St Martin, Laval, Qc. H7V3P4, itei.ca
Camellia Sinensis, 309, Emery St, Montreal (Qc) Canada H2X 1J2, camellia-sinensis.com
France
l'École du thé, 7 Rue de Nice, Paris, www.ecoleduthe.com/paris/
Palais des Thés, www.palaisdesthes.com/en/tea-school/
Italy
Eastern Leaves, Via Macedonio Melloni 32, Milano, easternleaves.com/it/pages/tea-academy
India
*Asian School of Tea,*18-B Creek Row, Kolkata-700014, West Bengal, www.asianschooloftea.org
Japan
Global Japanese Tea Association, Wazuka, Kyoto, gjtea.org
Urasenke Internation /association, Urasenke Tankokai Federation, Kyoto, Japan, www.urasenke.or.jp/texte/aff_org/uia.html
Spain
Global Japanese Tea Association, Madrid, gjtea.org
Thailand
*Asian School of Tea,*151 Moo 4 Thasala, Muang Chiang Mai, www.asianschooloftea.org
UK
European Speciality Tea Association, University of Chester, NoWFOOD, Parkgate Road, Chester, CH1 4BJ, specialityteaeurope.com/tea-certification-programme
USA
World Tea Academy, New York, www.worldteaacademy.com

TEASHOPS
Australia
Australia Tea Masters webshop, 107 Ryrie Street, Geelong, VIC, 3220, australianteamasters.com.au
Long's Tea, 9 Dora St, Hurstville NSW 2220, www.longstea.com.au
Lupicia, QV Shopping Complex, 14-16 Artemis Lane, Melbourne, VIC, 3000, www.lupicia.com.au
My Tea House, Shop 4&5 129-133 Military Road Neutral Bay, NSW, 2089, myteahouse.net.au
Quali-tea Sydney, Shop 12 Ground Floor, The Strand Arcade 412-414 George Street, Sydney, NSW, 2000, www.quali-tea.com
Taka Tea Garden, 320 New South Head Rd, Double Bay, NSW, 2028, takateagarden.com.au
Zensation Tea House and tea shop, Shop 160/806 Bourke St, Waterloo, NSW, 2017, www.zensation.com.au
Belgium
Biochi Fine Tea Lounge, Lange Koepoortstraat 43, 2000 Antwerpen
Le Fossé Fleuri, Rue des Fossés Fleuris 45, 5000, Namur, lefossefleuri.be
Unami, rue du Postillon 2, 1180 Bruxelles, www.unamitea.com
Bulgaria
Tea House Plovdiv, www.teahouseplovdiv.com
Canada
Camellia Sinensis, 351 Emery St, Montreal (Qc), 7010, Casgrain Av, Montreal, Qc 624, St-Joseph East St, Quebec, Qc, camellia-sinensis.com/en

Cha Gloriette, B56b-4300 Steeles Ave. E, Markham, Ontario, L3R0Y5E, www.chagloriette.com
Cha Yi maison de thé, 165 Rue Eddy, Gatineau, QC J8X 2W7, chayi.ca
Great Wall Tea Co, 810 Quayside Drive, New Westminster, British Columbia, greatwalltea.com
I Cha Tea, 4-235 Spadina Ave.,Toronto, Ontario, M5T2E2, www.ichatea.ca
Le bruit de l'eau, 10, rue de l'Évêché Est, 1er étage, Rimouski, QC, G5L 1X4, lebruitdeleau.ca
O5 Rare Tea Bar, 2208 West 4th Avenue, Vancouver, www.o5tea.com
Pluck, 89 Research Rd, Toronto, M4G 2G8 Tel: 416-882-7787, pluckteas.com
Pugs-And-Pigs, 331 Ch de l'Île-du-Sable, G0X 2J0 Sainte-Anne-de-la-Pérade QC, www.pugs-and-pigs.com

France

Cha Yuan, 7/9, rue des Remparts d'Ainay, 69002 Lyon9, cours Vitton, 69006 Lyon
Cha Yuan, 18, rue Sommeiller, 74000 Annecy, www.cha-yuan.com
Jugetsudo, 95 rue de Seine, 75006, Paris, www.jugetsudo.fr
Les Thés sur Terre, 47 Rue Franklin, 69002 Lyon, www.lesthes-surterre.com
Loréne Millet Cave à Thés 7, rue Fontange, 13006 Marseille, contact@lorenemillet.com
Nuage Sauvage, Vietnamese wild tea, 34bis rue Bichat, 75010 Paris, nuagesauvage.fr
Ogata, 16 rue Debelleyme 75003 Paris, ogata.com
Palais des Thés, tea shops all over France and webshop www.palaisdesthes.com/en/
Plaisirs des Thés, 29, rue d'Italie 13100 - Aix-en-Provence, www.plaisirsdesthes.fr
Saveurs et Harmonie Comptoir de thé, 24 rue de la Colombette, 31000 Toulouse, www.saveursetharmonie.com
Tea & Ty,16 rue Victor Hugo, 35000 Rennes, 21 rue de la Villette, 75019 Paris, teaandty.com
Theine, 4 rue de l'Arche Sèche, 44000 Nantes, ilovetheine.fr/fr/
Unami Maison de Thé, 8 Rue Saint-Jacques, 59800 Lille, www.unamitea.com/fr/

Germany

Anmo Art Cha, Bendemannstr. 18, 40210 Düsseldorf, anmo-art-cha.com
Bamboo Tearoom, Friesenwall 29, 50672 Köln, www.bambootearoom.de
Bohea Teehandlung, Niederbarnimstraße 3, 10247 Berlin, www.bohea.de/
Chaya, Budapester Str. 38-50, 10787 Berlin, www.chaya.de
Nan Yi Tee, Westfälische Straße 66, 10709 Berlin, nan-yi-tee.de/
Paper and Tea, Bleibtreustrasse 4, 10623 Charlottenburg, Berlin, www.paperandtea.de
Tea Addicts, Auf der Bojewiese 58A, 21033 Hamburg, www.tea-addicts.de
Tee Geschwendner, tea shops all over Germany and webshop, www.teegschwendner.de
Teewald, Martin-Luther Str. 37, 01099, Dresden, teewald.com
Tushita Teehaus, Klenzestr. 53 (Fraunhoferstr.), 80469 München, tushita.eu

Greece

To Tsai, Al. Soutsou 19, Athens, tea.gr/el

Italy

Eastern Leaves, Via Macedonio Melloni 32, Milano, easternleaves.com
Teacup Milano, Via Caminadella 18, 20123 Milano, teacupmilano.com
La Via del Te, Via della Condotta 26/28r, Firenze, www.laviadelte.com

Japan

151E, Chuo-ku, Fukuoka Kego 1.15.51.1F, Fukuoka, Japan, 151e.biz
Chanoha, shops in Ginza and Tamaplaza, chanoha.info/english/
Hibiki-an, 36 Shimonoto Yuyadani, Ujitawara, Kyoto, www.hibiki-an.com
Ippodo, Kokusai Bldg. 1F 3-1-1 Marunouchi Chiyoda Ward, Tokyo 100-0005, global.ippodo-tea.co.jp
Nishinotoin Tea Shop & MOTOAN Tea House, West side of Nishinotoin, South of Oike, Nakagyo-ku, Kyoto
Sono Organic, 42, Koda, Kikuma-cho, Imambari, www.sono-organic.com
Thés du Japon, 3-14-6 Yanaka, Taito-ku, Tokyo, www.thes-du-japon.com
The Tea Crane, 424-2 Kasugacho, Kamigyo-ku, Kyoto, www.the-tea-crane.com
*Tokyo Saryo,*1 Chome 34-15 Kamiuma, Tokyo, tokyosaryo.jp/

Tsuen Tea, Uji Bridge, Uji, Kyoto, tsuentea.ca

Korea (South)
Smith Teamaker Café, 417, Apgujeong-ro, Gangnam-gu, Seoul, smithtea.com

Latvia
TEAritoria, Caunes street 4, Riga, Latvia, LV-1006

Poland
Chá Camélia, Rua das Escolas Novas 605, 4485-122 Fornelo, www.chacamelia.com

Portugal
Chá Camélia, Rua das Escolas Novas 605, 4485-122 Fornelo, www.chacamelia.com

The Azores, Portugal
SDASM, Quinta S. Gonçalo - 9500 - 343 Ponta Delgada, S. Miguel Açores, email: info.sdasm@azores.gov.pt

Spain
Tea Ritual, Carrer Monges,6-Bajos 07001, Palma de Mallorca, www.tearitual.es

Switzerland
Chemin sur la voie du thé (opening soon), Grand Geneve
Länggas Tee, Länggassstrasse 47. 3012 Bern Switzerland, www.laenggasstee.ch
The Queen Camellia Tea House, Kapellplatz 7, 6004 Luzern, www.camellia-tea-house.ch
Yulu Teahouse, Zürichstrasse 8/Innenhof, 8610 Uster, www.yulu.ch

Taiwan
Digni Tea,18, Lane 183, Section 1, Heping E Rd, Da'an District, Taipei City 106
Lin Mao Sen, No. 195-3, Section 2, Chongqing North Road, Datong District, Taipei City, Taiwan, linmaosen.com
Meimen Six Senses, teahouse, No.69, Lane 107, Linsen N Road, Zhongshan District, Taipei, www.youtube.com/watch?v=uLKT_T9KziE

Thailand
Monsoon Tea Company, 328/3 Charoenrat Rd, Chiang Mai

The Netherlands
Cha x Art, Eerste Constantijn Huygensstraat 78h, 1054BW Amsterdam
De Eenhoorn, Oudestraat 101 - 103, 8261 CJ Kampen, eenhoorn.eu/nl/thee/
Evermore thee, Coolhaven 158A, 3024 AM Rotterdam, evermorethee.nl (shipping only within EU)
Formocha, Brouwersgracht 282, 1013HG Amsterdam, www.formocha.nl
Moychay Tea Culture Club, Rozengracht 92H, 1016 NH Amsterdam
Oficina, Jan van Galenstraat 147, 1056 BN Amsterdam
Ravensteijn Thee, Hinthamerstraat 160, 5211 MV 's-Hertogenbosch, no webshop
Simon Lévelt, Around 60 shops throughout the Netherlands, www.simonlevelt.nl
Tea's Delight, Kinkerstraat 58, 1053 DZ Amsterdam, teasdelight.com
't Japanse winkeltje, Nieuwezijds Voorburgwal 177, 1012 RK Amsterdam, no webshop
Thee van Sander, Bagijnestraat 15, 2611 AT Delft, www.theevansander.nl

UAE (Dubai)
Tchaba Tea, Aspen Lounge, Kempinski Mall of the Emirates
Tchaba Boutique, JW Marriott Marquis Hotel, Business Bay, tchabatea.com

UK
Comins Tea House, The Quarterjack, Bridge St, Sturminster, Newton and 34 Monmouth Street, Bath, cominstea.com
JING Tea, 18-19 St Christopher's Place, London, W1U 1NN, www.jingtea.com
Katsute 100, 100 Islington High Street, London, N1 8EG,147 Brick Lane, London, E1 6SB, www.katsute100.com
Mei Leaf Teahouse, 99 Camden High Street London NW1 7JN, www.meileaf.com
My Cup of Tea, 5 Denman Place, London, W1D 7AH, mycupoftea.co.uk
Pekoe Tea, Old Leith Central Train Station, www.pekoetea.co.uk
Postcards Teas, 9 Dering Street, London W1S 1AG, www.postcardteas.com
Quinteassential UK, Red Hill House, Hope street, Chester CH48BU, quinteassential.co.uk
The Chinese Tea Company,14 Portobello Green Arcade, ,281 Portobello Road, London, W10 5TZ, the-chinese-tea-company.com/pages/tea-house

USA
29B, 29 Avenue B, NY, NY 10009, www.teadealers.com
Jin Yun Fu, 40 W 25th St, Showplace #224, New York, NY 10010, www.jinyunfuteashop.com
Floating Mountain, 239 West 72nd Street, 2ND Floor, New York, NY 10023, www.floating-mountain.com
Kettl, 70 Greenpoint Av. Floor 1, Brooklyn, Ny 11222, kettl.co
Luv Tea, 37A Bedford St., NYC, luv-tea.com
Puerh Brooklyn Teashop, 174 Grand Street, Brooklyn NY 11211, www.puerhbrooklyn.com
Red Blossom Tea Company, 831 Grant Avenue, San Francisco, CA 94108, www.redblossomtea.com
Rishi Tea & Botanicals, 185, South 33rd Court, Milwaukee, WI 53208, www.rishi-tea.com
Samovar Tea Lounge, 411 Valencia Street, San Francisco, samovartea.com
Seven Cups, 2516 East 6th Street, Tucson, AZ 85716, sevencups.com
Sipping Streams Tea Company, 374 Old Chena Pump Rd., Fairbanks, AK 99709Alaska, sippingstreams.com
Téance Fine Teas, 1036 Grayson Street, Berkeley, CA 94710, www.teance.com
Te Company, 163 West 10th St. NYC, www.tecompanytea.com
Setsugekka NY, 80 E 7th St, New York City, NY 10003-8415, www.setsugekkany.com
Smith Teamaker, 110 SE Washington St., Portland, Oregon, smithtea.com
Song Tea & Ceramics, 2120 Sutter Street, San Francisco, songtea.com
Tea Source, 2908 Pentagon Dr, St Anthony, MN, www.teasource.com
The Boulder Dushanbe Teahouse, 1770 13th St., Boulder, Colorado, boulderteahouse.com
Trident Cafe, 940 Pearl st, Boulder, CO, 80302, www.tridentcafe.com

TEA WEBSHOPS
Australia
Cloud Nine Teas, cloudnineteas.com
Nishio Japanese Green Tea, www.japanesegreentea-nishio-australia.com.au
Tea Land Australia, tealand.com.au
Valley Green Tea, www.valleygreentea.com.au
Yamaguchien, www.yamaguchien.com.au
The Steepery Tea Company, thesteepery.com.au
Austria
characteas.com, www.characteas.com
Belgium
Tearista, earista.eu (E.U only)
Curiosithee, www.curiosithee.be
Canada
Soocha, www.soochatea.ca
Zhen tea, www.zhentea.ca
China
Amoy teas, amoyteas.com
Bitter Leaf Teas, www.bitterleafteas.com
Exquisite Leaves, exquisiteleaves.com
Morima Tea, www.morimatea.com
White2Tea, white2tea.com
Tea in Town, teaintown.store/shop/
Yiwu Mountain Tea, www.yiwumountaintea.com
Yunnan Sourcing, yunnansourcing.com
Czech Republic
Tea Mountain, www.teamountain.cz
France
Terre des Thés, www.terre-des-thes.fr
Nunshen, nunshen.com
Germany
Siam Tee, siam-tee.de
Deerland Tea, www.deerlandtea.com
Teecultur | Café Onlineshop, Marktstraße 11, 74172 Neckarsulm, teeladen.teecultur.de
India
Dancing Leaf, www.dancingleaftea.com
Dorje Teas, dorjeteas.com
Forest Pick, www.forestpick.com
Ketlee, www.ketlee.in
Nuxalbari Tea, nuxalbaritea.com
Tea Gardenia, www.teagardenia.com
Japan
IKKYU, ikkyu-tea.com
O-Cha, www.o-cha.com
Koto Tea, www.kototea.com
Sazen Tea Co., www.sazentea.com/en/
Obubu Tea, obubutea.com
Forthees Sonogi, forthees.com
Yunomi Tea, yunomi.life/
Hojo Tea, hojotea.com/en/
Momo Tea, www.momotea.co

Malaysia
Hojicha Ya Teas, hojichaya.com
New Zealand
Maitea, www.maitea.co.nz
Zealong, zealong.com
Switzerland
Nio Tea, nioteas.com

Taiwan
Beautiful Taiwan Tea Company,
www.beautifultaiwantea.com
Taiwan Tea Crafts, www.taiwanteacrafts.com
Taiwan Sourcing, taiwanoolongs.com
The Cha Tong, www.thechatong.com
Thailand
Monsoon Tea Co., www.monsoontea.co.th/
Tezumi, www.tezumi.com
The Netherlands
Chamoods, www.chamoods.com
Crusio Thee, www.crusiothee.com/nl
Het Zuyderblad, www.hetzuyderblad.nl
Hotsoup, www.hotsoup.nl
UK
Grass People Tree,
www.grasspeopletree.com
Karma Tea Co., www.karmateaco.com/
Kiani Tea London, www.kianitea.com
Rare Tea Co., rareteacompany.com
Suki tea, suki-tea.com
What-Cha, what-cha.com
Unravel Tea, www.unraveltea.com (shipping only within the UK)
USA
Crimson Lotus Tea, crimsonlotustea.com
Floating Leaves, floatingleaves.com
Liquid Proust, www.liquidproust.com (shipping only within the USA)
Mei Mei Fine Teas, www.meimeitea.com
Purple Cloud Teahouse,
purplecloudteahouse.com
Robertson Tea, www.robertsontea.com
Tea Drunk, tea-drunk.com
Tezumi Tea, www.tezumi.com
Unytea.store, unytea.store

VIDEOS AND DOCUMENTARIES ON TEA
China
Puer Tea: Ancient Caravans and Urban Chic, by Jinghong Zhang,
www.youtube.com/watch?v=FmukEgBrprQ
India
Glenburn Estate, the making of Darjeeling tea,
www.youtube.com/watch?v=ri8ShJu5Eek
Tea in the Land of Thunder, by Arbor Teas: Field Notes from Darjeeling,
www.youtube.com/watch?v=jqXPGvXkaKQ
The Makaibari Tea Estate,
www.youtube.com/watch?v=bzgGQcz75vo
Japan
Kagoshima Chirancha Oritaen tea farm, Japan,
www.youtube.com/watch?v=fcj13dwDTQw
Nagasaki Tamaryokucha farm, Fukudaen: Tamaryokucha,
www.youtube.com/watch?v=pGROi-2qmMM
Tsuruko's Tea Journey,
www.youtube.com/watch?v=-TToWb_JcHY
Malawi
Lost Malawi Tea, by Rare Tea Company,
www.youtube.com/watch?v=OsroewAbybA
Nepal
Jun Chiyabari,
junchiyabari.com/index.php/videos/

VARIOUS OTHER INTERESTING LINKS TO WEBSITES AND SUCH:
Jan Pavel Pottery, www.janpavekpottery.com
Pots and Tea, www.potsandtea.cz
Mono Japan Haruka Matsuo,
shop.monojapan.nl/collections/haruka-matsuo
Popalini and Jezando ceramics studio, North Devon, UK, www.popaliniandjezando.com
Solo Kolektyw, www.solokolektyw.com
Tea Log, www.tea-log.com
To'Ak chocolate,
toakchocolate.com/pages/our-story and
www.youtube.com/watch?v=3iWAevvWEaA
Woven roots tea crafts, tea ware, tea tables, tea, www.wovenroots.com
Yellow Nose Studio, www.yellownosestudio.com

Bibliography

- Heiss, Mary Lou en Robert J. (2007) *The Story of Tea: a cultural history and drinking guide*, Ten Speed Press, U.S.A
- Heiss, Mary Lou en Robert J. (2010) *The Tea Enthusiast's Handbook: A Guide to Enjoying the World's Best Teas* Ten Speed Press, U.S.A
- Lydia Gautier (2012) *1001 Secrets sur le thé*, Prat éditions, France
- Lydia Gaultier et Jean-Francois Mallet (2006) *Tea Exotic Flavors and aromas*, Stewart, Tabori & Chang, Editions Minerva, Switzerland
- Andrew Dornenburg and Karen Page (2006) *What to drink with what you eat?* Little, Brown, and Co, U.S.A
- Peter Klosse, Angélique Schmeinck en Jacques Meerman (2015) *Het Nieuwe Proefboek*, Fontaine Uitgevers BV, The Netherlands
- Fabio Petroni and Gabriella Lombardi (2014) *Tea Sommelier*, De Agostine Libri S.p.A, Italy
- Gold & Stern (2010) *Culinary Tea*, Running Press Book Publishers, Philadelphia, U.S.A
- Norwood Pratt (2010) *Tea Dictionary*, Tea Society, U.S.A
- Timothy d'Offay (2017) *Easy leaf tea*, Ryland, Peters & Small, U.K
- Timothy d'Offay and Michael Freeman (2018) *The life of tea*, Hachette Book Group, U.K
- Tony Gebely (2016) *Tea: a user's guide*, Eggs and Toast Media, Maryland, U.S.A
- Gascoyne, Marchand, Desharnais, Américi (2014) *Tea, history, terroirs, varieties*, Firefly Books, U.S.A
- Jane Pettigrew (1997) *The tea companion. A connoisseur's guide*, Apple Press, U.K
- Kakuzo Okakura (1964) *The Book of Tea*, Dover Publications, U.S.A
- Wu Juenong (2017) *The Classic of Tea*, Shanghai Press and Publishing Development Company, LTD, China
- John Griffiths (2011) *Tea, a history of the drink that changed the world*, Carlton Publishing Group, U.K
- Wes Marshall (2016) *Wat je als wijnliefhebber moet weten*, Karakter Uitgevers BV, The Netherlands
- Hubrecht Duijker (2015) *Welke wijn waarbij*, Kosmos Uitgevers, The Netherlands
- Victoria Moore (2017) *The Wine Dine Dictionary*, Granta Books, U.K
- Coe & Coe (2007) *The True History of Chocolate*, Thames & Hudson, U.K
- Maricel E. Presilla (2009) *The new taste of chocolate*, Ten Speed Press, U.S.A
- Harold Mc Gee: *Nose Dive: A Field Guide to the World's smells*, (2020), Penguin Press

RECOMMENDED BOOKS ON TEA

Above list plus books written by:

- Alex Ahearn (2019) *Please bake it. Simple gluten-free, and vegan recipes with tea pairings*, U.S.A
- Alex Ahearn (2019) *Flowers + Tea, poems with matching teas*, U.S.A
- Simona Suzuki, (2017) *Japanese Tea: a Comprehensive Guide*, Japan (Independently published)
- Tyas Sosen (2019) *The Story of Japanese Tea: a broad outline of its cultivation, manufacturing, history and cultural values.* Japan (Independently published)
- P.J. Graham (1999) *Tea of the Sages: the Art of Sencha* University of Hawaii Press, U.S.A
- A.L. Sadler (2008) *Japanese Tea Ceremony: Cha-No-Yu.* Tuttle Publishers, U.S.A
- Henrietta Lovell (2019) Infused - *Adventures in Tea* U.K Faber and Faber Publishers, U.K
- Erika Rappaport (2019) *A Thirst for empire: how tea shaped the modern World* Princeton University Press, U.S.A
- John Griffiths (2007) *Tea: a history of the drink that changed the world* Carlton Publishing Group, U.K
- Virginia Utermohlen Lovelace (2017) *Three Basic Teas and How to Enjoy Them*, U.S.A (Create Space Independent Publishing Platform)
- Michelle and Rob Comins (2019) *Tales of the Tea Trade: The secret to sourcing and enjoying the world's favourite drink*, Pavilion, U.K.
- Lisa See (2018) *The Tea Girl of Hummingbird Lane*, Scribner, U.S.A
- Jinghong Zhang (2013) *Puer Tea: Ancient Caravans and Urban Chic*, University of Hawaii Press, U.S.A

Acknowledgments

This book would not have appeared in its current state if not for the help of many others.

Special thanks to:

Willem Toutenhoofd
Van Zussen
Alex Ahearn
Monica Griesbaum
Dameshk Wijesinha
Sarah Rebecca Kersley
Natasha Tastachova
Harold Pereira
Nicole de Werk
Karin Luiten
Paul Jongsma
Annemiek van Leeuwen
Willem Huisman
Karlijn Dapper
Deirdre Deprettere
Robert Verwey
Hazel Lee
Thees Peereboom
Paul Römer and his team at Uitgeverij Terra